Knight of Faith

The letters of
Norman Percy Grubb

Volume 1

edited by
DeeDee Winter

authorHOUSE™

1663 LIBERTY DRIVE, SUITE 200
BLOOMINGTON, INDIANA 47403
(800) 839-8640
WWW.AUTHORHOUSE.COM

First published by AuthorHouse 2/27/2006

ISBN: 1-4208-8878-1 (sc)

Printed in the United States of America
Bloomington, Indiana

This book is printed on acid-free paper.

CONTENTS

FOREWORD

In 1968 when my Christian life was shipwrecked and on an ash heap, I met and fell heir to Norman Grubb. As I listened to him speak for the first time I could not have told you a thing he said, but inside my spirit was leaping! During that first visit I remember sitting on the floor at his feet, not knowing anything to say or ask - only receiving a smile. This started the healing process that would bring me home within to the person of Jesus Christ.

That day was the beginning of a beloved, invaluable friendship evolving through letters and visits which spanned the next 30 years. During that time as I listened, learned, and watched Norman, I not only saw his acts but also began to understand his ways. Eventually I came to walk beside him in the spirit of understanding his commissions - the heartbeat of his calling became my own.

Second to his willingness to give of himself, sitting for hours and listening to our problems or trials, was his correspondence. He started each morning at his typewriter, promptly at 4 a.m., answering those same problems in the form of LETTERS!

To the thousands of us who lived in self-condemnation, not knowing what to do with our temptations, or how to conquer our sins, Norman's call to "see through" these circumstances to God and his "Oh, Dahling, its just a little mist on the mountain" seemed all too simple. We were suffering the loss of all things - marriages, money, children, even ourselves - as we, moment by moment, lived the 'dark night of our souls.' His vision and strict discipline to trust a God who could be nothing other than love, compelled us to take that leap of faith into the unknown and call into being those things which did not exist (Romans 4:17); thereby bringing total light, freedom and deeply serious purpose into every condition and situation in our lives. After our first meeting, I immediately wrote to him and this was his reply:

Dear little Linda,

I think this is the first letter I have ever received from you, isn't it? I am so pleased you have written. It seems to have taken time to get here - or I would have answered.

Yes, dear, I shall keenly look to seeing you in April. Pauline will give you dates, and perhaps you can arrange with her so that we can get time just by ourselves. I am only in Hopkinsville, Kentucky, before coming to you, and go on to Iowa.

Dear, you may not think so, but it is good that you have had these tough times! I praise Him. There's no other way to find and live in the light than by first feeling the reality of the dark.

You are not in Rom.7, dear, you only think you are, and what you believe is a fact to you. You are only in Rom.7, when you wrongly believe that you should be better, and I rather think you have some of this mistaken idea because you kind of bemoan that "the flesh is weak," and of course it is; that's all it is. And "not much faith," and word and prayer life nil. Excellent! You can have no faith, nor can the word and prayer be alive to you. Humans just remain negative human have-nots. But that's just what turns your attention away from that wretched "law" of Rom. 7 which will tell you "you ought" if you still think you ought. But when you learn and accept that you ought not, because we humans are not meant to be or have anything...then you can say, "Of course I'm weak, of course I have these failures, of course Bible and prayer are dead to me." At that point you say, "Now Lord, You are Yourself in me, and You Only are any quickening in me, or anything" and You are Yourself in me, the real Self, though I may not feel a thing and feel as dead as ever." As you "recognize" Him in faith, though feeling nothing (and don't try to improve yourself or pick yourself up, or feel as if you ought to be something - Rom.7) then in God's own way, He will make Himself real to you.

So, I'm just glad you wrote, dear, and glad you have these dark times in order to learn this great lesson that you have "the sentence of death in yourself, that you should not trust in yourself, but in Him," in you. (2 Corinthians 1:9)

Ever lovingly dear,

Norman

In that letter I found a man who daringly challenged the recommended, acceptable, and respected doctrines of the day. He set my course to find the living Christ in me - "The mystery of the gospel once hidden, now made manifest, which is Christ in you, the hope of glory." (Colossians 1:27)

He was truly a man "out of season" - a "revolutionary" who brought a message that will forever be an eternal rebuke to the one who is satisfied with a recommended life of security and performance living for Jesus or under the letter of the law. So may it be said of Norman, our present day reformer, as was said long ago of another reformer, Martin Luther:

Great men need not that we praise them; the need is ours that we know them. They are our common heritage. Whether we stand where they stand or tread another path, we are the richer that they lived.

He was very human, this hero of ours, fiery-tempered, passionate, imperious, loving withal, warm-hearted and generous, with quickness of perception and subtle *English* humor.

Full of contradictions, he had the frankness and carelessness of genius, and what he was he fully revealed without concealment or diplomacy. He was unsurpassed in his human sympathies, simplicity of character and transparent honesty.

Martin Luther - The Man and His Work.
The Century Company, 1910, 1911

~~~

The hallmark of Norman's life is borne out in the scores of us whom he took aside to "explain the ways of God more perfectly." Only through this book and the endearing love that comes from the hearts of those who shared their letters of a personal relationship with him will one begin to understand the quality of love that came from his pen. To understand others one must understand himself, and that he did, as those who knew him will attest. He was gifted with a Spirit intuition that guided him to catch the heart of the man. So whether we were in the wounding or binding up of his tongue, whether he gave criticism or compliment, we knew beyond measure that we were loved.

I am honored to have been asked to write the Foreword to this book of letters that will reveal the most remarkable insight of a man who lived an extraordinary life of giving it away to others. May God bless you as you read and may the Eternal One who indwelt His humble servant Norman Grubb... be revealed in you.

Linda Bunting

INTRODUCTION

Books of letters have always been of great interest to me, because in reading them I get the real essence of the person.

This book began in my heart during the many times I visited Norman Grubb and his granddaughter, Sandy, in their home. In almost every room were stacks of correspondence with people from all over the world. During our thirteen-year friendship I personally received over one hundred letters from him. They were, and still remain, golden nuggets of encouragement, wisdom and excitement at the move of God within His creation, but most of all they were love...Great Love.

Norman personally answered all of the correspondence he received. Those who had him as a guest in their home recall hearing him pecking at his typewriter (using only his two index fingers) during all hours of the day or night. He was as famous for his bad typing as he was for his illegible handwriting. He had a very warm style of writing and had "lovers" all over the world calling each "my darling" or "precious" which affirmed the recipient and revealed the love of Christ in a new way.

I knew that many thousands had been recipients of these living epistles during his more than seventy-five years of corresponding. We had been encouraged, blessed and sometimes chastised, but always with the purpose of Christ being formed in us—and always with the reality that Galatians 2:20—the <u>fact</u> that Christ is living our lives—was the truth about each of us—and every believer.

Norman was our friend, our mentor and our encourager. He saw us as his equal in Christ and in turn made us see ourselves so. He taught us to be people of faith by directing us to look not at life's circumstances but to God and what He was about in those hard places, because God was the "real," not the circumstance.

As I filed the letters according to dates, as much as possible, I agonized about the numerous letters I did not have—in the thousands for each year he corresponded. I finally came back to the truth that God had preserved the letters He wanted published. Because of the volume, phrases were often repeated. Plus, in his "latter-years commission" to bring our union with Christ to "the whole church and the whole world" he wrote repeatedly in letters what held his heart and was in his own words "a fiddle with one string." Also, because of the volume, I have decided to

present the letters in three books—Knight of Faith, Vol. 1 & 2 and

My Dear C.U.M.B., Norman Grubb's Letters to the Cambridge University Missionary Band 1922-1989.

In reading the material I was overwhelmed at times by the scope of Norman Percy Grubb. There was hardly a subject he did not touch and knowledgeably explore. His spiritual insights encompassed the *totality* of life. He possessed great wisdom on how and when to take issue, as well as a graceful manner in which to do so. About five years before his death I asked him if he had told me *everything* he knew about God, because I certainly did not want him to "leave" without doing that! He looked at me in a quizzical way, smiled and assured me saying, "Why, yes my dear, I think so", indicating *surely* he had.

I look back at the naiveté of my question and his guileless answer in amusement now. In these letters I have come across a number of issues and thoughts I never heard him discuss. Of all the books of the Bible he taught that we have on tape, the *Song of Solomon* is not to be found, nor did I ever hear him talk on it. Yet, in one letter he encourages a woman as he weaves her life in and out of those verses, culminating with the fact that when she is filled by her true marriage to Christ, she can then be concerned and consumed for those around her. This is only one example of the wealth to be found in his letters.

Norman's interests embraced a remarkably broad spectrum. He could converse on any subject from religion and current events to science, literature and sports. His was always a unique perspective tempered by life experience: success and failure, victories of faith, and also great heartache. His wonderful wit and English sense of humor lightened our hearts at every turn.

I gathered the letters in this book from many sources. I first sent a letter to those on Norman's mailing and conference lists explaining my desire to publish this book and requesting any of his letters they would be willing to share. I also asked for any special memories each might have of Norman as well as a salutation they used in writing him. I received many responses; some even included copies of their letters to him. In addition, I asked each one to help me by sending my letter to anyone they might know who had corresponded with him. In one case, I corresponded at length with a woman for over a year before she finally trusted me enough to send her letters containing intimate details on which Norman had counseled her. Norman loved sharing his, as well as others' letters, with those whom he thought might benefit from them. Many of the letters I received were "shared" copies. And finally, he gave me some during the times I spent in his home.

Each chapter begins with a word from those who knew Norman—a word either to him or about him. The letters range in dates from the 1940's through the 1990's. Some were dictated to his daughter, Priscilla, when he was bedridden and no longer able to write. His punctuation was "creative" and his sentences impossibly long. They are, for the most part, exactly as he wrote them containing many of his British phrasings, punctuations and spellings. I have edited only for repetitiveness or privacy.

By the grace of God, as you read these letters, you will reap an expanded understanding of God, humanity, life and life's problems - understandings not normally heard in Christian circles. May you fully discover the wonderful truth about yourself - the *you* "fearfully and wonderfully made" and containing the Life of the Living God, Jesus Christ.

For those of you who may not know Jesus Christ and His saving life, you <u>also</u> are "fearfully and wonderfully made" and contain "the Light, which lighteth every man that comes into the world." (John 1:9) Only say "Yes" to Christ to bring His Light and Life to *birth* within you.

NPG HISTORY

Norman Percy Grubb was born August 2, 1895 to Harry Percy Grubb and Margaret Adelaide Crichton-Stuart. He was of "prominent British lineage" but found no gain in his earthly heritage. His boyhood years were spent in the village of Oxton where his father was an Anglican clergyman. Although he was raised in a Christian home and in the Church of England, Norman was presented with a question as a teenager that he could not answer. "Do you belong to Christ?"[1] seared his soul. Through this event he came to know Jesus Christ as his Saviour.

When World War I began in 1914 Norman soon received his call-up and commission as a second lieutenant in the British army. His goal was to be a good soldier not only for England, but also for Jesus Christ by bringing the gospel to his fellow soldiers on the battlefront.

He spent the next few years defending Britain's commitment until he was wounded in France and sent home to recover. For his service he received the Military Medal. His return to England to recover from his leg wound would set the course of his life.

While in the hospital he was visited by Gilbert Barclay, a chaplain and a son-in-law of C.T. Studd, founder of the Heart of Africa Mission, later to become the Worldwide Evangelization Crusade (WEC). Reverend Barclay left a small booklet on his bed called "The Heart of Africa." As soon as he began to read it, Norman "heard an inward voice as clear as I ever heard in my life. 'That is where you are to go.'"[2] He immediately wrote to Mrs.

Studd of his call. Little did he realize that this call would also include a wife, Pauline Evangeline Studd, the youngest daughter of Priscilla and C.T. Studd.

After the war he attended Trinity College in Cambridge. As usual he began sharing his faith at every opportunity—going door to door to speak to individuals and participating in a students' Bible study and prayer group known as the Cambridge Inter-Collegiate Christian Union. It was here in 1919 that the Holy Spirit gave him the vision for Inter-Varsity Conference (now Inter-Varsity Fellowship) to have bible study groups like his in every college and university.

One semester before completing his degree, the Lord impressed upon him that now was the time to fulfill his call to Africa. Thus began a life-long pattern the Lord had for him–earthly credentials were not to be his. In 1919 Norman and Pauline were married and immediately set sail for the Congo to join C.T. The journey took three months by boat, train, flat-bottomed river steamer, truck and then the final three hundred miles by foot and bicycle.

One of Norman's often-told stories was of almost losing his fiancée, Pauline. He told her he was afraid of losing out in his "call" because he loved her more than he loved God. She responded that she would not marry him because God would be first in his life, God's work second and she third. And she wanted to be third in no man's life. This was great agony for him, until the Holy Spirit revealed to Pauline through Philemon 15 - "For perhaps therefore he departed for a season, that thou should receive him forever"[3] - that she was to marry him. The strength of her "No" became the strength of her "Yes." He always believed that it was her wisdom and stabilizing force that enabled him to build the Worldwide Evangelization Crusade (W.E.C.) as he did.

Norman remained in the Congo until 1931. Along with bringing Christ to the Africans, his work included translating the Bible into Bangala, their common market language. Norman and Pauline had four children. Their first child, Noel, born in the Congo, died on his first birthday. God later gave them Paul, Priscilla and Daniel.

Not long after arriving in Africa Norman found himself in the second great crisis of his life. He discovered that he could not love the Africans (who called him Ngrubi, shortened to Rubi by fellow missionaries) as he knew God wanted him to. It was then that God revealed to both Norman and Pauline Galatians 2:20, "I am crucified with Christ: nevertheless I live; yet not I, but Christ liveth in me: and the life I now live in the flesh I live by the faith of the Son of God who loved me, and gave Himself for me." That night in the jungle he made a headstone saying, "Here lies Norman Grubb" and he took by faith what the scriptures said.

However, he remained in a "crisis of faith" for two years until the Holy Spirit made Galatians 2:20 fully alive in him. During this time he met Rees Howells and was invited to visit him at the Swansea Bible College. While there Norman saw and heard God living in and speaking through a man. In observing Rees Howells he finally understood the fulfillment of Galatians 2:20 for himself.

Within a few years God brought him to the third and final crisis of his inner life. So severe was it that he even doubted the existence of the God to whom he had given his life and served with his whole heart. His answer came in reading Andrew Murray's "*Wholly for God*" and was expanded through several others who would become his "friends" for life—William Law, Jacob Boehme, Soren Kierkegaard, John of the Cross, Meister Eckhart, Walter Lanyon, Teresa of Avila, Henry Suso, Plotinus, Richard Rolle, Lady Julian of Norwich, Walter Hilton, John of Ruysbroeck, Thomas Troward, Evelyn Underhill, William Kingsland, Jesse Penn Lewis and Rufus Jones.

In his autobiography "*Once Caught, No Escape*" Norman says, "...there has been for me a vital difference between the second experience of discovering Christ living in me, and this third revelation of Christ all in all. The second experience left gaps where I did not yet see Him in everything everywhere, and all a form of Him, whether negatively of Him in wrath, or positively of Him in grace as light; and so there were separations, and callings on Him to be this or do that, in place of affirming that He is in fullness of His action everywhere...to be settled into this union which is unity, I had to go through a 'dark night of the soul' which affected no outward things, but the very inward vitals of my 'I and Thou' consciousness."[4]

~~~~~

The Worldwide Evangelization Crusade was unique in missions. Being a "faith mission" they told only God of their needs. They did not raise money or appeal to man for the work, but all trusted God at each turn for His supply. When C.T. died Norman and Pauline took over the mission's leadership. He remained International Secretary until his retirement.

The years that Norman led W.E.C. were years of great growth and expansion built on the foundation of their Four Pillars - sacrifice, faith, holiness and fellowship. One of the mission's outreaches was to the United States. In 1957 it was decided that Norman and Pauline would move their family, which had grown to include their son Paul's two children, Sandy and Nicky, to America.

In the years prior to the move, on trips to the United States to speak about the mission, he made numerous contacts in churches, Bible colleges, universities, home groups, other missions and Christian fellowships such as Faith At Work, Camps Farthest Out and International Christian Leadership, who host the Presidential Prayer Breakfast. An amazing thing began to happen. When speaking about the work, he also told of life changing truths of the "replaced life" he knew. People began to "catch" what he was saying as the Holy Spirit revealed to them their union with Christ.

In the midst of an active mission life Norman also wrote a number of biographies of men and women of faith and booklets telling of mission life, as well as several books and booklets detailing his theology as the Holy Spirit expanded his understanding of God. His passion was always as Paul's - that "Christ be formed in you."

As the work in America expanded, turmoil and tensions began for Norman within the Mission and the Spirit clearly showed that "retirement" was to be the way for him. He was relieved of his duties in 1965.

As with many great men of the Bible in their latter years, when their life's work seemed over, God had a new work for Norman. He called it "God's redirection" in order that he might bring Paul's "mystery of the gospel, Christ in you, the hope of glory" to many he could not reach through W.E.C. Norman had shared the truths which God had given him in Galatians 2:20 for thirty years, but few in W.E.C. really understood. And even though God gave him years of tremendous fruit with countless ones coming to fully understand their union with Christ, his heart remained broken over his beloved W.E.C. until his death, reminding me many times of Jesus as He cried over Jerusalem, always beseeching God that they would know what he boldly called "Total Truth."

The last thirty-plus years of Norman's life were spent traveling eleven months of the year to conferences and home meetings for a week or a night. One of these homes was that of Pauline Catlett of Louisville, Kentucky. For many years she had been teaching the Bible to a group of young married women, as well as hosting missionaries from all over the world who would also share at meetings in her home. Norman Grubb was among those who came once a year.

Linda Bunting attended the Bible studies and recalled the first time she heard Norman. She said she could not have repeated what he said, but that for the first time in her life someone made her feel that there was something good about her. She slowly began to see the truth that it was Christ living her everyday life—washing the dishes, feeding her children, folding the clothes, driving the carpool, etc. In her own personal hardships Norman taught her how to believe God for their resolve—how to live by faith.

In 1974 Linda asked Norman if there were others he visited who understood the truths he had brought to her. Out of this came a weekend house party at Linda and John Bunting's home of forty "knowers" from across the U.S. That first weekend of fellowship became a yearly gathering and grew from forty in their basement to three hundred in a large tent set up in the backyard. It continues today with an annual gathering the second weekend in September.

One of the attendees the first year was a successful businessman from Illinois, Bill Volkman, who wanted a way to communicate what people were sharing. He began a magazine called "Union Life" which he published for almost twenty-five years. He also established a conference center in Wisconsin for summer retreats. God began to open many new doors through the magazine and the quickening of the Spirit in people's lives.

In several ways life had become increasingly difficult for Norman. He did not drive and his advancing age made it impossible for him to travel by plane or train. Pauline was very ill and needed additional care at home. God once again provided, as He always had.

In 1979 Norman's granddaughter, Sandy, heard the call of the Lord to leave her life in the business world and return home in order to help with her ailing grandmother, Pauline, and support her grandfather in whatever way she could, hoping to extend his years of ministry. Pauline was bedridden, and although their daughter, Priscilla, lived with them, she was unable to undertake her care. A W.E.C. missionary from England, Susie Wheeler, came to nurse Pauline. Sandy made it possible for Norman to continue travelling until his 95th year and functioned as his companion, chauffer and personal secretary. Pauline's "glorification" came September 15, 1981.

In 1986 God once again brought division into Norman's life. The Union Life fellowship split due to doctrinal differences. Those who remained with Norman gathered in January 1987 to seek the Lord's direction. Within a short period of time it became apparent there were two strong opinions—those who wanted to start another magazine and build a retreat center and those who felt God calling them to have no organization, but be a living organism. Initially Norman wanted to leave an organization such as he had built in W.E.C., but he came to realize that God's "new thing" (Isaiah 42:9; 43:18) was truly new and freedom from what had been.

In 1989 doctors discovered that Sandy had lung cancer. As she underwent treatment she continued her duties for Norman until the summer of 1992 when the cancer metastasized to her brain. During this time Norman's legs had begun to give way and he had fallen several times. Sandy had to make a very hard decision.

Although she had spent the last dozen years supporting Norman in whatever way she could in order that he continue his ministry, she now had to insist that he no longer walk without assistance because she could not afford to have him fall and break a hip. (Although Norman had the physical difficulties of weak lungs, frostbitten feet and a "bad" leg from a WW I injury, he was not what he called a "body fusser." Many times when asked how he was, he would reply, "Oh, I don't know; I haven't noticed.") He became wheelchair-bound and bedridden, but remained mentally sharp until just prior to his "homegoing" on December 15, 1993. Sandy's life was completed fourteen months earlier, October 2, 1992. Losing her was one of the great heartaches of Norman's life.

SPECIAL MEMORIES

After Sandy died Norman's life became even more isolated and lonely. I continued to visit him for a week every few months. Norman was ever his gracious, kind, loving and always appreciative self. When Sandy was told that she had only a short time to live, she asked me to be the executor of her estate.

Afterwards as I went through the house sorting things, I noticed that many pictures had no identification on them. One by one I brought them to Norman. I labeled them, as he delightedly identified each of the people and recalled the rich history of the photographed event and reveled in the memories of those he had known, worked with and loved. Some photos took him as far back as eighty years. That day remains etched in my mind as one of my most treasured memories.

During those days I enjoyed many special times with Norman. In the mornings as I got up early and took his coffee into him, I sat on the side of his bed and we talked about a vast variety of subjects. It was also a wondrous event to sit with him on a sunny afternoon in the woods next to his home as he marveled at God in His creation. He would describe God's attributes as he observed these simple things—trees growing tall, straight and sturdy; the faithfulness of the sun to rise each day; the ants busily carrying on their assigned tasks; the breeze to cool; and the unique design and color of each leaf and flower. He opened my mind and expanded my awareness of God in so many new thoughts and realities— God as all and in all.

THE FINAL DAYS

The last time I was with him was about three weeks before his death. He asked Linda Bunting and me to come and be with him while a W.E.C. missionary, Elliot Tepper, from Betel in Spain was to visit him along with about ten of the men from Betel's fellowship. Our friend, Sylvia Pearce, accompanied us.

When we arrived we found Norman somewhat confused for the very first time. We were concerned that after traveling from Spain his visitors would not be able to have a meaningful time with him. But as they came into his room he was immediately fully alert remembering their visit a year earlier and even speaking to each of the young men individually by name, which was amazing as Norman rarely remembered anyone's name! They stayed about an hour. As Norman began to tire, Elliot asked him to pray and they took their leave.

He prayed a beautiful and very personal prayer. As soon as he finished and they left, he again became confused. I was reminded of the many times over the years when I had seen him sharing in homes around the country. In his late eighties and early nineties traveling was very wearing on him. Many times, tired or ill with bronchitis, when it was time for him to speak the Spirit within him would rise and he would talk for an hour or two in a strong clear voice. In these times we all readily saw the "same Spirit who raised Christ Jesus from the dead" dwelling in a mortal body.

I received a call from Norman's family on the morning after he peacefully passed away late the night before, December 15, 1993. His nurse, Cheryl, reported that his breathing had become labored and he had whispered, "Abba Father," just before the Lord came for him. He was buried in Philadelphia next to his beloved wife Pauline. His son Daniel, an Episcopal minister, officiated at his burial.

A close W.E.C. co-worker and friend, John Whittle, told Stewart Dinnen, also of W.E.C., shortly after Norman's death that he had only recently come to see that God had given Norman a commission after W.E.C. and that was to bring Galatians 2:20 to the whole body of Christ. After reading the volume of letters over the years, I have been awestruck by the realization that his "Total Truth" message was his commission all along—from that day in 1920 that he believed Galatians 2:20. Building W.E.C.—as great as it was—was really secondary to fully building the believer in Christ. Movements will pass. Missionary groups will pass. Organizations will pass. Civilizations will pass, but the truth of Christ and the *full* work of His cross—its meaning and reality for mankind—will never pass away!

~~~~~~

My heartfelt thanks to...Linda Bunting for your willingness to help in any way and for your wisdom at many turns in this endeavor—especially for convincing me not to put myself under an unreasonable time frame for it's completion...Judy Dunn for being available over the years and especially in the final push as you worked side by side with me in typing, proofreading, formatting, advising me from an executive secretary point of view and making it "your" book also (without you I could have never finished this project)...Doug Eblen and Sam Dunn for each of you following the leading of the Spirit to call me and suggest what has become the book's title, Knight of Faith...John Bunting for always upholding and encouraging me with your sure conviction that this book would have a mighty impact upon the body of Christ...Harriet Wearren, Carol Lingard, Bette and Tony Ketcham, Marian and Ray Sandbek, Judy East, Deanna Winter, Liz Lowrance, Linda Hagman, and John Collings for your advice, typing and proof reading...Darlene Breed for your professional editing skills led by the wisdom of the Holy Spirit... my husband, Gary, and my daughter, Kim, for your willing and ready hearts to assist me in what ever way you could and your interest in my progress. You are God's greatest gifts...and finally, to the man who provided me with such rich material as you went about your everyday life of love for your Lord Jesus Christ, Norman Percy Grubb.

As you read Norman's letters my prayer is that you will read them with your "heart," feel as though he has written to you *and* let anything that seems foreign to your understanding be sorted out by the Holy Spirit. The letters were chosen to express Norman's theology, background, personality, care and concern—revealing his Scriptural approach to life, yet showing his warmth, humor and humanity. I have included a broad range of letters from deep theological essays to simple love-touches and practical exchanges of information. You will find surprising and challenging thoughts that take you beyond the norm and transport you to a different dimension. May you come to know, love and appreciate, or maybe fondly remember, Norman Grubb—this remarkable container and expressor of Christ—as I did. Blessings...

"There is an element in the gospel of Christ
so disturbing
that the world will forever reject it,
but never forget it;
and the Church will forever waiver between
patronage and persecution.
Yours is the present,
for the world will ridicule or crucify us;
but I think the future is ours."

"The Gold Cord" ......
Brother A. Vida Schudder

ଓ ଶ

BELIEFS

As you can imagine Norman repeatedly urging me to believe Col. 1:27 "Christ in you, the hope of glory." When it dawned on me, it was a sort of second conversion.

Dr. Wallace Haines International Christian Leadership

~~~

I never can thank God enough for what his life meant to me from the first time I sat under his ministry to the ministry of his last few years. I considered what God showed him is what the evangelical world badly needs to experience.

John Lewis 'SOON Gospel Literature Worldwide

~~~

Your book, "God Unlimited" ...expresses so well what I have always believed within, but never found elsewhere in print.

Brigadier in the Salvation Army

~~~

Then I remembered some of the things you said and they began to apply to ME, and I realized what you meant by TRUNK-MINDED INSTEAD OF BRANCH-MINDED, and somehow, I began to relax and be a SPONTANEOUS ME.

ഇ ൞

Ibambi. March 13, 1950

My Dear Ray;

How I wish I could drop over and sit and yarn with you on the things of the Spirit. As I often told you, you were always such a help and stimulus, because you have the gift of digging out spiritual truth. So often we just spend so much time talking of the work of the Lord, but not so much on Himself and His ways with us; but that was your interest and you sort of turned on the tap in me! That has moved me to sit down and knock this off this morning, before the day's meetings start. We have so often talked of "Christ in me", and God has been leading me on. I had a fuller glimpse than ever before, when down with my beloved friend, Rees Howells at Swansea College, who has just gone to be with the Lord, of the Person Himself living in me. I saw Him, the Spirit, not a power or influence, and not someone who does something to me and changes or sanctifies me, but The Person in Himself come to show me where I am for ever, on the Cross and in the tomb of Jesus, and that He has come for ever to live His own life in me. He is the One who thinks in my mind, sees thru my eyes, wills in my will, loves in my heart, and acts thru my body. This is old truth (as all truth is, hidden from ages and generations, but now made manifest!), but it came, He came in yet more living reality in me. It seems to me that in our earlier experiences He is occupied in revealing to our fallen selves what Jesus is to us in justification and sanctification; He removes my guilt, He purifies my heart, He gives me power; but it is still me, my, mine! But then He comes to show us that the true meaning of our original creation, and our new creation is not I, but Christ. It is a mystery, a paradox, because we never thru all eternity lose our personality, as the Buddhists erroneously say, we are always conscious selves, yet we voluntarily and eternally lose ourselves in His allness; Christ our life, Christ all and in all.

I saw this yet more fully two weeks back when I picked up Madam Guyon's book, "Spiritual Torrents" on one of our stations. There she speaks of the soul being so "lost" in God, that it is consciously "deified" in other words it loses consciousness of itself and only sees Christ in place of self, living, thinking, acting as He pleases, yet it is really thru us. It is not we wanting to feel Him, or know Him, or love Him; that is still a self wanting something; it is just He, that's all. We lose sense of ourselves. He IS, that the one entire truth; all else, even my very self-existence, might be false (although of course it isn't), but He IS. And so I just recognize HIM living and working in place of me. It is beyond feeling or desire; it is just HE, everything is just He within and without; for I went on to glimpse the greater truth than Christ in me or Christ my life, which is I in Christ and all in Christ. I saw that Jesus put that first when He said, "Abide in Me and I in you", not the other way around, and I begin to have my eyes dimly opened to all the mass of emphasis in scripture (Ephesians, for instance, on 'in Him"). I see that all is in Him, always. All people (Acts 17:28); all things, for by Him they consist (stand together) (Col. 1:17); all circumstances, for He is the beginning and the end. And above all, His body is in Him, for they are the fullness of Him that fills all in all; and finally God's preordained plan is that all things are to be gathered together in one in Him. So, just as I see only Him in me, not me at all, not really even Him in me, but just Him Himself shining thru, so I see Him only everywhere. All circumstances are He; He is our circumstances. We are no longer blindly stumbling along in a place called the world, we are in Him, and all the world is in Him, even the devil functions in Him and in the end works out His purpose and glory, (Acts 2:23, 4:27-28); so we see devilish works (which are true enough), or devilish people, but God, crucified still, perverted still in His creation, but God working in all, pleading, convicting, working in all men and things, until Rom. 8.19-24 and Rev. 21:1 are fulfilled. Therefore life and death and suffering and all things are in Him, Rom. 8: 35-39. We enter into the prayer of Paul in Eph. 3: 16-19, for an enlarged comprehension thru the indwelling Christ ministered to us by the Spirit (16, 17), of the universal Christ, height, length, breadth, depth. Nothing moves us, for all is His love, Himself, all, we cannot be outside it, there is only one true realm of living - "in Christ". And we gradually learn to see Him only in all things. And in all people, especially of course in His own body. What a time I find it takes to see and reverence Him only in my brothers and sisters, and to recognize that their individual characteristics are the variegated garments of the One Spirit, and their lacks (to my critical eyes, which are only really a burden to me because they respond to the same lacks in me) are in His gracious ever-transforming hands and He is hard at work on them, as He is on those in me, and my faith in Him in them, not my unbelieving criticism, is the contribution He would make thru me to their transformation.

And that brings me to one point about which you have often argued with me, and I need to climb down! About faith. I see you are right that, on the above basis of Christ being ALL in me, the faith in me is His faith

(Gal. 2:20). It is His believing in Himself operating within me, and that makes it easy to believe, because it is not my believing, but His in me.

I must stop, as I have already been interrupted. God has broken through again with a stream of souls. Just thought I would share these thoughts and light with you all.

Norman Grubb

~~~

June 22, 1956

Dear Miss Watson:

Thank you for your long letter just arrived. I am so glad you felt free to unburden your heart so fully.

Of course you are forgiven and cleansed- I John 1:9, and Hebrews 9:14. That old liar, the accuser of the brethren, is getting at you with his false condemnation. You only have to stand square to the Word, where it says that those who repent, confess and have faith in the cleansing Blood are in the sight of God as those who have never sinned. He forgets, so we are entitled to forget also. Praise Him. Of course do not let the devil stop you using your remaining years to the full in ministry and witness. That's exactly why he accuses you. He cannot stop your loving Father forgiving and accepting you, but he can stifle your witness. That verse I John 3:20 is good. Satan can disturb our hearts with false condemnation, but God is greater than our disturbed hearts. He knows the truth of our repentance and faith. He knows the fact of the atonement in Christ, so we are not to be influenced by our falsely disturbed hearts, but by our simple faith in His declared Word.

The unforgivable sin is distinctly said to be sin against the Holy Ghost. That is not some outward sin committed partly in ignorance (Paul said he obtained mercy because he sinned in ignorance I Tim. 1:13); that is the deliberate refusal by the heart to accept conviction of sin, until finally our consciences are seared with a hot iron, and we cannot feel conviction. The very fact that you do feel it is conclusive evidence that it is not that sin. We see what that sin is also in Hebrews 10:29 when we are told of those who tread the Son of God underfoot and count the Blood an unholy thing, and crucify Him afresh (Heb. 6:6) and put Him to open shame. Now that is open and deliberate contempt for Christ and His Blood, denial of Him, and open ridicule of Him. Such things have been a thousand miles from your attitude.

I think you have done right to make open as well as private confession and of course you have long put this thing away out of your life. If yours was the unforgivable sin, we are about all in the same box, because we have all done things since we were saved of which we are ashamed.

Finally, I think one can always silence the devil by casting one's self without reserve upon the mercies of God. Don't fear hell or judgement, but only fear less you don't trust Him. Say to Him that anyhow you will trust and love and follow Him, even if He did cast you out. The new heart does not love Jesus and Heaven for its own benefit, but just loves Jesus and glorifies Him, even though He sent us to Hell - as God did send His own Son for our sakes. "Though He slay me, yet will I trust Him."

Be free to write again, and I will be glad to answer if this still does not meet your deep need.

Sincerely yours in Christ,

Norman Grubb

~~~

August 7, 1956

My dear Joan,

Many thanks for yours just received. I am answering at once because I shall be on the move with conferences until early September, and so far as I know at present, will be sailing September 14. Of course I shall be coming through and spending at least a day with you. I trace a little wobble in you in your concern about my various theories and my extreme views! Who has been getting at you? You ought to know me well enough by now to know that I hold a host of weird things, but I am not such a fool by God's grace as to spoil a testimony on the vital things that do matter by dragging in a lesser point of controversy where I know it would divert attention. So you can still get me in at your old St. Clements!

Don't be too alarmed about bits of news you hear about us in U.S.A., God is doing a wonderful and unifying work. There are problems but that is what we exist for, to see God pull us out of hot water. I will tell you all about it on our next 3:00 A.M. conference!

Warmest love to you both, you know how much your love and friendship have meant to me through the years. Excuse this short line.

Ever your old friend,

Norman Grubb

~~~

27th November, 1956

Dear Mrs. Hadley,

I suppose I would call myself a "free-lance" in theology, not being attached to any particular school of doctrine, or denomination, whether Calvinist or Armenian. Our WEC is strictly interdenominational, and contains folks all the way from the Pentecostals and Holiness to the Baptists and Episcopalians. If you care to get it from a Christian bookstore my last book, "The Liberating Secret" goes pretty thoroughly into the light on God's Word, as He has given me to see it.

Now in answer to your question, the Scripture makes clear that what Christ did once in Calvary and the Resurrection, He did once for all. In that sense all who receive Him are justified, sanctified, and perfected for ever. That is why I say that it is not so much a "second work of grace", but a fuller recognition and acceptance in mind and heart of what we are in Him and He in us. We may call it a "second blessing" if we like, though it is not a Scriptural term. It is "second" only in the sense that usually we see Christ as the remedy for our sins first - Rom.1:5, and then for sin and enslaved self second, Rom.6:8, and what we recognize and receive is born witness to by the Spirit. Thus no born-again person really has two natures. That is impossible, but he may not have recognized and entered into the liberating experience of what he has become in Christ.

But you use several expressions which are not exactly Scriptural, such as "old man of sin", "eradication of every root of sin". Probably we mean the same, but never having been brought up in any special school of teaching, I have learned to soak myself in what seems to me to be the most exact Scriptural wording and Scriptural emphasis – most perfectly given in those Roman chapters, and in parts of Galatians and Colossians.

As to your final question on the saint losing his salvation. Yes, I think there are Scriptures which warn us of that possibility. But there are also Scriptures which emphasize our eternal security in Christ.

6

Therefore I believe we should hold both. I don't think the Scripture is meant to be logical to the finite mind. Truth is dialectical. To our finite reason we can only see the thesis and antithesis of everything; we are still in the realm of duality, the Tree of Knowledge of good and evil. The final synthesis is in the invisible, in the resurrected Jesus, where Truth, subjective and objective, is in its final form still beyond our reach.

I wish we could meet for a talk, but anyhow we meet in Jesus Himself. The Person is the place of unity where often our interpretations of our relationship to that glorious Person may differ, and anyhow is never more than the partial truth.

Perhaps if I come your way, we can meet for fellowship. I greatly appreciate the fellowship with you all.

Norman Grubb

~~~

October 1, 1958

Dear Constance:

I was very glad to hear from you again. You will be surprised at the rapidity of my reply, but the first reason is that I leave in two days for a month's tour in the Mid-West, and secondly that your honesty challenges me to write.

God will bring you through, just because you are in the light with God and man. Hypocrisy is the one thing that Jesus so utterly condemned, and I believe you are honest to all the light you have. So thank God for that.

God has got to work on in you, until He can finally make you accept the fact that you have been crucified with Christ. You see your attitude to God and Christ is still spiritual selfishness, and that is why you are in the dark. The point to you is not how much you fail and grieve Him, but how much He has failed and grieved you! You speak of having been so much "in love with Christ that it is as though I had lost a lover". But true love is selfless. It is not considering what it gets out of its love-bond, but what it gives. The love of Christ is selfless, and in so far as His love is shed abroad in your heart, your only concern will be how much you can please Him. If He appears to fail you or let you down that does not affect your love for Him, or trust in Him, if it is the pure love of the Spirit flowing in your heart towards Him. You simply love Him for what He is, no matter what happens to you.

7

Your love for Christ has had self in it. Your disillusionment with the world made you turn to Him and love Him more that the world; but it was still selfish love, because Christ was more to <u>you</u> than the world. But Christ living in us means a love for God (Christ loving Christ!) in which all that matters is what I am to Him, not what He is to me. And it is those self-roots that God has to dig down and root out of all of us. That is why He is taken you this drastic and painful way: to expose the hidden subtlety of self-love and to bring you to the place where at last you recognize that the new life means that you have died out to yourself in Christ's death, and Christ alone is your new self, your new love in this new life.

That is the purity of God's own love, though it may not appear so to you at the moment. It is purely selfless. It is perfect love towards you, He only caring for your own interests, and doing what is the very best for you; and that very best and highest is to take you the thorny pathway on which self dies to itself.

In this new life, it is not a matter of how much you feel of the Presence of God, how much assurance, etc., you have. You just disappear so far as responding to your own reaction is concerned. You lose yourself in the basic facts that the real self in you is the perfect Christ. You just "see Him" with the eye of faith, though you may feel nothing.

Constance, God will bring you there. I say it again, because I know that you are being honest with yourself, with Him, and with me. Keep opening your heart. I appreciate it, and it stimulates me to answer it. So I shall look forward to hearing again.

My love to you,

Your friend and brother in Christ,

Norman Grubb

~~~

November 5, 1958

My dear Pamela;

I got back two days ago from my month's tour, to find your two interesting letters. Of course you are "coming through" with God. He has a strong hand of love and has a tight hold of you, despite your wriggles! I see you, with the eye of faith, not as you appear to be to yourself with your inner struggles, but as you actually are in spiritual fact, the dwelling place of the living God, through the Eternal efficacy of the precious blood.

Thank God for the very signs in your own letter of a more conscious return to Him. You are still on the wrong foot, and that foot is your reactions, your self. That is what the Bible calls the soul (self) life in contrast to the Spirit life, and the Bible tells us that we have to learn to discern between the two. (Heb. 4:12); and I don't believe we can learn in any way except the painful one. We all have to go through it in some way or other; I did for several years. At last we cross over our Jordan, and forever discover that my true new Self is not I at all, but Christ in me; and I learn to live by His reactions in me in place of my own. He is pure love and a pure lover of the world, His enemies; and when He lives His life in us, He can take us any way in self-sacrifice for a world of people eternally empty until they find Him. In this way, your concern for the way you think God may have treated you, or your examination of your own feelings and attitudes towards Him, will be sunk, immersed, drowned in God's-other-love flowing through you.

Actually this is not a gradual faith, but a continually repeated act of obedience. That is to say, you deliberately reckon on the fact that Christ Himself is your real Self within, and you meet all the stirrings of your self-reactions by replacing them with this act of faith. Then what you continually practice becomes a habit.

Yes, I think that there was that mixture of self-pleasing in your seeking to please God, and that is what God is burning out of you by your experiences. We all have it at the start, and our human love one to the other, man for woman, etc., is riddled with it. The proof is that you have any feeling of bitterness for the way you think God has treated you. Pure love just loves God- period. However, He appears to "behave", it makes no difference to pure love.

Now I think that's the lot this time, but keep writing. It is helpful and stimulating to talk over these ways of the Spirit. My love to you in Christ,

Affectionately your friend,

Norman Grubb

~~~

November 7, 1958

My dear Mike and Sue;

It was good of you to stay over so that we could have a time together. I wish it could have been longer in which we could have gone still deeper into our united commission from its different angles, and unlocked our hearts still more to each other.

This morning I came across what I think is a remarkable article from "Christianity Today" - the most thoughtful religious paper put out over here. Its title, "The Christian and Atomic Crisis", won't attract you particularly, but the essence of the article is tremendous. Its point is whether the Christian message is the end in itself, or whether it is a convenient means for giving the world its ideal social ethic. I have never seen the subject treated in so masterful a fashion.

You see, it seems to me that you are much more daring adventurers of faith, because you are taking a dive right into the center of world problems in your activities, but at the same time you are "living dangerously". All that the humanist wants is to take advantage of high religious standards to produce a convenient social ethic, as this article points out. To him the relationship of man to God is irrelevant: only that of man to man matters. Now I know that you have your roots right down in Christ as the only answer in this world and the next, and that in the final analysis personal commitment to Christ and the direct will of God work out in the individual and the world is the only reason for the existence of the human race. So I think you have a tight rope walk in using the Christian ideals to meet human problems, and yet at the same time not to slip down to the delusive level of substituting human betterment for the Lordship of Christ.

I believe that servants of Christ in your situation can do a thousand times more than we with our limited outreach. You reach thousands who have only the skimpiest idea of or who are antagonistic to vital Christianity. It is never easy to remain loyal to Christ Himself as man's Saviour, and there is always a cross in doing so, and our time together stimulates me to hold you to the highest in prayer. You are the real pioneers!

Don't bother to answer this, but if you can spare a quarter of an hour, read the article through.

Much love to you both, and thank you ever so much for coming to see us,

Ever yours affectionately,

Norman

~~~

December 13, 1958

My dear Elizabeth,

Thank you for your letter. You say many interesting things in it as usual.

Yes, we have one mind and heart in our mutual desire to go to the bottom of things. I have always been like that. I have never been satisfied with a superficial explanation. I believe we ought to have an informed faith, and that is what the Bible has given us. I went through a year of intellectual darkness as I pursued my investigations, even after I was Secretary of the W.E.C., and it seemed to me that there was no proof of the existence of God. I was in a strange condition of loving and having loved for years One of whom I wasn't sure He existed!! I came back, as one always does, to a faith which has foundations which have never been shaken since. That was about 1933. Outside the Bible, I have never found anything to satisfy me deeply except some of the writings of the mystics, especially those with a more philosophical as well as devotional approach, such as the master of them all, Jacob Boehme. I have drunk deeply from him and others. As a consequence, one is always seeing more light; and before I finish one book, I am dissatisfied with it, and have to write another to expound missing points in the previous one! So I am hoping around Christmas to do some more writing.

You raise a deeply interesting point about the consciousness of power for service. To my mind, the key in all our relationships with Christ is a clear differentiation between soul and spirit. In the soul life we have our emotional reactions which are variable. The Spirit is just ourselves and Himself, one Spirit. Here we just <u>are</u>, no matter what we may see or feel. Therefore, I don't think that a "consciousness" of full power is anything to do with the fact of full power. I don't think we ever come to full rest in Jesus until there has been a final divorce in our understanding between soul-reactions and spirit-facts. I "saw" the Holy Spirit as the executive of the Trinity as I fellowshipped with my beloved friend, Rees Howells. I just saw Him in operation, leading and using him, and I "saw" that He was the same in me, and had been through the years, but now I recognized Him in a completer sense. Our emotions will always bother us, because we are emotional creatures. Our emotions subservient to the Spirit are the channel by which we have a Christ-consciousness, peace, joy, etc. But because we so respond to the emotion, and so like to be emotionally satisfied, when we meet with those who can give us an emotionally charged testimony to the power of God in their lives, such for instance those who have the gift of tongues, there is something in us that desires the same emotional completion as they have had. At least I find that. But I have learned that I am not to be moved. He is in me "mighty in me toward the Gentiles", and there I stand. If you ask why we feel powerless in the face of an evil force, I say again that that is a question of feeling. I have no business even to feel the evil force, but rather to recognize my union with an enthroned Christ "far above all". I stand in Him, and affirm Him, and declare His victory, whether I see an immediate change or not. I am not to be influenced by what I see in the outward eye, but with the fact of a Christ in operation by faith. I wish we could meet and talk a little further on that!

How helpful and interesting our correspondence has been all these months, and I always enjoy getting a letter from you, and get something vital from it.

Affectionately yours in Christ,

Norman Grubb

~~~

June 2, 1960

Dear Standford,

How good to hear from you, and such a thorough heart out pouring too. I'm answering at once, as I'm on the move in two days for about a month, and don't want to leave this unanswered.

Of course I also agree with Bro Bakht Singh on NT church principles, and Hay's book is good, except for his unnecessary attack on the Pentecostals. But I also must admit that there are not many signs in our Western countries of God's seal being vigorously upon groups such as you mention. They tend to be self enclosed, instead of remembering that a church exists for the unchurched. I find many splendid house groups here, but nearly all meet weekly for sharing and inspiration, but all go back to own denoms for weekend witness and worship. Maybe that's God's pattern because we have to say that he does seal His word in thousands of churches which we may not think conform to the pattern of NT church order. I would advise you to go without pressure as far as God seals. Wonderful if you just gather with others for free fellowship. You <u>are</u> the church. I don't believe the NT church is fixed local assemblies, meeting at set times "going to church", with membership,

12

pastor, etc. The church is the invincible body everywhere, and when a few meet with no organized setup—that is the church.

My love to you, and glad to hear from you.

Ever yours,

Norman

~~~

June 16, 1960

Dear Mrs. Hopper,

I am glad you have written and opened your heart again on these problems. Your root trouble is that you have not believed God's Word in which it says that when Christ died, you did die with Him- according to Romans 6, for instance- not that you have to die sometime or other, but that you did die then.

But you will say to me, why then does the old self-life apparently so often crop up again. The Bible answer is that when you died with Christ, it was not your self-life which died. It was the spirit of self-centeredness, which is Satan himself, who dwells in all of us from our natural birth. In Christ we died to that spirit controlling us. In Christ again we have risen, our same selves, but now with a new Person, a new Spirit dwelling in us, the Spirit of Christ, the spirit of self-giving.

Our self-life is always there, that is just our human selves. What matters is who is controlling and motivating it. In the old life it was the satanic spirit. In the new it is the Holy Spirit.

Being real humans and therefore with all our appetites and faculties open to any solicitation, when we were in the old life, we were open to appeals from the Spirit of God through the Bible, preaching, ethics, etc. We made occasional responses by prayer or good resolutions. It was not really we; it was a kind of surface response. We were really controlled by the wrong spirit.

Now in the new life, we are equally open to all forms of solicitation, and the anti-Christ selfish world and Satan tempt us to use our appetites and faculties in a wrong way, and sometimes we respond and sin. That does not mean that Satan has taken us over again, but we made a temporary response and have to come back to be cleansed. Basically, we remained with Christ living in us.

When you have taken this position by faith, then you learn to see the great fact of Christ living in you and you joined to Him, branch

13

to vine. You do not look at yourself, but at Him; when you do turn away from Him and follow temptation into sin, then you come back in repentance and faith, get cleansed, and walk on with Him.

So I suggest that if you understand this and see it in the Word, you get before God; once for all affirm that you did die in Christ and that is not to be questioned again; and that you now begin to walk as risen with Him, in whom He lives.

Write me again and tell me how God speaks to you about this.

Sincerely yours in Christ,

Norman

~~~

June 28, 1960

My dear Irv,

I shall need to get some fellowship with you on an awkward spot that has arisen, and yet I don't want to make it more awkward than I have to.

You know I am basically a "fundamentalist" (as I believe you are and Bruce, etc.), and I've never moved an inch since my student days from accepting the Bible as the Word of God, even though I'll admit points I cannot explain, and that one cannot always say which is symbol and which reality. Because I so profoundly believe that a Christian faith which is not finally anchored on the authority of the written word gradually slips off into error and heresy, I was led in my college days to found the movement which is now known world-wide as I.V.F. (I.V.C.F. over here), although it had to mean an open separation from the Student Christian Movement, and has remained so ever since. For the same reasons, and with the same convictions, I wholeheartedly spent my whole life in WEC activities.

However, that has not meant that I believe that the correct proclamation of the Gospel is to wave the Bible in people's faces, and demand that they believe every word of it. I believe in the Christ of the Bible as the true Gospel, and in presenting Him alone as Way, Truth and Life; and I delight in fellowship with all who have Him as their center, without necessarily asking and demanding that they cross every T as I do concerning the scriptures. It is for that reason that I have loved, and do love FAW with all my heart, and propagate it everywhere.

But I do recognize the risk that someone in the ranks of the movement which does not demand an orthodox doctrinal stand, may come out with something which really cuts across the plain teachings of the scriptures and then the fat is in the fire! I had an example of that in my first CFO camp last year, when I had to speak out in protest against a forthright address on Universalism—and I received no further CFO invitations since!

Now all this leads up to an alarm signal when one of our workers this week brought me the July issue of Eternity, and in it a long review by Barnhouse of Sam's latest book on the Holy Spirit. (I'll be glad if you can get hold of a copy and read it for yourself). Barnhouse on the whole is very positive and approving of a lot of the book, but he does show plainly serious proofs of Sam's wanderings from scriptural foundation particularly where he comes right out with the inspiration of the Spirit coming through Hindu, Moslem "prophets", etc., as much as thru Christ and the Bible. Now you know that no Evangelical missionary would ever accept that. It is the heresy of heresies to us! It was pointed out to my co-worker by her Presb. Ministers wife, who with her husband is very bitten by FAW and loves the mag. She was shocked to see this review - and that Norman Grubb could be linked with the author of a book like that!! There was also a remark in the book on Evangelicals "consigning millions to hell" which has the same un-scriptural flavor about it.

Now I love Sam, and have the deepest respect for him as one who has been used far, far beyond me in winning men to Christ; and I know that his emphasis is the Holy Spirit and experience, and not theology and the Bible. But you see it is difficult when statements which run clean counter to the Bible are put in print by one of the FAW leaders, and the book pushed by FAW.

(I have learned, by having my fingers burned, to be much more careful what I print in a book than what I say on the platform!)

So what do we do? It would be the utmost tragedy if a rift came in FAW between "conservatives" and "liberals". How much we need each other. FAW manifests Christ in wonderful love and fellowship, we conservatives need you, and at the same time may make our contribution in faithfulness to foundations. We need each other! But the position does become difficult when something like this happens. We are already under some fire for "reaching out" beyond normal conservative circles, and I've rejoiced with all my heart to be welcomed at all by such as FAW and ICL, and I've taken no notice of questionings (which have not been serious incidentally, mainly because the FAW mag has such a glorious positive ring about it); but such a thing as this by Barnhouse in print could make the situation more serious. Of course I get out of it at present by saying that Sam (just as myself) is not a member of FAW staff, and therefore FAW are not responsible.

Well, Irv, you know how I love you and Bruce and all, and how totally one I am with you, so I just thought I'd write you this personally, and may be follow it later by some personal fellowship with you about it. Please don't think that I'm making some public fuss about this, or taking it further, but I thought I ought to open my heart and mind to you on it.

God will show the right way.

Ever yours,

Norman

~~~

My dear Mrs. Malone:

It is a great encouragement and refreshment to get your letter. Of course, it always spurs me on when I hear directly, as from you, of those who have found "the liberating secret." I don't find reason to change what I have sought to share in those books (really remarkable that you have read all of them). Yet, as you know, it does not fit with the general teaching. I do not find it necessary when seeking to share this, to use definite terms like "the two natures," which are anyhow not in the bible, and yet have become such fixed doctrinal definitions for so many, that you immediately raise a barrier if you call them in question. I don't find it necessary to make negative attacks on any viewpoint or conviction; but rather to present positively what I see to be the truth of this union life, and to bring some of the many Scriptures there are to bring witness to it. I find by this means that the Holy Spirit kind of circumvents peoples' doctrinal prejudices, gets round behind them as it were, and before folks know where they are, the walls of prejudice are down, and the walk on the open road has started! Everywhere in this country there are people in churches, house meetings, etc., eager to catch at this secret, and many who have found the liberation you are rejoicing in. In the main I find the trouble is in the misunderstanding of the human self, and of course that traces right back to the concept of us being two-nature. The beautiful truth, as you say, of us being containers of either one God or the other, and never both, is the key to liberation. For such long years folks have down-graded themselves, and you say yourself you are only just beginning to rise up to the self-acceptance and self-appreciation level. But thank God, many do rise up, and cast off the old garments, often hardly realizing what they have cast off! Of course, I do believe that with thousands of God's people our hearts are in advance of our heads, and we can live on levels of victory which we could not adequately explain to others, or explain erroneously. So I hope you will go ahead not combating any mistaken ideas, but by-passing them and swallowing them up by sharing the liberating truth which is yours now in experience, and with the Scriptural backgrounds you can give for it.

I'm not surprised that you've come the long way into this. That is no mistake. I'm sure we have to have a healthy dose of frustrated self before we can be conditioned for finding the allness of the Divine Self – He all in all – then the paradox of the released human self, in the terms so perfectly outlined for us in the three-fold process of Gal. 2:20.

So thank you again for writing. As you get clarification on the third level – the Father level of I John 2 – the ascended life, the glory of our own liberation will move into the background, as we enter into the full meaning of the activities of the liberated self as God's authorative and redeeming agent. I am thinking, writing and talking more on that level these days.

My love in Christ to you, and I will always be glad to hear further from you and talk these things over further.

Ever in Christ,

Norman Grubb

~~~

Sept.10.60

My dear Marguerite,

I only wrote and sealed the envelope of a letter to you last night (not yet posted), but will not re-open, just simply add this. Thank you for your wonderful letter. I don't know whether it was the Spirit or flesh, but I do get a surge of thankfulness and encouragement when someone like yourself passes on that there has been blessing – although of course I know the only "gold, silver or precious stones" in a thing only so far as GOD HIMSELF did the speaking.

I am distressed at the further news of your letter that Lon is thinking of contesting the lawyer in Fran's estate. The Lord's servants have <u>no</u> business meddling with the world's finances, as if an odd few hundred dollars were anything to God! We drag God and faith in the

17

dust by such actions. And I am <u>ashamed</u> that any of us should have presumed to try and involve Sam in it. I don't wonder he turned it down. But I blush. If any man takes thy coat, give him thy cloak also. We preach the Sermon on the Mount to peoples of distant lands, but how do we carry it out at home? No indeed. Let us be deeply thankful that God led Fran to give these sums to His work. God loves that lawyer, and has to shew him, as He has us, that covetousness is darkness and death. We are not here to shew him we are covetous also, but that God gave His Son for those who defrauded Him. But thank you for telling me.

Much love and many thanks,

Norman

~~~

April 26, 1963

My dear Beverly;

I am so glad you have begun to share with me some of your heart and life experiences. I only wish we could talk face to face. I would judge that you were troubled by a real affection for that psychiatrist. I really wish you had given me some of the "many details" which were hurtful at that time and you think would sound foolish – but they would not! They are the stuff of life. I wonder if you have had real fundamental battles on the line of the affections and sex. They are not things to hide up. God made us all like that, and there is nothing stronger in us. We all have our own natural physical desires on this line, which are also God-given, and it is no easy thing when God has not given the normal outlet of marriage; and sometimes there is real guilt hidden away in lives when there has been battle and failure on these lines, which we have all had at times in our lives. I know women who have felt free to treat me like a father and open their hearts to me who have had years of guilt through defeat in these ways (and men even more so of course) and to share with some one is a step in the right direction.

God is bringing you to your only resting-place – God. Don't be foolish enough to listen to fears. You may feel them, that is quite natural, but you say to yourself, No indeed. I don't accept fears about trusting myself wholly to God. Is there something special again that makes you fear to give yourself completely. Be honest on this, both with yourself, with God, and with me. In GOD ONLY is your resting-place, accepting what you are NOW, and where you are, as He living His life in

His own way in you. Just dare to believe that – He united to you – and praise Him.

Now write again soon. You can write as privately as you like to me. God is taking you thru to a large place.

My love in Christ,

Norman Grubb

Remember you are always wholly in this Lamb. He has joined Himself to you and you to Him, so just dare to recognize this. Don't "give yourself" to Him, just recognize that He has you whether you like it or not!

~~~

Sacramento, Calif.
March 26, 1965

Helen my dear,

So you hit the spot with your fundamentalist friends! There again, there is a true fundamental foundation on which we are all built and from which we don't move, the "rock which follows us" into whatever queer alleyways we wander; <u>but</u> Christ has become the Fundamental Fact, and the Bible fundamental in revealing Him. But to find Him thru the letter is a breaking open of the shell to get at the kernel, and the acid test is whether we are "shell" people who centre our attention on the wording and our pet interpretation of it, or "kernel" people whose interest is the Living Person and our interpretations of the Uninterpretable Person are open to infinite variations within the guidelines of the Scriptures.

Thank God, there are many "fundamentalists" who are reaching out to these wider areas, though, like ourselves, remaining unaltered fundamentalists!

I love you and Freed and your precious group and my heart was bound with yours. Meanwhile I have been with some more priceless groups or individuals, and I have told each about you. I have got to link us all up!!

Ever lovingly, both to you and all of you. I am thrilled God brought us into each other's lives.

Norman

~~~

19

4.9.1965

My Dear Leslie;

Finally, your leap, not into theology, but into faith! I greatly like
your linking all of God's callings to Jesus to faith exercised by Him as a
human. I never have had any doubt in my mind, and have often talked
that way, that every phase of His affirmations of his Sonship, of Him
being the fulfillment of God's Word through the prophets, of His death,
resurrection and finally ascension, were all exactly the same, leaps of
faith as we make. It is only this that makes it thrilling and real to us,
and still inspires us to follow along. I am impressed that in His Last
Supper talk, John 14:17, He makes no reference to His resurrection. He
was "through" on that. But all His thought is around the coming of the
same Person into the disciples as was in Him. This is the product of the
ascension, and the priesthood of Melchisedek. And He now fulfills this
priesthood, not only in us, but by us to others. We share that priesthood
- that is Hebrews 11. But I also like your thought, quite original to me
that it was Melch who taught faith to Abraham or at least in its deep
implications. Good. Spread this quality of faith abroad.

Answer my questions. Much love.

Ever yours,

Rubi

~~~

January 14, 1966

Dear Bill

Thank you for yours today.

You are a cautious bird! When we talk together, I have no idea what
"registers" and what doesn't! It would greatly interest me to know.
Maybe you can't exactly say at the time, "This isn't registering, it's still
phony to me." And I can hardly expect you to spare time to write me
later what has registered. But it would be interesting. Though I'm wholly
with you in there being a time-lag to find out what is of N.P.G. and
what of God. Actually, all truth we get is through others (the Bible was
written by men), but it becomes ours as it registers with us, and I don't
go about saying or writing that I got this from so and so (except for
Bible quotes) I just give it out as my own because it has become my own.
God knows where the credit really goes to someone else.

No more now, but shall be hoping to hear from you.

Ever yours,

Norman

~~~

Jan.25.66

My dear Bill,

What a corker, but full of interest. This can only be a line, as I leave tomorrow morning.

I am first of all interested in Carol's own definition of what God has given her. I see she does not call tongues the proof of the baptism. But actually what she has got thru tongues so outweighs - everything else that she really means and teaches that without "it", you are not really "there". Now this is real to her, and dynamic, and we must each be ourselves in the Spirit; so I think the only thing at present is to recognize that this is the heart of her ministry. I am sure God blesses her to many, and will do so; yet we have also to regard it as a limitation for the many of us who have not gone this way. We are bound, I think, to find our true levels of fellowship elsewhere.

In answer to your question which takes some answering. I believe the Scripture can only be taken as a whole. If tongues was the essential, it was bound to be a major subject in the epistles – but is hardly mentioned. ALL is CHRIST. Yet tongues is there from Pentecost onward, is of God, is a gift AND often may be the evidence of our inner union as at Pentecost. Therefore I respect all who have that gift, consider them as having a gift beyond myself, but will not confuse it with the reality of the union. Of course the Mark 16 passage is questionable on the authenticity of that whole passage (as you know). But apart from that, it cannot make tongues as essential, or taking up serpents would also be!

I go a little farther than you on the "second blessing". I believe it is rare for anyone to have assurance and inner witness of the union at regeneration; therefore for most there is a "second blessing" when there is the specific faith for the union (though it has been a fact since regeneration) and the witness attesting it.

I don't have much to say about "demons". It seems to me any resistance to the Spirit can be called demonic. I believe some have a real ministry in casting out (and discerning) demons. Not up my street.

I still hope I shall get up to Boston (and thus see you) in early May. I always have the Boston "flock" on my heart. Keep in touch with them – for me!

Write again soon. Love to Anne

ever lovingly,

Norman

~~~

</div>

<div align="right">

Aug. 26.67

</div>

Dear Bill,

TREMENDOUS. Yours came yesterday. I am wholly with you that this is of God. I might have questioned it if you were just starting this out in the blue just on theory; but the strong point is that you have proved that you are being given a ministry of the Spirit, so you have all the authority of facts. I wonder in a way, if I may say so daringly, God is giving it to you to kind of pick up the torch from me in my old age, and carry it to a practical completion in hundreds of lives, where I more just throw out the union fact for any to pick up who wish to.

I like the name "Discovery" because it is not too ambitious, boastful, "we've got it" style of thing. I think we have to be very careful from the beginning. There is no new truth. We bring no new thing. We are simply given to underline certain aspects of the total life in God. In a way it will be better to disguise it (as your title does). You won't get to first base if you give any of God's people anywhere the idea that this is something extra special which the church of Christ has missed and it is now revealed to us. God forbid! It can best just be called some common title like "the victorious life", "the full life in Christ as we see it", or some such. And you will have carefully to avoid giving the impression of being something disruptive like "tongues", and keep off the grass of treading on pet clichés like "two natures" or eternal security, etc.

And we're not out to form any kind of new "sect", but just to exist to shew people the implications of the Union Life, as we see it (for we all only " know in part".)

<div align="center">

Love to you both, and praise,

Norman

~~~

22

November 8, 1967

Dearest Marian:

Thank you ever so much for calling and now for the enclosure from "Christianity Today." Interesting, but I've never really bothered about the speculations and investigations of the theologians. I had my dose at Cambridge, and decided that what mattered to me and the world is how to relate the Word of God to my own personal life, taking its message and its historic facts as they stand. I'm not surprised to find their questionings coming full circle, so that they are beginning again to "condescend" to accept John on his own terms and not imply him to be a liar, when he claimed to be a personal participant in so much of what he related and what he heard Jesus say. The pride of man and "the wisdom of this world" do waste a lot of time.

Thank you so much, my dear, for your concern for my health, pretty well again now. I took some of the yellow pills.

Ever affectionately,

Norman

~~~

Jan.21.69

My dear Alfred,

I have sought rather muddily to express some of my thoughts on "Help....." I think down at bottom I feel we are in danger of giving in to the false accusations of the world or liberal churches – that we Christ-lovers and gospel preachers don't care about peoples material needs, when the truth is that we so see the supreme need to be for Christ to come into people's lives that these outer needs are of merely secondary importance; but that we do also (as all we missionaries do) minister to their material needs. Evangelical missionaries have been way beyond any humanitarians in bringing medical and educational help to the less privileged people.

Still less, as I say, do I accept as a reason for giving help, that governments pressure missions to undertake economic projects and that this should be regarded as a pressure to be taken off missions. As I say, I believe we should totally reject any implication that this is a pressure we should be concerned with. Is not this the "broad road" that the church began to descend in Constantine's days?!!

23

So I fear less we are running away from "the offence of the cross" in any recognition that missions or churches should bow down to governments in this.

I can only therefore see "Help...." As a specifically service ministry, but with dangerous outreach where it goes beyond helping evangelical churches or missions to develop the economic status of its members.

When it advocates getting help from Government funds or other such solely humanitarian sources, is it not nearing what we talked a little about – the meaning of 2 Cor.6.14-18? Does it not obviously mean that the main result of starting such projects will be the financial prosperity of those in it, and the elimination of all Christian emphasis except what is always there through Christian business men in businesses. Is not this exactly where CBMC so healthily stands? Not for building business for profit, but for individual witness by servants of Christ in business?

Now I am very prone to take a bit between my teeth and run off with the buggy, so maybe I am doing this here – but I just share what I see.

Please don't think there is any need to answer this. You have just allowed me to share my thoughts as your friend in Christ, so I have done so.

Ever affectionately,

Norman

~~~

June 6.71

My dear Ed,

I don't know if you are back yet from your Congo tour, but anyhow I thought I would write. I have recently returned from a tour and this morning had time to run thru the pile of Mags, brochures etc.

Among them I first came on your issue of "The Spirit and the Word". I read this May-June number with greatest delight – and relief! I found how wholly I can go along with you in your general "sons of God" and "Inchristed Men" article.

But then how my heart fell, when I dug further into my pile and found two other envelopes consisting of four other books and brochures by Saxby and others presenting the whole position of those who hold "ultimate reconciliation" or by whatever is the correct title, and including also your own magazine in which you wholly align yourself with them and give your own detailed presentation.

So I fear it does come down to it being not just a personal viewpoint, but a publicly preached doctrine.

I know it is no good saying anymore to you about it. I have known this presentation of what you and they believe for fifty years, and since I first came to see and read about it (I Know of Saxby but can't also remember whether I read his books), I came to my own conclusion that I must stand to the revealed truth of the Bible in its general most obvious teaching and declarations which have been found to be so through the centuries by the vast majority of Bible-believers, and as the plain simple reading of Jesus in the Gospels, Paul, John and the rest seem to present to us.

I am not saying there may not be deeper investigations which some feel called to make (such as in the word "eternity"); but I am saying that it is not for me to distort or disturb what is the generally accepted and experienced gospel of our salvation by investigations and conclusions which have to be sought out with great intensity and presented by the gathering together of all kinds of varied Bible statements, and which cause dissention and disturbance among God's people. To hold a personal viewpoint is one thing, but to present it as a doctrine to be received by all is quite another, and I have now to say that you are committed to this latter.

It does not take away from my real love for you, and my thankfulness for all of Christ that is ministered by the Holy Spirit by you; but it does seem that it makes it difficult for us to present in any combined sense the truth in Jesus in which we don't cut across each other. (For this same reason I had once to walk off the platform at the Pittsburgh Bible Institute conference when one brother followed me by declaring what you are now holding as the truth.)

So this with my love, though of course I would also add – with my regrets.

Ever in Christ,

Norman

~~~

25

June 14. 71

Dear Richard,

You kindly suggested that you would like me to see your latest MS.

You do not actually ask me to correspond with you over this, and therefore I hope I am not presumptuous in writing; but you were very gracious about what I wrote of the former one.

I would like to say that I think your differentiation between Flock and Fold is magnificent. Real light, and I had never seen this before, and didn't realize that there had been a mistranslation in John 10.16. I think you have presented a vital truth here which the Lord's people need to face – the liberty implied in the sheep "going in & out" under the direct leadership of the Shepherd, and the subtle bondage of being bound by manmade restrictions in holding to earthly securities through manmade denominational restrictions.

But here again I take upon myself the role of critic – with all the risks involved! In your last I boldly mentioned that you did not seem to me to follow thru in a way which geared the testimony and your church affiliations to people's questions and problems of to-day. Now I feel exactly the same here. It could be read into what you say that no one really in the clear in a walk in the Spirit is bound to a specific denomination. Yet I don't believe you can really mean that, because whatever a group is, small or large, if it continues to function as such, is a group with a name and therefore a denom! But it is tremendously true as I move around this country, and of course you know likewise, that tens of thousands of the Lord's people are dissatisfied with their present denom. affiliations, yet don't know what they should do.

Now to me the practical answer I give is that freedom is inner, not outer, (just as Paul says you can be a slave and yet the Lord's freeman in 1 Cor.7.22). Therefore a puzzled person should not necessarily leave a denom. church if that is where God seems to have put them and they have a witness; but that they should be free in spirit, and not bound to the laws or so-called duties of that local church. They do not "have to" keep their set timetables, or attend their set meetings or branch activities, or just give where their local church urges them to give. Some may therefore come out (as I have technically been a "come-outer" these 50 years), some may stay in or be put out - but all can be Flock-member and not fold-adherents.

So my comment is that (though you may mean it purposely) you do not bring this great Scriptural revelation down to the workaday situations of your readers, but leave them wondering, questioning, and possibly under some false condemnations!

The same over where again I think you are truly Scriptural about a local church having no one-man leadership and the snares which have come in through the "pastor" position in nearly all churches. But what practical solution are we to offer the thousands of the Lord's people? The honest truth is that where there has been the greatest example in our era of a church fellowship built on the non-pastor position, the Brethren, we can by no means say that they beyond all others have been God's chosen agents this past century, nor that they manifest a less "Fold" mentality. In one instance only, I always feel the bondage in their Sunday morning worship, because the first part <u>has</u> to be bound to no messages except those which centre objectively on Christ crucified, and <u>has</u> to centre in "the Lord's Table".

So again I would say that if you merely lead readers with what you correctly (in my view also) point out as the proper leadership for the local church, but don't give any guiding lines to the thousands who are not related to a church governed in this way, you leave them, puzzled, uncertain what to do, and many in condemnation. Whereas I would add that, recognizing human fallibility, the simple fact remains that God has used and is using the normal pastor-led churches, and generally speaking those still are His chief agencies for the birth and progress of His people; so I would say that readers can continue where God has placed them, through recognizing it is not the perfect pattern, or some may find a fellowship nearer to that pattern; unless in your presentation, you are really meaning that believers should move out and find or form more Scriptural fellowships; if so, it would then be more practical to say so.

So I feel, Brother, that this first part of your MS has a great living and much needed message and I wish that, if not yet fully in book form it could be published in pamphlet form, with (in my opinion) some more practical conclusions added.

As to the second section relating to the Kingdom. You give a completely clear presentation of the interpretation of the Kingdom being The Millennial Reign, and that God's present purpose is preparing the "overcomers" to reign with Christ in it. I think in my day D.M. Panton was the chief exponent of this in Britain. I have never personally come to any final conviction on this, though I have always noted what you now point out about the full meaning of the word "resurrection" in Phil.3.11, and of course have known the general convictions held. This has limited what you say here to Christ's coming and our participation during the Millennial period. Personally my absorbing interests are more in the ultimate destiny of Christ and us as His body which I think more fully occupy Paul's heart, mind and vision as in Eph. 1 (and this in the whole letter), in Romans 8, co-heirs, and in 1 Cor. 15, the Son rendering up the kingdom to the Father and He as "All in all". I feel that is the ultimate glory which fills the vision of Paul, John in 1 John 3.2, and leaves the reader with the sense of the ultimate glory and wholeness of the body joined to the Head, whereas the "partial rapture" tends to leave an emphasis of "regret" – actually the last phrase in your MS.

But here of course there is room for differings of conviction, to which each has a right; and you do most effectively present by this means the implications of discipleship - "If thou wilt be perfect"...., only perhaps that also needs some bringing down to this interpretation for folks living in the modern business and suburban world.

So the second half of the MS is more specialized, though it may be the specific calling of some, such as D. M. Panton and maybe you, to present this to God's people; while the first half is magnificently true for all, and indeed I shall plagiarize and often use this "Flock-fold" revelation, as I already have to one or two!

So I've just knocked this off, brother, as a retired man of leisure who has time to do so. You did not ask for it and no reply is needed; but I still hope that that first half may become available for Christ's church, and maybe, too, the message of the whole.

Excuse my typing. Ever in Christ,

Norman

~~~

Aug. 18

Betty & Smitty dearest,

Thank you again for your loving remembrance. You have so kept these love-links these years though we don't meet.

I know about the Way and have an idea that some of their viewpoints are off-centre as we interpret the Scriptures. But I have a close friend whose only son and daughter and their families have been fulltime in The Way for years and seem established in it and really love the Lord. It has bothered my friend much, but in the end we say the

Lord knows what He is doing, and let us be thankful that our children are Christ-lovers even if unorthodox in some viewpoints. But then many think we are!! So KEEP PRAISING. God's ways are PERFECT.

My much love,

Norman

~~~

Dear Brother Bob,

Indeed I remember you and our links of fellowship and most vividly of all coming to your home together with our darling Anna and I know she has kept touch with you thru the years- like you, I have a great love for Anna and we keep very close to each other. Marvelous how she has grown and moved into that total liberty in Christ in which she inwardly knows she is not Anna, but Christ in Anna's form, and in that realization, she moves freely among all, not holding back her love for others, including us, nor theirs for her, for she has liberated affections.

I wish we could get together further, brother, because I can see you accept false downgrading and condemnation of yourself. You are not a babe in Christ, you are a whole man in Christ, but we are controlled by how we inwardly see ourselves. Nor are you "Mutilated" by past years and their supposed effect on you. Why is that so? Because in our Gal.2.20 union with Christ, we are not we, you just Bob, or I Norman, but we are Christ in our human forms. But we have to exercise our God-given gift of faith and boldly affirm spiritual facts to be facts. When we do that, and begin to affirm and recognize who we are- He in our form- then we cease suspiciously looking at our human selves, condemning our flesh (mostly mixing up temptations which Jesus Himself had in all points, with sins which are the actual committal – and we don't keep doing that!!). No, we boldly accept that we are God's assets, not His liabilities! We are His precious human means of manifestation, every bit of us precious. Our appetites, faculties, minds, emotions are HIS precious agencies. Tempted often, but that is our springboard for the faith which says, No, I am crucified with Christ, He is the Real Me. And we replace our fears, feelings of weakness, or even more our feelings that we have not "arrived" in Him (which I think is your special snare! Feelings are outer soul-emotions. But we are spirit joined to Him – one Spirit, and there we do not accept the invasions of our feelings, nor accusations that our past upbringings have "damaged" us, etc. No, we are wholly what God always planned for us to be. See what Paul says of God from his birth - Gal.1.15. So you and I!

So you see brother, you have been caught up by the lie of a separated human self and its reactions, instead of being what you are- a unified self, where He is your Real Self. I have known this for long about you, dear brother, because you look at yourself as a weak human self, instead of Christ the Real You, have been afraid of shewing affection, and maybe afraid of your wife's accusations instead of boldly affirming you have only one mated love, and your body is faithful to her; but you can go out in your affections to others, where the real bond is not body, flesh or sex, but it's our oneness in Spirit.

I wonder if you have had a copy of that small book I wrote called "Who Am I". It talks of all this. I will gladly send you a copy.

Loving you in Christ and so glad you have shared your heart which permits us to share with you.

Norman Grubb

~~~

Oct.21.71

Dear Gloria,

I have just come back from a five weeks tour in the West and to a pile of mail- which it is a privilege to receive and answer! But now yours came yesterday, and it must have priority over others!

Dear, thank God you stand like a rock. By no means be moved. You stand for revealed truth in the Scriptures on the new birth and the fallen condition of all men ("children of the devil" - 1 John 3.10: "ye are of your father the devil", Jesus' words in John 8.44: we all without Christ have in us "the spirit that worketh in the children of disobedience" in Eph.2.2: and so on). You cannot give an inch on that. It is true that as we have our being in God (Acts 17.28), there is an inner light in us all which tells us what we ought to be but can't be without Christ; that's the nearest to Mr. Allen's saying (falsely) all are basically good.

The same, dear, with your stand for the full inspiration of the Scriptures as against him saying he did not accept some of Paul's writings. Yours is a <u>right</u> narrowness.

So, dear, having got it clear and firm that you cannot move an inch on your basic convictions, the next question is whether you should continue in the fellowship in which you "appear" to stand alone (I say "appear" because I am sure that your stand does also strengthen others who think alike but maybe don't come out and say so), and which you find drains you.

I don't think I can answer that, dear. There are times and people who are led to come out and join in a fellowship based on the truth; but there are also those who see it as God's call to stay put as a witness. Have you consulted on this with others in the church fellowship who you said had the Pentecostal experience? Are there others disturbed like you?

If you remain in flat opposition and probably rightly feel you cannot continually oppose your minister, it seems you should leave. But I would advise putting this straight back on God and now (and I with you in faith) looking to Him to give you some clear word; you meanwhile continue as you are. How about that?

Actually, if God hasn't given light before then, we can have a chance of talking together at Callaway. That will be good. But meanwhile you know I will be delighted if you feel it can help to talk it over further by letter, as now.

Much love to you,

Norman

~~~

14.12.71

Dear Leslie & Jill,

You spur me on to send a line. I'm just home after five weeks and to a mountain of mail. But you're always so provocative!! Thanks for fine budget, including one you sent Elwin. Thank <u>God</u> you keep jabbing at us all. Don't let us off, and don't limit the outpourings. You are God's forward man for WEC in this area.

Now you ask me about my heresies. What we call evil is freedom misused. You cannot have a person, whether God or man, unless he stand between alternatives and must choose. What he chooses he becomes. So God <u>cannot</u> lie (Titus 1.2), amazing to say there is something Almighty God <u>cannot</u> do. But as First Person (really Only Person) He stood between the choice- self-getting or self-giving. His choice is eternally fixed. A liar is a self-getter, He cannot be that. He is fixed as self-giving love.

Now He creates persons which means freedom of choice. Satan chooses the opposite, and being the opposite to the Fixed One in the universe, we call his choice evil, sin etc. The human race gets caught up in that same Satan-choice.

God is responsible for creating persons which means freedom. He is not responsible for the wrong choice, but for the possibility of that choice. But all are still in His being, the only being (Acts.17.28); so He has always "determined" (in the nature of things) that the wrong choice should have the wrong effects. Thank God it does, because that produces the suffering (the sorrow of Gen.3.16,17), and that drives us back to God. He wills that those who harden themselves are hardened, but always in hopes of them coming for mercy (Rom.11.32). And suffering is not outward conditions, but the way we take things. All we have is our reactions.

So God very conveniently uses the devil as His agent to take a great human family who are to be His eternal sons and managers of His universe (co-heirs of Christ who is heir of all) through their <u>necessary</u> training by going the <u>wrong</u> way and discovering the wrong use of self; for no one is ever efficient in their profession before they first know how <u>not</u> to use their tools before they are confident of how to use them. It was God Himself who put Adam & Eve between two trees, instead of giving them just one, because He must have sons who know and have experienced evil and good. Then having tasted the bottom and come to the top in Christ, no more bottom thank you (except for occasional visits maybe!).

And God Himself took full responsibility by appointing His Son as Lamb before He created us (1 Pet.1.19,20) not responsible for our choice, but responsible for creating persons who can and must choose. So He fixed the way to maturity by suffering (Heb.2.10, 5.8); and every single thing that happens, evil or good, is His perfect will <u>unto redemption</u>. We are real men of God, real reliable sons thru eternity because we are honoured by coming the hard way; and now being in it for <u>others</u>.

Nuff said. God has known His own business from eternity to eternity, including good and evil, which He knew about before we tasted it (Gen.3.22); but we got the divided two-power outlook thru the Fall; but we put back evil in grace, with the single eye, as God's determined means of making light to shine <u>out of</u> darkness. The cross looked like the devil; Jesus saw it as His Father's cup. That's the standard. He always saw <u>through</u> material distorted appearances to Reality. God in action in and through all things.

This will leave you a bit more confused than when we started- but I'm glad you have a <u>sharp wife</u>. Get her to interpret!

Love you both, and praise God for you,

Ever yours,

Rubi

~~~

May 22.72

My dear Lanny,

Thank you for your letter which has just caught me before I fly on Wednesday. If you did want to write while I am in England, which might not be likely, but in case, my fixed address will be

Bulstrode

Gerrards Cross

Bucks SL9 8SZ

England.

As to the new pastor, I more and more think that it isn't even God's plan that normal churches should be given too much "in depth". We know, don't we, that there is no way to the positive except by the negative, in other words we have had to experience the wrong way before we are conditioned to desire and find the right. So we must know we are sinners before we need or find a Saviour. And when redeemed, we must find that works and self-effort are a broken reed before we can even conceive of, still less enter into a replacement of self-effort by Christ. Death and resurrection are painful!

So I think that if a pastor sought to build a normal church by emphasis on our kind of message, he would soon have a revolt on his hands. I believe it is more God's way to have pastors who can give the gospel and get folks saved, and then build them in the first steps of the duties and standards of Christian living of which we find so much in the epistles, Sermon on the Mount etc. All will then start by thinking they must somehow practice these and get their disillusionment. Then, while there may be pastors who can take folks some way further, or can back those who seek to do so, like yours, but it is such as <u>you</u> among the brethren who are God's shepherds to give them the richer pastures. In other words let's be thankful if you have a good evangelical pastor and who know something of the victorious life; and you and others beside

33

him for what God has given us. Keep me in touch with how the Lord leads you to the new man.

Ever yours,

Norman

~~~

Aug.6.74

Dear Lanny,

Thank you dear ones for remembering my human birthdate – very loving and thoughtful of you – good thing we have eternal life flowing in our spiritual veins!

Glad you've had this vacation. Remember we have at our present disposal the wealth of the universe, as princes in God's household; and with Him at our disposal.

This is what He revealed to Jacob when He said that line to him as He had first prevailed over Jacob's persistent self-reliance and self-scheming. (God wrestling with J., until He finally got him to the point of seeing self schemes of escaping Esau were hopeless by putting his thigh out of joint, and Jacob suddenly recognizing that it was none but God Himself refusing to let J. go by this wrestling with him; and now by appearing to want to leave J., sparking J. to turn all his persistence, instead of sticking to self-effort, to not letting God go, till finally Jacob was conditioned by desperation to hold on to God in place of the former desperation to hold on to himself. Then He could open J's understanding to who he really was – not a helpless self-reliant schemer, but one who had now "gained" (really of course by God "gaining" him to the discovery of who we eternally <u>are</u>) the recognition of his being a prince in the household of God; or rather more still, a human who had God at his disposal, and who had "gained" the right to know it, and thus prevailed over any apparent reluctance on the part of God to be always wholly available to Jacob; God serving him now, not he serving God; and thus also in the overcoming situation in his next morning's previously feared meeting with avenging Esau!! Yet always thru the rest of his life (Jacob still "leaning on his staff" in blessing his sons at his dying moment) being reminded by his limp that the recognition of human weakness is the basis of the recognition and application of God's strength to our human affairs- a persistent human self with that human persistence, which is an endowment of being a human person in God's image, being now a power-line for God's working for and by us! In other words, dear ones, you can look and take from God all you <u>materially</u> need for the kind of material provision you want for yourselves and your lovely children!

Blessings on you. Wish I saw the chance of another good day with you.

Love to you all,

Norman

~~~

June 29.75

Merry darling & Eldean,

Lovely to get your further letter and enclosures. Poem is good and edges near the ultimate fact - which is we ARE God in our human forms - not just "like Him" - a lot to swallow till the full light dawns. So with what you write, darling. Don't say you "want" to be used, yielded, etc. No, you ARE all that. This "want" business means I am really still accepting the lie of me being a "failing" separate self, and then I live under the burden and illusion of "wanting" to be like Him or used, or yielded or some such rubbish!! Darling, He HAS taken you over, nothing to do with <u>what you may think of yourself</u> and <u>your reactions</u> as if regarding yourself as separate. NO! Only see by faith (and inner witness which follows) that HE is the real you, and your humanity the form of <u>His Self-manifestation</u>. Your "pressures" of <u>feeling and acting so just human are our practicing</u> ground where we say, "I'll be a little quicker next time in seeing Him in me and Him in everything and everybody".

Love, please keep it plain that I by no means can be certain of that Sun. aft. I am Wayne's guest and so have to conform to any plan he has, also I don't know whether I will still need that afternoon for getting more of my facts together (all days are alike to me as work days!!). Thank you, dear for offering for me to come to you.

My much love,

Norman

~~~

Ap.27.76

Dear Brother Eldean,

Thank you for your letter. I much appreciate this fellowship with you as well as with our dear Merry.

Yes, I am happy about Jim. I caught it from our talk that he is not a "formal" pastor but is looking for the vital movings of the Spirit among the people, and I believe willing to pay the price, for there is always death before resurrection, and there will be those, like the "false brethren sent up from Jerusalem to spy out and steal the liberty in Christ" which the Galatians had, who will strongly oppose anything except dead orthodoxy. We can search the Scriptures and yet never be in living touch with its Author (John 5.39,40!) and I think Jim will go quietly and easily with the Spirit among such a large group, and HE will come thru in His own way and time; and you will be among the prophets and intercessors of faith who foresaw the need and had the faith.

But you've got me beat on the Cana "sign". Curious that Paul never referred to Christ's sayings or doings on earth (2 Cor.5.16), but marvelously revealed Christ in the Spirit to us. I take it there are always all kinds of allegorical truths we draw from parables and miracles (again like Paul over Hagar and Isaac - Gal.4.24). I just see in it the bold presentation of our liberty in the Spirit to be ourselves and obtain from God what is needed in normal human social living to experience His goodness and material provision. And we can stretch that out without limit.

Ever with my love to you both,

Norman

~~~

Nov.5.76

My dear Leslie,

I've just been reading your excellent report on the Muslim World Conference. But is not our approach on a fundamentally erroneous basis? You can't start by comparing Christianity and Islam because there is no such thing as Christianity. It is natural man's false invention to affirm and perpetuate what he calls the Christian religion, which is only another outer cloak for his unregenerate self-affirming self - the old Judaism repeated, which Paul gave the true label to in Rom.10.3! And Islam is just the same – a natural man's attempt to cloak and preserve his fallen self under some relationship to his Creator sufficient to appease his conscience, and yet leave him to his own final cloak of self-righteousness.

But we know the only "Christianity" is described in John 3.8 – an indefinable brotherhood of people of the Spirit thru union with their crucified & risen Saviour, scattered throughout the human family.

Therefore the whole attempt to line up and consider Christianity with Islam as in this conference report is dangerous offbeat heresy. Nor do those who go out to bring the new birth to Moslems need to "know" what Islam stands for (except maybe as a bit of useful external knowledge), because it is on a wholly false fallen basis.

Surely this needs re-emphasis after all this hullabaloo about this "onward march of Islam", which is no more to Christ and His redeemed body than is communism – just one of those things God blows on in due time! Surely we need to emphasize, and specially to our Weccers, that this "Christianity" which these Moslems claim is decadent and perishing is just their Aunt Sally, a figure of straw, and in its outward structure is as doomed Islam.

That's all, but just a cry once again for us to retain our total spiritual balance, and see only with the eyes of the Spirit and the One who sits in heaven and laughs. I really deeply question this false inclination to a false condemnation of the people of God which infected Lausanne and even our blessed Billy Graham. We know <u>no condemnation</u>. God's redeemed servants have <u>perfectly</u> taken the gospel to the world in each generation by the only methods available to each generation; and now the Spirit of God IS marching on, as you so gloriously keep presenting to us in your true voice, my beloved Leslie and Jill – your LOOK.

Wish you would read this to British staff and recruits and MTC!

My love as ever,

Rubi

~~~

Sept.2.77

Thank you darling, for yours. Yes I've been on the same track as you for years, getting fresh glimpses of light from many sources, but I'm always glad that my foundations all my years has been the Bible, centred in Christ, so I never have cause to deviate from that, but both draw sustenance (and plenty of it) from many sources, yet not be moved where

I see them not to be locked in to the Centre. Friends have recently lent me Starcke, some good stuff, but being more centred in the Impersonal than in the Personal Trinity, and I see that danger, for instance my friend, a bachelor, (and I see tendencies in Starcke on sex) boldly claims total freedom is promiscuous sex. So I equally totally repudiate such perverted liberty, rather finding the true freedom in God my freedom, yet who is Himself a servant to other-love, and of whom it is said, "He cannot lie". The Anglican prayer book has that right "In whose service is perfect freedom!" So I still love my brother, but make it plain I am at a totally opposite pole to him on freedom! The same when I read Walter Russell's Secret of Light. I get a lot from it though he is not an orthodox Christian; but when his wife who now publishes his books writes contemptuously of the atoning Blood (while Russell never did), I stand square against her. So I agree with you, we can wander all over the place and savour all sorts when we know our solid foundations – and we can accept (and learn from) or reject as may be.

So, lovingly,

Norman

~~~

Sept.20.79

My dear Bus,

Many thanks for yours of to-day. Thank God for the clarity in which you present our basic truth – God in His human forms. I checked in the Greek your "All things and in all is Christ" and I find you stimulatingly right - and I think that translation a new sharp weapon for our use. The word "is" is not in the Greek, so it actually reads – "All things and in all – Christ". Still more startlingly total. Thank you!

Yes, we are off in three days. Humanly looks like lean pickings – two main bookings have now rejected us, another will only take me, etc. – but The Spirit is not easily put to sleep!!

Yes, I'm glad of your joining our "Board" – you might think it came from me as knowing you longest – but it didn't! You and I have dug together into our UL "deep things" from our J. Boehme days before most of our present ULers were out of short pants!

Much love,

Norman

~~~

March 27.80

Dear Joan,

I only returned from a tour last night and found your letter, or I would have answered at once. Thank you, Joan, for your honest sharing. It is so helpful when we can be in the light with one another.

No, I stand completely where you and all evangelicals do on sin, repentance, the blood. Actually it comes out strongly again in the book I am just completing. You don't want to be loaded down with printed matter, but as you raise this question, I wrote this pamphlet on temptation which covers the same subject, if you would glance at it.

The same with universalism, I stand where evangelicals stand on the reality of a lost eternity, as in Rev,20.12-15 – though the emphasis of my message is more 2 Peter. 3.9 and I Tim.2.4.

Unitarianism is a new one! Of course I stand with you all on the Trinity.

Thank you, Joan, for the many times you have given me the privilege of fellowship in your church.

Lovingly in Christ,

Norman

~~~

May 12.80

My Dear Bill

You raise an important question in your letter of to-day of sin in relation to soul & spirit. I see it like this, and have again written on it in this coming YES I AM. Spirit is exclusively our I am, spirit is self consisting of knowing, loving, willing. This is true of God as spirit, and man in His image.

Soul and body are merely impersonal agents, nothing but expressors of spirit. So good and evil can only be the Spirit of God or the spirit of Satan expressed thru our spirits. In that sense, therefore, you are right in saying I have changed my position from humans having one or other nature to our having no nature.

So when we start our human life enslaved to the spirit of error, we spontaneously fulfill his lusts in our human spirits expressed thru soul and body. Temptation, then, is from the Spirit of Truth drawing us to "good works" to which we may temporarily respond but of course remain slave to the spirit of error.

As this is reversed by our Last Adam by his substitutionary death and resurrection, we by our free response of faith have the spirit of error replaced by the Spirit of truth in us, and, as we move in to respond wholly to the union relationship via Rom. 6-8 and Gal. 2.20, we are totally expressors of the Spirit of Truth. <u>But</u> that union does not destroy or dissolve the paradox of duality (I have a chapter on One, yet Two – a Paradox). So now our same human spirit, our self, is tempted by the spirit of error, for the whole world lies in his dimension, "the prince of this world". These temptations come by the drawings on us in our variety of soul-body faculties. Such drawings entice our human spirit in its union relationship, yet remaining dual within the union, to forget its union reality, and usually to want to follow the enticements, but recognizing as only pullings on our outer soul or body, we don't fight them but replace by affirming who we really are; and Christ as us, in us, makes the temptations agencies of His self-manifestation. Occasionally we go farther, as in James 1.15, and then it is our human spirit which consents to the temptation, marries it, as it were and that brings forth a sin. The human spirit has had a touch of that "filthiness" of 2 Cor. 7.1. That is where we say we do "have sin" and need a confession and cleansing of 1 John 1.9.

It is <u>only</u> spirit that sins, for soul and body are only impersonal agents, for only spirit is will and makes choices. The reality of the human spirit within the union with the Divine Spirit is seen clearly by Jesus' "not My will, but Thine be done". So human spirit sins and is cleansed, the conscience cleansing of Heb. 9.14.

We still have a weakness in our union reality, when we don't wholly recognize soul & body is now wholly HIS in every faculty, and not a kind of left-over in sin or "flesh" hands. Indwelling sin of Rom. 7 is replaced by Indwelling Christ of Rom. 8, and in that respect we are wholly Christ-expressors – 1 Thess. 5.23. Flesh is now His means of manifestation – God manifest in the flesh. So we walk in freedom, without anxious watchfulness over our "flesh" responses. We are KEPT. But, we recognize with Paul, our bodies are still unredeemed, corruptible, and therefore responsive to flesh drawings. But they are the impact of external drawings on us. Human spirit does sin and can sin (but not impersonal soul & body). We can talk about our perfection, because the Bible does in such as Matt. 5.48 and 1 John 4.18, but I prefer to say He is my perfection as me, just as I prefer to say I am Christ in my human form rather than just I am Christ! There is an area in which we have been so accustomed to flesh yieldings, both in our unsaved and saved lives, that we tend to be slow in boldly affirming and recognizing all of us – soul & body as well as spirit being so liberated in Him that we are not afraid of our emotional or physical responses. We are daringly free to express love. And that is where I have sensed a hesitation in presenting the liberated walk, where we do so clearly present the liberated union. It is on this level we can move into vicarious intercession often at loss of our own reputation, for we have no soul-body to preserve any more than we have spirit.

I think we have sometimes overstated our union reality as if we can't or don't sin, because we have mistakenly confused our human spirit as if kind of dissolved into His Spirit. This may be our experience when we are in God's final dimension of James 1.13 but we now, as did the Saviour in total form – live in the tempting dimension and shine there as "Lights". I think that both covers what I would say now, but we can profitably go further in Wisconsin.

Much love and I love our open fellowship.

Norman

~~~

Mar.17.

Dear Don,

So glad the Spirit has been giving you light. As to your question about who are false prophets. John says those who don't acknowledge Jesus as Lord – I John 4:1-3. But I can add the cross is always the center. Any teaching which does not have its basis on our identification with Christ crucified and ourselves both dead to sins thru His blood (1 Pet.2:24) and dead to sin through His crucified body (Rom. 6) are always false. So don't fear. Go ahead and trust the Lord to keep you.

ever with my love,

Norman

~~~

Dothan, Ala
Ap.7.83

My dear Stewart,

A week ago I wrote you in much gratefulness for your letter and your bold continuance in preparing extracts from the books. And you also made a loving appeal to me to take notice of the concern of some of you in what appeared to some as over-statements in the recent books, so that you would say that 95% of the book are "bang on", but the other 5% cause the concern.

I have already written you and expect the letter will just have reached you; but now John Whittle sends me copy of yours asking permission from CLC to make these extracts, and also saying Lutterworth agree at the price of 5%. May I say that if you go forward, any such expense we will see, or if I have gone to the Lord, those who follow me will do the same.

But hearing from John moves me to write and seek to explain further why, so far from pulling back on this 5% which disturbs, I have to say it is just this 5% which is the core of what we call "Total Truth", or "Total Reality". I only wish we could talk it out together, and perhaps that might later be possible, because both of us are open to what God reveals to us as truth. So let me further say this:

You raise the point of whether we skirt over "moral responsibility". Stewart, that is almost laughable to us! Our whole reality is based on our living by and expressing moral absolutes, or immoral ones! We see ourselves as branches of a tree whose fruit we just bear – the two trees and two fruits of Rom 6.21.22. Branches having no nature of their own, merely spontaneously manifest the fruit of their vine (true or false). So we who are now new creatures in Christ look back with absolute clarity at ourselves as absolute expressors of the nature of self-loving self! Those "lusts of our father we did"! John 8.44. We simply expressed his nature. Eph.2.1-3. We could be "pulled" (tempted upward) to some temporary response to the Holy Spirit, but back we went to our normal immoral absolute. It did not take much "responsibility" to walk in those Satan-sin ways!

And now the glorious reverse! Knowing ourselves (by our faith-commitment to such truths as Gal.2.20, based on that body-death of Christ in 2 Cor.5.14 & 21, and thus receiving the inner witness of 1 Jhn 5.10 to our new being as Christ our life, our oneness with Him, we as He as the "righteousness of God" even as He was as us "made sin", we as "the light of the world", as lamp by which invisible electricity becomes visible light, we "in Him and He in us", as iron put in fire becomes the glowing iron-fire), we walk spontaneously as He in our forms expressing His other-love nature, as we used to walk spontaneously as Satan in our forms expressing his self-love nature. Thus now we live in the moral absolute, that love that fulfills all law; and the "heavy end" of any responsibility rests on HIM, who chose us, joined us to Himself, and now "causes us to walk in His ways" (Ezek.36.27). Human responsibility in the form of self-effort has totally ceased (for it would be a declension to Rom.7). His yoke is easy, His burden light. Temptation, yes, plenty continually, and accepted as negative asset without condemnation, and then freely turned into replacement by who we now are, thus being He in our form – darknesses which valuably shew up light. (I have talked much on that in YES I AM and other books). So you see, to have an enquiry about "moral responsibility" conveys to us the realization that those making the enquiry don't really <u>live in</u> their replaced reality, of Christ as they in place of Satan as they – or they would not ask it. They would <u>know it</u>.

And, Stewart, this is the "inner knowing" I long that the Spirit should reveal to our Weccers; and the best and most glorious uptodate evidence is in Neil Rowe's letter on "Union Life Bane or Blessing" in the Weccer; for it shews we can go a long way in professing and knowing to a point the reality of Gal.2.20, and yet not having finally had the total revelation of the reality of the new liberated "I". Then such questions simply do not arise. We are occupied with "Being".

And thus the same about the question you raise of not admitting mistakes in spoken words or positions of faith. You refer, almost sarcastically, to that great man of faith, Rees Howells, (and but for him there would not be the WEC in its present enlarged form, or it would have to have happened by some other agent, not by me). I am bold to prophecy that the day is now at hand when the people of the Spirit will really grasp by this new exposition of "The Intercessions of Rees Howells" just coming out by Doris Ruscoe, that they had in him a prophet's voice for our generation, just as they had a soldier-saint's voice in CT Studd, and both of whom died rejected!

From him they will learn that intercession has always its "death", the first fruits on the alter, which gave a chance to those who don't know the secrets of the Spirit to make their foolish accusations. But then they will see in that total stand over the Dictators and the battles of faith fought each night thru the war, that walk of faith which has produced this staggering world spread of the gospel of to-day.

In short, positions of faith are taken by those who catch the mind of the Spirit, and thru travail speak those words of faith which can never be withdrawn without making God a liar; and there's no such thing as a mistake for which an apology has to be made. How I blushed for our USA WEC when they declared some position of faith for some reinforcements, and then in our own Mag aplogised later that they must have made a mistake. No indeed, we Weccers need some tightening up of our loins of faith. Paul knew that well enough when he turned his apparent refusal of a prayer three times repeated into a glorious declaration of an answer which has been the triumphant voice of God to millions thru the centuries (2 Cor.12:9,10).

So again, Stewart, I am so glad to be talking this out with the one in WEC who comes so close to our liberated glory, and with whom I have a true love-relationship, and thank God for the miracle of you as Internat'l Sec. (and I'm delighted to see you were the man of faith in foreseeing it, you are like Rees Howells!). I have faith that some of the 300 or so who have asked for YES I AM, and to whom I am so glad to have sent it, will have their inner eyes opened by the only Eye-opener to these ultimate 5% truths which alone put the whole in focus. I still have to mourn that my own Weccers hold us at arm's length in this "Union Life" truth, and but for you and hardly more than one or two others, keep stony silence when I have fellowship with them, obviously shewing that though I am thankful for their love and personal acceptance, they never make one enquiry into what they know is my present absorbed ministry and occupation, either to find out what it is that is disturbing to them, or seek to put us right. Meanwhile I can only say the rivers are flowing in ways which make it plain to us that it is the embryo stage of a church-wide commission. But I can finally only say what I said in a P.S. in my last week's letter, reason or attempts at Bible expositions can never make the eternal paradox of the fixed union reality factual in life, only the Knowers know.

So, lovingly, and just thankful that I can talk my heart out to you,

Norman

PS Further, on "responsibility". Of course it is <u>we</u> who "do" the lusts our former father, and now "bear" the fruit of the Spirit. But it is mainly the product of the Spirit-drive in us, and thus moment by moment spontaneously. Thus we work out Phil.2.13 by 2.12! If in doubt, we await and receive a "divine" push – and all of course according to His word. Temptations as assets, not liabilities, I have already mentioned. We don't live sin-and-temptation-conscious, or "anxiously abiding". We live subconsciously Christ-minded (that new mind of Rom.8.5-9, and 12-14). We live positively, as being what the Scriptures exhort us to be, not as "I ought to", but as "I am"! <u>That</u> then <u>is</u> fulfilled moral responsibility, and of course it is an "of course"! We <u>can</u> go into a sin, and then just as quickly into 1 John 1.9 and straight out into the cleansed conscience of its last phrase and Heb.9.14; but we live positively by 2.1!

~~~

England, July 23, 1983

My dear Warren,

I was glad to get your letter sent on to me yesterday. How greatly I delight in this mighty drive of the Spirit that that has thrust you into such bold action in taking our "total truth", under your terms of "Life in the Spirit" and Christ-life Institutes to the whole world, particularly of your "charismatic" brethren. It is tremendous and marvelous to me, as an unthought of large scale expansion of our worldwide churchwide "Twentieth Century Reformation" of the "Christ in you as you" completion of "the Mystery" available to the whole body of Christ (Col. 1:24-29). I am thrilled to hear of your Christ-life Institute already in operation.

It will be good if we can get a day or two together, and I would like to outline to you what I think I see to be in focus about this Adam-Christ truth (and it is wonderful how close we are together in our understandings in Spirit).

Christ is the Last Adam replacing the first. Paul says that in 1 Cor. 15:45. He gives that full weight in his Romans 5:12-21 summing up of our new birth experience – Romans 3-5. Here is plainly set forth the disobedience of the first Adam and its consequences on us, replaced by the abounding grace of the obedience of our Last Adam. This is on our <u>positional</u> level of righteousness imputed by faith, and thus our privileged <u>positions</u> in the Royal Family and Inheritances with all its prerogatives.

But this statement, gloriously announcing our position under the headship of our Last Adam, and "first born among many brethren," does not touch the basic <u>condition</u> issuing from the basic nature of either the first or last Adam, and thus our natures as derived from them. This now proceeds on in Romans 6-8, from the question "Shall we continue in sin that grace may abound?" We now have, exposed to us and expounded, the inner reality of the two Adams in their humanity (spoken of by Paul in I Cor. 15:47 as the one man earthy and the other, second man, as "the Lord from heaven"). Then the gathering together of other Scriptures explain that humans have no nature of their own, but are "vessels, branches, temples, slaves, wives, etc," and are indwelt and operated (with their willing consent) by a Deity Nature – by the false one of "the god of this world" as in Ephesians 2:1-3, or by the Spirit of Truth in His "divine nature" (2 Peter 1:4).

This is seen so remarkably clearly when the human Jesus received the Spirit in the form of a dove at His baptism, and heard the voice saying, "Thou art My beloved Son." Then that Spirit of Truth compelled Him to face the "spirit of error" for forty days to confirm His total choice and rejection of the false one. Then, as He started His public ministry, He said it was by "The Spirit of the Lord upon me to preach the gospel..." And when confronted by Calvary, it says, "Who, through the Eternal Spirit offered Himself" (Hebrews 9:14). And then, of course, the resurrection by the Spirit. And His final great supper conversation, telling His disciples that this Same Spirit would possess them as He sent Him from The Throne, which was, of course, realised at Pentecost. Thus the spirit of error operating his nature as us (John 8:44) is replaced by the Holy Spirit of Truth operating His nature as us, through the body-death of Jesus, as depicted in 2 Cor. 5:14, 21, and brought into effect in the terms of "dead to sin" in Romans 6. (And its full consequences in Hebrews 10:5 and 10-14), and thus also the body-resurrection.

So then as we move into our presentation of total "life in the Spirit," or "Union Life" or whatever term, we present on the Justification level the glorious change of Adams as in Romans 5:12-21 as the positional fact of our regeneration, culminating in that Romans 3:5 passage. And then we move on, as our total central Spirit-revelation, as given to Paul in Arabia (Galatians 1:17, resulting in his 1:8 and 11,12 statements, and culminating in the Galatians 2:11-21 crisis, with 2:20 at its center). Thus revealing that neither Adam operated by the false concept of a nature of his own, but the first Adam by the spirit of error masquerading as his independent self (until exposed in Romans 7), and the Last Adam by The Spirit of Truth coming in the form of a dove.

So I believe we really see and say the same, when linking the replacement of the first Adam by the Last as the glorious positional fact as realized in our justification, and then continuing on to the revelation of how we humans operate as our permanent condition of living by The Christ in us as our nature, that glorious Christ being The Last Adam Himself a "quickening Spirit" (I Cor. 15:45) by the Spirit who entered Him, and now indwells us. And as you say, "The real me is Christ" in the paradox of "I live, yet not I, but Christ lives in me" and thus my human "me" continues in that paradox, as now my liberated human I am free to be myself, yet really it is HE as me, and Paul puts it in terms of "and the life I now live in the flesh, I live by the faith of the Son of God".

So I thought I would just run over this early morning outline on my splendid British tour, where there is now a glorious breakthrough with a number who really know who they are by the Spirit and are spreading it. Just came from a great weekend in a college of about 150, many from the arising house-churches.

Much love to you and Robbie,

Lovingly,

Norman

~~~

Dec. 14.83

Dear Joyce,

Ours is a specialist God-given ministry to which Paul referred as his "second ministry" in Col. 1. 24-28, centering on Christ in us.

Yes, we do believe and accept what the Scripture constantly refers to concerning a personal return of Christ with His saints. But when asked why we don't emphasize that, we answer as General Booth did to the same question, "I haven't finished with the first coming yet"! We are also much geared to Paul's Roman epistle, where he does not refer to the Second coming, but does speak of the groaning creation awaiting the "manifestation of the sons of God". Maybe that is how He will manifest Himself when He does come, for it says as much in 2 Thess.1.10; note the preposition "in".

Warm greetings in Christ,

Norman Grubb

~~~

Dec.26.83

Dear Don,

Union Life sent me on your letter and questions, but I have not been able to answer before as I've only now returned from a three months tour of meetings.

That I Cor.9:23 saying of Paul's is concerning those who are called into God's service - the whole chapter is concerned with Paul and the others in their ministry.

Therefore his statement about being a "castaway" (Lit. "disapproved") refers to the possibility of being set aside in the ministry and as a fruit-bearing branch. Jesus says that in John 15, which again has nothing to do with salvation ("now ye are clean." v.3), but then as a fruit-bearing branch (v.16) we can fall away and be no use in our ministry, and "men" (v.6) won't turn to us for spiritual ministry.

As to making a decision, certainly when you inwardly know by the Spirit that you and He are one, then you have the mind of Christ (I Cor. 2:16), and can be bold to follow what HE indicates to you as His way for you, though you will always also welcome counseling from others - but the decision is between you and the Lord.

My love in Christ

Norman Grubb

~~~

September.10.84

Fran darling,

I have sent you some of the correspondence of our recent happenings, so I wanted to add what the Lord is shewing some of us very clearly and with much joy. We do not see disunity. It is not in our vocabulary anymore than it was in Jesus; in John 17, and in Paul all thru his epistles, esp. in 1 Cor. 1 etc! So what we are seeing is that the Spirit gives different ones of us a variety of emphases and convictions, and that all that matters is that we all go right forward in full faithfulness in the way God shews us, not looking for any to change unless God gives a change, but rejoicing that thru these six or so years the Spirit has deeply confirmed us in our special revelation for the whole redeemed church of Christ in us as us; and we all go forward bringing our "total truth" to all parts of the church and believers as put within our reach or in our further world outreaches.

All this combines in giving us great joy in seeing varieties in which in some details (but not in the central truth entrusted to us) we may see differently, but all that that means is it is HIS way (as in Jerusalem in the early church!) of fulfilling our known and accepted worldwide commission. So we "lift up our hearts" and praise. We have always kept to the principle of the least amount of organization and freedom from controls except by the Holy Spirit, giving each his liberty of ministry, and with no financial bindings among us, but each wonderfully being supplied by the Lord Himself by whatever channels He provides. So we go ahead loving each other, each as Christ in our forms, precious to Him and therefore precious to each other; and recognizing the right of each to teach and minister as given by the Spirit through the Word; and hopefully "by love serving one another", as we are in the world "among you as He that serveth".

With my love as ever,

Norman

~~~

As from Arlington, Texas
Feb. 1985

My dear Stewart,

You know how I love you, (and indeed you me!) and delight in you in your Holy Spirit ministry, and have done so all these years.

But it looks as if I may be in trouble with you by your "both concerned", but also loving letter which has just reached me here.

So I must say categorically that neither Union Life nor I personally condone sin. Absolutely No. Indeed the opposite is true in us even now dealing with the very opposite - overemphasis on sin such as calling depression and things of that kind as sin!

But where I have to stand equally uncompromisingly clear is that what you refer to as my "no nature" theory we are more solidly convinced - all of us - that we have the right Scriptural basis for saying and being wholly committed to affirming as truth that we humans have been created in God's image, in His being (Acts 17:28) to manifest ONLY ONE NATURE (2 Pet.1.4). We are vessels, branches, temples, slaves, body-members, but in every instance only express the nature of Him whom we contain, and only HIS nature. It is obvious to us, for instance, where Paul says in our fallen condition we bore fruit "of which we are now ashamed". But now in our redeemed condition, "ye have your fruit unto holiness". And a branch only bears the fruit of its Vine. It has no nature of its own - which Vine (Rom.6:20-22)? And we are never anything but branches-not vines. And independent self is THE LIE. Satan himself was always God's good and purposed agent, but was self-deceived in thinking himself independent, and he slipped that deceit (Rev. 12:9) into us humans. And thus the lie of self-acting, self-relying self. And this was Paul's great revelation in Galatians, and fully analyzed in Rom.6-8, where his misery in Rom. 7 was his mistaken idea that his self-responses in the flesh were his; but at last he "discovers" they were Satan's (sin indwelling me): and Paul was the one to whom it has been revealed that there was this second "operation" at Calvary, (symbolized by the broken bread as well as the shed blood in the Lord's supper) - the "body death" of Christ where His body represented ours was "made sin", for our body expresses Satan's sin-nature: and thus in His death, out went that Satan-spirit from His body as ours, and in the resurrection in came His Spirit of truth, and thus into our body. Thus we humans, never having a nature of our own, were "walking Satans" (Eph.2.1-3), and now when we have moved by faith from Rom.7 into 8, we are walking Christs (2Pet. 1.4) - "made the righteous of God" (not merely imputed) because He had been "made sin" as us (2Cor.5.15,21).

And thus, as in Rom. 8:2, we walk free - our God-created bodies always were "OK", but misused, and now by grace thru Calvary, rightly used. We get ourselves back, and the new basis of our daily living and ministry is not "our responsibility" but His keeping of us and the drive of His Spirit "causing us to walk in His way" (Ezek.36); just as formerly we were 'well-kept' by the Satan-spirit of self-loving self, and very easily were "caused" to walk in his way! Glorious liberty. Of course we are continually tempted -that is our privileged condition as James says, giving us practice, not in taking condemnation for temptation, but recognizing the right of Satan to tempt, and then without condemnation having our right to affirm who we are, Christ in our forms, and thus we expressing His love overflowing hate etc etc. Temptation thus being asset in fresh manifestation of Christ as us, in place of liability - thus James 1:2

Thus because of the joy of our new-found liberty, statements may sometimes appear in quoted letters, or what not, in the Magazine which the many who do not understand our key to liberty (indeed the majority of Christ's body) see suspiciously as condoning sin. We just have to put up with that, and are certainly in good company when we read what they called Jesus and Paul as light on sin (Rom.3:8 etc!).

I only wish you could meet and know the numbers of folks over this nation with marriages mended rejoicing uninhibitedly in their new walk. Many have been severely tempted by diverted affections, but instead of being filled with false condemnation, have recognized temptation (which is not sin); and then have turned a flesh affection into an intercession for Christ formed in the other, and the victory resulting. I wrote on this in a chapter under "Infatuation" in YES I AM. But I know victories like this have been misunderstood and spoken against.

So I can only tell you, Stewart, that I and so many of us are altogether continually thrilled with these total "trophies" of total liberation. I had one by this same mail, which I am tempted to send you, but it is long, a very famous Bible teacher who has had the depths of independent self opened up to her and what a revelation of a letter! So I'm afraid I'm a 'goner', and a greatly increasing number of us: and I always watch and search carefully to see if our Bible foundations are solid, and I think they are.

Stewart, you will have to let those who want to, if they are in charge of publishing, if they wish to insert something which I suppose hints or speaks out about the supposed danger of us in our "Total Truth" message which we shall be increasingly and unceasingly making; and I'll be sorry for them, and I'm sure they will grieve the Spirit, and only increase interest in our witness. We <u>well</u> know the church of normal evangelical believers will oppose us for we touch the core when we say we humans never had an independent self-acting self, but ON WE MUST GO. No, our position is <u>not</u> "central" - It is EXTREME, as it always has been when the Spirit is moving out and on. I would my loved Weccers were still extreme, as was CTS. I <u>know</u> and I believe you know that so many of our Weccers will claim to know and live Gal.2.20, but those that do leap forward as totally equipped, sufficient, enabled apostles of to-day (I <u>wish</u> we had not so weakly dropped our "Crusade" terms and its soldierly implications): and our very praying would be more totally praising and affirming and confident of our ability as in 2Cor.3.6, but I don't find that ringing note in many, though you know I greatly rejoice in you being who you are these days in WEC.

And we know we shall go on loving and backing each other, and believing for each other as thru all these years, even if there are areas in which we don't use the same terms.

Just lovingly as ever,

Norman

~~~

Aug.19.85

Dearest Evelyn,

Thank you for writing and it is good that we do share. You see you have come out plainly with what we have all been "guessing" and seeing indicated in the Mag and by the various authors recommended, that you all do say we have a 'human nature' in addition to the two "divine" natures.

So I have to sorrow in one respect, dear, and yet greatly rejoice in the other, and see what others of us were much quicker to see that this is ALL God. How I learned that lesson with my CT Studd. What a raging fire for God, hard to follow except when caught up in the same fire (like Moses on the Mount who could walk in fire that wd burn the Israelites); and when in his extremes of dedication he took shots of morphia to keep him going in getting to the lost souls, and then produced the booklet with the swearing title of "Don't Care a Damn", practically all left him, his oldest backers in Britain (such as F.B. Meyer whom he had led to the Lord), and most of the "Board" and all the missionaries at home, saying he was led of the devil. Pauline and I, not easily but then plainly said, "This man is burning out for souls, while others sit on their haunches at home: and we stood with him. We learned then the great lesson of milk or meat ways of seeing – Heb. 5:13, 14. The 'milk' judge by appearances, the 'meat' "discerns" the <u>motives,</u> and that is where the Spirit is. And how surely right we proved in the enormous expansions of WEC-CLC today. How thankfully, though not easily or without pain, we learned that "meat" lesson, and came to see what James said in James 4:11 – beware of judging your brother – for he is expressing the nature of God, and you judge that nature if you judge him. But while we still add that 'human nature area', we judge that. We don't say it is Satan, but we won't say it is God, so it's "just human". The cutting edge is blunted, as it is by most of God's people. Then we get "judging".

So there it is, dear. While you see that human nature, then you see it. But it is not what Union Life has taught, and is finally made clearer then ever in YES I AM. That does not make it right, of course, except that we believe it is a true interpretation of Scripture. And I have to say that, just as with us WEC years ago, that dividing sword of the Spirit (as in Heb. 4:12) limited us down to the few who stood along with CTS, how the Spirit has mightily resurrected a mighty army, though with loss of some at that time; so now I see, and we see, there had to be this dividing edge between those who see only two natures in Scripture, either Satan spirit of error or Christ Spirit of truth; and we humans only, though

52

gloriously, have a "being" (not nature) from God (Acts.17:28), all the glorious <u>quantity</u> like all the potential of a computer, the quality of what is expressed by our being - the vessel, branch, body-member, slave etc., but the quality is the divine nature. So then after moving in by faith into that "Body" death of Christ in 2 Cor.5:14 & 21, and Rom. 6 wrought out in 8.2, having learned the lesson of the deceit of 7.11, as though we had an independent human self-nature, then at last we are FREE TO BE, and accept and operate ourselves as HIS expression. So on we go gloriously, and I only wish I still had my Evelyn and you other dear ones with us.

Loving you anyhow and thanking you for much precious fellowship thru the years,

Lovingly

Norman

~~~

Nov.20.85

My dear Chris,

It's glorious to read of that liberating light pouring in, but you need to keep it clear that only our human spirit is our person, and only spirit sins, not soul. Soul only is clothing manifesting spirit-mind by reason and spirit-love by emotions. Temptation comes through soul where the primary enticement is of James 1:14, but it is ONLY spirit - our God-made self - which makes the final choice where temptation becomes sin (v.15) - and 2 Cor. 7.1 - filthiness of <u>spirit</u>.

But that does not take away from the ecstasy of revelation you had of your freedom in spirit-union. It only adds to it the ultimate authority of us as persons - spirits as HE IS SPIRIT. And that includes what you very finely say about speaking that "word of faith", and the authority and creativity of that word - which of course is my spirit-ego verbalising itself, as in Gen. 1:3.

But don't stop till you've got this clear both from Scripture and inner witness. It is vital, because only then do we act as God, with soul-body as vital means of outer expression, but not the essential ego!

I won't say more now. Also don't let us drop our present soul-spirit discussion until you and others are totally clear. Even Watchman Nee had this wrong.

My much love to you both

Norman

~~~

53

Dec.16.85

My dear Fred,

Yours has just come. Good to talk things out. As to the sin question. Yes, I have always stood by Rom.5:13, and said that in final analysis all we humans in our human self-boasting (I'll be the best president etc etc) is really SIN. But I see I must not call it that, as Scripture doesn't. We should only be seeing sin, sin, sin in all round us, instead of distorted sons (prodigals!).

Then this carries on thru to our redeemed activities. We don't call Moses a sinner when he'd gone all the length of Heb.11:24-26, and then killed that Egyptian! So obviously both Paul and Jesus left room for calling it what you like - "babes" (I Cor.3:1) but not sinners as in I Cor.5:1,2. And Galatians "foolish" in their return to indep. self, but not sinners as he called by implication the Judaizers of Gal.5:12 & 6:12, 13 and 2 Cor.11:3,4 & 13-15. Jesus the same when He was always chiding the disciples for not having faith, but obviously responded to appearances in unbelief as on the boat in the storm - just "Where is your faith?"

So this always seems a thin line. I met it greatly in my Ruanda contacts from which Roy Hession wrote his "Calvary Road" and I my "Continuous Revival". The fine point where we condemn ourselves under temptation and at what point do we say we have sinned? Such a radical attitude that we quickly call temptation momentarily responded to as sin has a real cutting edge, and I found much benefit from my Ruanda contacts and consequent ministry. But I don't see it like that to-day.

So I see we have to walk a tightrope in this, and sin is only nailed as sin where there has been a conscious choice in it - Jas.1.15. I think that is the fair open, liberated outlook we have on ourselves and thus on each other. That leaves plenty of room to point out any indication of indep self (but we must be careful first that we walk in Matt.7:1-3). I often refer to Jesus when the disciples urged Him to call down fire on the Samaritans who wouldn't let him stay in their village. He didn't point out their indep self spirit, but affirmed their true Spirit and left the Spirit to shew them the difference! Lu.9:55

Love to you,

Norman

~~~

54

Jan.15.86

Dear Dieter,

Thank you for your excellent letter just come. It seems to me that you are being 'sealed' of God as HIS disseminator of what I like to call our "Total Truth" in Germany and Europe. I am sure Dan is right in saying it is the TWENTIETH CENTURY REFORMATION. The reason is before our era and such men as Freud (tho an atheist), the church in general was not investigating or seeking to discover the true meaning of the "self". Now that day has come and all psychology centers round self-activity (but with the lie at its base when the "self" has not started at the Cross), and the revelation of that so-called independent self really being Satan in forms and the real self-Christ as us. I dig into that in the YES I AM book. That little KEY is precious and goes out in thousands. Of course translate and print anything you are led to do.

Yes, I know Ian Thomas, has a good ministry way beyond the normal evangelical. But there is a final total "leap" which very few see or accept, even among victorious life teachers and writers, and that is this 'no human nature' but only formerly Satan as us, and now thru Calvary Christ as us. This is our RADICAL basic truth of our "reformation". But it is bound also to be met with opposition. It was the "believers" of those days, not the pagan Romans, who crucified the GIVER OF TOTAL TRUTH. And so to-day. Many great teachers and writers come up near to the edge, but that FINAL leap of faith (as my loved Kierkegaard called it) is still rare and the life is ONLY self in satan form or self in Christ form, and no intervening independent human self. That's THE revelation. So it would be good if the Spirit is "thrusting" you into total dedication to this total truth, and as I say, wonderful if you are linked with us. And wonderful when you are linked with these young learners.

No, Bill Bright of CC is great, but does not accept this "total" of the natures, nor even my loved InterVarsity which the Lord led me to found in 1919 when at Cambridge. Great world witness but not on this level.

My love in Christ and will be glad to hear from you again.

Norman

~~~

55

Ap.21.87

Dear Brother Dieter,

Yours has just reached me on a tour of meetings and fellowships, and I have just been in your old home-town of Houston! Thank you for sharing God's ways with you as I read your testimony. How the Lord <u>corners</u> us by this and that until at last the Spirit breaks thru, as you describe, and He has beautifully brought you back and out of earthly occupation with the glory of making the sacrifice for Him in your present "high calling".

I am so glad the Lord has given you this living link with Bill Volkman and it would be wonderful if the Lord did lead to a visit by him and a seminar. There <u>is</u> a further and final "recognition" in the Spirit beyond the "Be BORN Declaration" and all those positions of "committal" to Him. We have nothing to commit, because we are only just vessels, branches, temples, slaves (Rom.6 last half), and all those illustrations which drive home that we humans never lived our own lives of self-expression. No, that self stuff is actually Satan's self-activity as us – even though it is the "good" part of that false tree of good and evil. It is "evil good"! So we don't commit a self-acting self to Him. No, we just recognize that the Self-operator has been changed in us, and we merely expressions of Him – IN us expressing light! It is radically different from the stresses of committing ourselves to Him and making declarations of our allegiances to Him etc. It is <u>HE who has committed Himself to us</u>, just as Adam & Eve chose to accept Satan 'committed' to them, so that their lives were expressing his lusts, not theirs (John 8.44); and now we are branches by which the Holy Spirit produces His fruits– Rom. 6:2-22.

I can't say more just in a letter, but it <u>is</u> more, and radically different from what is usually presented to us and by us as the "victorious life", even by precious men who do take us some distance. But there <u>is</u> a TOTAL distance and our links together are God's ways by which the Spirit can bring you that further final leap, even as He has brought us and what we now share in "Union Life".

I am so glad of having these living contacts with you and am altogether hopeful you will be able to continue the contacts with Bill until you can be together.

Lovingly in Christ

Norman Grubb

~~~

Sept.4.88

Rhonda dear,

Yours has just caught me before my granddaughter and I start a 2 ½ months touring thru to the West next week.

Yes, dear, I wouldn't bother your head by such things as "sins of the fathers", nor even about "spiritual warfare". Life is so simple when it is only and always just HE as me. You ARE Christ in your Rhonda form, and then all that comes to you, like your husband losing his job, has come to Christ as you. So you are right when you say life is just constant good practice in recognising and often 'feeling' the dark, but then, not fighting it (that's the danger of "spiritual warfare", for He finished that battle at Calvary), and so while we recognise those outer assaults on our emotional-soul life, we then say, "That's not me. That's Satan getting at me to respond as if I am an independent me. But I'm NOT. I'm Christ as me, and HE is perfect".

You speak of not being enough. No, love, that lack is only in your unbelieving self which feels dark or lack. You can't have more or be more than HE as you. Can you?

So with my love and I'm always glad to hear further from you and letters will always follow, though may take longer to answer!

Loving you,

Norman

~~~

June 22

Rhonda my dear,

Thank you for yours. Ok, there is "process". Light that "shineth more and more unto the perfect day". But we don't concentrate or even really notice growing. We live as "perfect now", BEING, and simply confronting the negatives, trials, pressures, as "sufferings" we accept, as Jesus did the cross: then as we accept, we find the resurrection there and others see it in our body form (2 Cor.4:7-12). Be a BE-ER rather than BECOMER! "Hath perfected forever them that are sanctified" etc etc!

As to tithing, you have it right. Babyhood may start by regular "law for" tithing and have its answers, as you had. Maturity is not a thing called tithing, but ourselves, as He, are the tithe, and it takes practical form AS HE AS US leads us this way or that. I tell folks when you have the Giving Spirit, as we have, keep all you can because HE will get out of you what is HIS outpouring to the world of need by you! I liked you paying your tax with your tithe!!

ever with my love and always glad to hear,

Norman

~~~

Dec.23

My dear George and Adaire, You dear ones, you just about put in most perfect fullest form what is happening. Thank you indeed. You just hit it RIGHT ON THE SPOT. Many Victorious Life teachers give a good dishful of Gal.2:20, and many are blessed, but I always knew from the first 'revelation' in Congo in 1924 that there was something radical about the "I am crucified" part of our great Gal. 2:20, and I saw but couldn't put it in clear form, and almost spoke as if we are Christ! So my earlier writings had not got it FULLY CLEAR THAT THE "exchanged life" is not exchanging Christ for <u>self</u>, which is the 'normal' teaching, but exchanging Christ for SATAN, and this beautiful created self BUT ONLY AS CONTAINER AND CHOOSER (John 7:17), and then ALL THE REST IS HE, HE, HE, but starting with the false "He" - that VAST, VAST LIE which has "drowned" still most of even the redeemed!

So, George, your letter is MOST HEARTENING to me. And yes, those "predictable" will phase out, but this RADICAL NEVER, though others may phrase it in other ways. ALL PRAISE.

All love and thanks,

Norman

~~~

Mar.2.89

June dearest,

Thank you, dear, for the bigger handwriting, but don't be bothered about that. I have various stages of magnifying glasses and can comfortably read anything. But this is clear!

I think I see suffering as outer impacts on us, as with Jesus in Heb.2:10 when it says outright the way of suffering as the road to perfection is straight from HIM, and then as in 5:7-9. The point to me

is that suffering is really solely <u>how we take it</u>. It is inward attitude.
All those 'horrors' such as that plane crash are really only horrors in
proportion as we are inner (subjective) people which of course is the
real we, and we know how to use "suffering" as the stiffening of faith
sinews leading always to "the joy set before Him", and to Rom.8.28. Alan
Parker's "Cross in the Heart of God" which he got from our greatest
Jacob Boehme implies that process for God Himself, which as it were
"forces" Him out of being the essential "fire" self we all are, by choice
(faith) into His eternal "light" self – Heb.12:28 and 1 John 1:5, but there
could be no eternal light-blessing in His eternal nature if it wasn't the
right use of His fire self. So I see all suffering from that different angle,
and free from – Why does God allow this? – by knowing it is ALL part
of the NECESSARY COURSE. "Joy set before Him" (Heb.12.2) does not
mean enjoyment feelings, but that deeper Spirit-flow of reality. So I
think we have to differentiate between outer "negatives" of outer trials
and sufferings which are part of our maturing (James 1:1-3 and thus
Heb.5:9) and we walk in and through them, and if we are "subjectives",
have got the habit of examining each situation until we see the purpose
in the suffering. Those are normal negs. But Satan's assaults are on the
FAITH LEVEL, and all that inwardly disturbs us by questioning, fears,
reactions etc is Satan getting at us with his self-for-self nature and
we "counter" by accepting his rights to attack us on this "god of this
world" realm, but then we "call his bluff" and transfer our "obedience
of faith" to who we are as Christ as us – thus all fits into the "more than
conqueror" process by which our great Paul ends up his great "victory
chapter" by lists of "horrors" assailing him as the very meat of his
overcoming faith. And then freed on that level, his real spirit-suffering
is in his Ro. 9-11, and on in 12-16 – intercession.

Heb.11 is the last word. Abraham, BELIEVED GOD, and is our
"FATHER OF FAITH" and Jesus, "Where is your faith"? and believing
simply means we ARE what He says we are. So SIMPLE! C.T. Studd
thanked God we are all born gamblers, and when we have sense we have
put our money on the right horse – Jesus Christ. And spirit life, as you
know dear, is just BEING and cannot be described. It is just BEING, once
we have travailed through Rom. 7, accepted honestly the desperation of
our self-failures, then the light dawns. Yes, yes I'm so glad you've got
that great great CONCLUDING UNSCIENTIFIC POSTSCRIPT - Kierkegaard
is so penetrating in thought that usually I start by not understanding
what he is saying, then a sentence or so later – "THAT'S what he is
saying!" and the light glows. How TRUE SUBJECTIVITY IS TRUTH AND

OBJECTIVITY IS CONVIENT ESCAPE. So if you can stick to Kierk, great riches, but it took me a year or two!!!

Let's keep on sharing,

Norman

~~~

Jan. 27

Darling,

Yours came this morning. I am so glad we have restless diggers among us. If we didn't we should atrophy or be easily knocked out by other diggers.

Curiously I saw _____ on TV while staying with Bette Ketcham. Don't know when I have really "Hated" with God's hatred (Mal.1:3) anyone, but I did "hate" that _____ and saw Satan in his human attractive but devil's form. And I read Jude 4-13. Precisely. And I see the need of such books as Hunt's Seduction. That is also why Alan's "Cross in the Heart of God" is so valuable for us all. No Cross in _____.

Darling, all "being" is fire – God's and man. The universe is fire on every level (for all is light and light is fire in right form).

But "being" (Acts 17:28) is NEUTRAL. Paul said "I am persuaded that nothing is unclean of itself". Right again.

But beyond "being" is the secret of the universe – The Person (of whom "being" is a product). But Person is in its essential nature, freedom to choose, for that only is "person". So God as Person - fire – chose in His freedom to be Other-love rather than self-love in His begetting of His Son, and by and thru His Son, all things. Therefore in God fire never became "consuming" (Heb. 12:29), but was transmuted into light (1 John 1:5) in which "there is no darkness". So He as fire is eternal light - other-love.

Lucifer was a "being" of fire created by Him, and nearest to Himself. But as a person he must be free to choose and God Himself has not power over person-choice. He may foreknow, but He can't predestinate beyond predestinating the consequences of choice. So Lucifer became an expressor of Deity Fire in its consuming self-for-self form which He our Deity God never was, who is "Father of our Lord Jesus Christ". So Lucifer becomes Satan as expressor of God as fire in its "evil" form of self-for-self and 'good and evil' come into manifestation – good as fire transmuted by choice into light: evil as fire turned into self and all consuming darkness – false light (Matt. 6:23).

Then God the Father had planned from eternity a billion family of sons whose created human "beings" could express by its person-free-choices His light, other-love nature, rather than that consuming self-for-self form of fire nature which He never was.

So there had to be choices as free persons in the Garden, and God "intended" what would be the choice in the sense of humans having to make the choice, and He foreknew they would try out the subtle (as in that TV show) type of pleasant self-for-self choice – Satan. So we humans became expressors of Satan's self-for-self nature which is God's misused fire-nature which in God the Father became eternal light. And by this means we humans have to go thru all the suffering of present world-being while we are captive to Satan's consuming fire-nature (though when we are changed into expressors of Christ's other-love nature, we can turn the suffering into blessing).

But good and evil are REALITIES, expressing the deity nature in its essential choices. (See Mal. 2:17 in the TV perversion).

Then THE MARVEL. Good (which is other-love in its ultimate form) will find a way of rescuing all humans who have been duped and tricked by Satan (as Eve-Adam in the Garden and in that sense are ignorant of what or who has really 'caught' them, but who have not yet made Satan's ultimate choice from the heart. But that choice can be made (as that Jude description), and those who do, do become "hated".

But for the vast majority of us, not yet in that ultimate choice but in partial ignorance, That Father-God has His way thru in the ultimate of other-love.

Certainly all humans have always known sin as sin. The written law on tables of stone only put it in clearer outer form. Did not God tell Cain "sin lay at his door". Was not Noah for 120 years a "preacher of righteousness" (2 Pet. 2:5 – wonderful touch of NT light on OT history of Noah). Did not Joseph say he could not sin against God in Potiphar's wife solicitation? And so on. Man has always known, though not in its essential sinfulness.

So what does ULTIMATE love do? It takes the reality and penalty of a human race captive to Satan in his sin-nature upon Himself, by His Son taking our human form (2 Cor. 5:19), which He could do as our Creator and thus representing all of us: live the perfect human life, not by Himself as human - impossible for a vessel - but by being possessed by His Spirit, thus Satan had no hold on Him in his humanity.

But then being of course totally hated by Satan-possessed humans in their highest 'religious' form (or false so-called philosophical form as _____) and put to physical death by them, He could die as representing all the human created race in their sin condition as captives of Satan - which was the Ultimate Love (1 John 4:9), and could and did go to that hell condition as they; but then as it was impossible for Satan to have any hold on Him, God could rightly raise Him up from that grave into a new kind of humanity, spirit joined to Spirit in some form of risen operation body, not yet known to us (1 Cor. 15). And this is what He did.

So by this means He could display love in its ultimate self-sacrificing form - as Intercessor. (Is. 53). By this means this 'gospel' of God's love could be presented TO US in winning form and give us the real spirit-life ("knowing no man after the flesh"), which we now live by faith (the value of Lanyon's book so sold on faith).

_____ is right that we do not operate by human obedience or disobedience. That's the very No Independent self truth. We are DRIVEN SELVES, expressing spirit of truth or spirit of error; but there is a final element of CONSENT in us. So there is good & evil product of personal choice, God or man, and each has its inevitable effects.

And now our marvel is that caught up by the Spirit of Truth we begin that same love-nature and our delight is to be intercessors, Lambs as He is The Lamb.

Darling, that's a rough answer. If it hasn't touched the point, let's hear further or when you see me, because my whole life has been a "gotta find out" ultimates and have no rest and give no rest until I do see on that next level.

LOVING YOU DARLING AND WITH YOU NEXT WEEKEND.

Norman

~~~

Ap.16. 89

Dear Joyce Sister,

Thank you so much for your encouraging word. Yes, you lay your finger on what has been real to me for many years - that I am to be a DIGGER to the roots. Karl Barth said real seekers are like Dogs who dig till they uncover the buried bone!! And I have found just that. The books I have been led to write seek to dig deep as I've been given to dig.

It took Paul all the travail of passing thru a "reckoning" in Rom. 6:11, thru, at last, exposure of that subtle lying self-effort way, because we have no self-acting "nature" of our own.

As to your question, the changes, which have to take place are in our outer "flesh" expression of Him as us. "Flesh" is our beautiful human selves with all its soul-body capacities. What Paul will speak of as "the infirmity of your flesh" (nothing to do with the deity NATURE which is expressing Himself thru our "flesh".) So that still has outer conformings to be experienced. Jesus Himself had to "learn obedience thru the things which He suffered"!! So all trial and temptation-pressure are "sufferings" which press us into further outer steps of flesh conformity – we are to be "conformed to the image of His Son". Inwardly The Spirit glows in and thru our spirit; outwardly there are ever enlarging conformities. So those outer chastenings are just for our outer improved expression of The Inner. So also James in 1:1-3.

Thank God you have been given to "see" much more clearly than most believers. KEEP GOING FORWARD AND ALWAYS GLAD TO HEAR FROM YOU.

Lovingly,

Norman Grubb

~~~

Oct. 11

Millie dearest,

I got your intriguing letter this morning about teaching James.

Yes, I would really like to build it together a bit more, but can't do that now. I think the essential secret is there when the folks get it clear that the heart of it is, first in our being begotten of God (new Birth) (1:18); but then after travail and failure in the self-life which have popped up in various forms of disturbed self-expression (1:21 first phrase): then we are at last conditioned to discover we are not only "begotten", but "engrafted" (1:21 last half) – which means the recognition of our Vine-branch union as a given fact as in John 15, but has first to be needed by our self-failures, then appropriated by faith (Gal.2:20).

Then the secret comes clear – that we <u>are Christ expressed in our human forms</u>. We <u>ARE</u> He as we. We then go to a mirror and see ourselves. So now when we look in a mirror we no longer see our human selves expressing that old self-nature of Satan, but expressing Christ, and <u>He</u> is our liberty and operates that liberty as His new law of the Spirit as us, and so we see ourselves in that mirror as He as us!!

Now then when all the "doubles" of James turn up, (double mind when needing wisdom; double attitude to folks as rich or poor; double tongue - 3:9-12; double motive in our prayer life – (4) etc.) we do not struggle as if we are double and take condemnation. No, we boldly say, "I am <u>NOT DOUBLE</u>, <u>I am single</u> – Christ in my form, with single faith for His wisdom; single seeing of all God's children equal; single tongue (which can be tempted by a muddie trickle getting in, but the fountain – Christ as me – is pure; single motive in my desires and prayer (4:1-4), not adulterer having an 'affair with Satan' though we may be tempted (4:4).

And finally we come to the bold declaration of 4: 7-9. Get clear in faith that I have cleansed hands, pure heart, and the devil has nothing to say to me.

So I think that is to me is the secret of James which I believe is missed. It is not a struggling to do good works, condemnation for failure book. No, it is the glorious life of practical outworking of our faith – position as Christ as, by just continuously declaring who I am – single, sole, not double and I AM the right ways of Christ expressed as me. I am that wisdom from above of 3:17, 18.

And then from then onward I meet all the doubles of that letter of Temptations with the laugh of faith which says Satan may make me feel like that, but that is his lie. I am Christ as me; I am love; I am purity; I am single-tongued; I am singly motivated; and as I boldly assert this by my word of faith, the Spirit bears His witness to me (4:7-10.) So it will be lovely, my dear, if you boldly plunge into James rather than in OT.

Yes it was lovely as always enjoying our wonderful precious fellowship. It is indeed true that the Spirit has brought us into a living Spirit-family which gloriously enlightens what might be a dull old age!!

I know and realise it is a problem with churches not giving this full gospel, but thank God if they even give a saving gospel; and we will pursue our calling of adding the complete.

Loving you, dear ones, and how can I thank you for all your love to us.

Norman

cs so

EXCERPTS

I surely wish to be open to any examination, like Berea, of whether what we say lines up with Scripture.

~~~

You hit that right again in terms of subjective and objective. That is what I saw most clearly thru our Kierkegaard and quite a bit further last year when you & I were digging into his "Concluding Unscientific..." together. I saw with Kierk the true meaning of that supposed dirty word "existentialism". I saw of course it is the ultimate truth. "Subjectivity is truth": and I saw that objective means that I bypass the disturbing necessity of going into myself to seek and find God's, not Satan's self-for-self, reactions in me to every situation: and that alone is true living, and Paul's "WALKING IN THE Spirit", while the others, as you say in Paul's terms is walking in the flesh. Yes I am passionately with you in the only true being is subjectivity – and that is what Kierk means by living "in existence".

~~~

It seems clear to me that the great number even of those who do 'see' far enough to affirm "Christ in me", and hopefully stand square on our Galatians 2:20 faith affirmation, while they say, "Nevertheless I live, yet not I, but Christ lives in me", are tangled up by the first phrase of the "I am crucified with Christ". I have had several letters lately taking that first phrase to be "death to self", and say so. (And actually that phrase is not in the Scripture!).

~~~

That Second Coming stuff has never grabbed me. I see spirit not matter – "the Heavenly Jerusalem" – "that city which has foundations", those "spirits of just men made perfect", that "Israel of God", not all this fuss around the musty old earth-city and rebel Jews. First coming was a shock and never dreamed of as He came, so also The Second. Anyway we are already members of the body, "seated with Him".

~~~

Freedom is never being anything. That is a kind of LSD delusion which runs us into nothingness. Freedom is the necessity of choice, for we are only consciously free because we stand between alternatives and have to choose and such choice makes us captive to our choice. So the eternal issue is presented to us – is freedom choosing self-interest and the bondage of self-gratification or is freedom choosing with God's other-interest and the bondage of other-love: and we find that heaven, for it is God.

~~~

Bill has now written that too much weight is put on choice, whereas in reality we hardly choose, we just ARE – a driven people, though of course we can temporarily deviate. He has written me so well on this about us basically not "choosing" but just "being", where our primary choice first fixed us, and even that was hardly a choice but just going where I couldn't help going when I had seen my need and saw the reality of Christ's love. I was caught and yet in the "mystery" of the law of opposites the paradox of my friend Kierkegaard, there does remain that amount of choice as in the final word of Revelation, "Whosoever will". Never beyond the dialectic, which as Kierk says puts passion into life!!

~~~

We are for ever humans and have human responses and are meant to, but they are overflowed by Christ in us; and indeed unless we were first living human persons with human reactions, we should not be the persons by whom He unveils Himself.

~~~

The first compulsion on Jesus after being baptized by the Spirit as a Dove was to spend actually forty days confronting that other spirit who caught Adam-Eve into response and disobedience but after fifty days could not "catch" our Last Adam. Jesus called Peter "Satan" when speaking by Peter's words, and He said He would not permit that same "prince of this world" to have anything in him – John 14.30.

~~~

"Good" satan is what is so subtle. That was how I came to Christ for salvation while reading as part of my philosophy book John Stuart Mim's phrase of "enlightened self-interest", I said that is precisely "me". All my life was geared to self-interest, whether it had good or bad appearance, and in that sense I sure was a "Walking Satan". Thank God because Adam-Eve did not make an irrevocable heart choice when they responded to the Serpent, we do remain within hearing and responding distance of God, and He can reach us by the law and does.

~~~

By "nature" we do not mean our basic human being with all its forms and potential, our selfhood of will, emotion, consciousness etc. We mean, not quantity of our being, but the quality, and that's not we, but the deity-nature expressed by our humanity. All Biblical symbols of our humanity point to that we are "vessels," but it is the nature of the liquid it contains, whether expressing wrath or mercy. We are "branches", but we express and reproduce the nature of the Vine – true or false. So as temples indwelt by and manifesting the Deity in it, our bodies temples of which Spirit? We are slaves of which owner (Rom. 6) and wives of which Husband (Rom. 7) and so on.

This we understand to be the secret of our liberty to function as humans (Rom. 6:16&20). It is much the same principle as the computer with its vast potentials, but only as it is programmed; or the way we freely practice the profession we first committed ourselves to attain, and which takes us over; then we practice them and call ourselves by its name - doctor, carpenter etc. So we all call ourselves Christians as practicing Christ.

~~~

That whole 'holiness' teaching means that some altogether new thing has to happen in us, removing 'something' from us which supposedly remains after new birth in our 'flesh', whereas Paul taught it as one total work of grace thru Calvary and the full meaning of Christ's body as well as blood death, clearing both sins out by His blood (I Pet.2.24 – "dead to sins", not sin), and then sin (Satan in his sin nature) by His body death (2 Cor. 5.14 & 21 linked to Rom.6.10,11) and thus our whole selves now rightly used by the Spirit, and temptation either way, up or down, as merely pulls on our God-created flesh.

Our whole total salvation was completed at one stroke, as Paul implies by his "know ye not" of Rom.6.3-6; and thus it is not some special 'taint' to be removed by some new act of grace, but only an entering in by the redeemed to their full inheritance ("possess their possessions" of Obadiah), by an act of total faith and total witness of the Spirit, which admittedly is by a second word of faith such as Gal.2.20 in nearly all of us, as apparently in Paul himself – so that our human selves, created perfect by God, have totally regained their misused selves to express Christ in place of sin (Rom.8.2-4 completed by 9 & 10, with Christ dwelling in us in place of the indwelling sin of 7.17, with the one exception of the physical body - but not moral or spiritual - remaining mortal). Thus what we are saying is radically different from the "holiness' second work of grace in 'entire sanctification' needing some second change in our redeemed selves. The pastor of the largest Nazarene church in USA, in Denver, told me that this inability to fit in the responses of the human self (flesh) after their "entire sanctification" doctrine is their weak spot, while our "teaching" clarifies this.

~~~

You speak several times of us "allowing" the Spirit to operate by us. We very strongly speak of BEING who we are and thus the Spirit IS in action by and as us, and there is no "allowing" in it. I just think that is what makes us and will make us continually anathema to our Bible-loving brethren. They regard us as going too far as BEING HE IN OUR FORMS, and thus calling ourselves God – precisely what they crucified Jesus for maintaining.

~~~

One or two comments. You are right about "cannot sin", and there is the Scripture. But the same writer puts in 1 John 1.8-10. In other words I have had to separate sin from sins. Sin is principle, and that is out forever – for Sin is Satan living in us as us. Sins are product, and as you follow thru with temptation in James 1.14,15, can turn up in our lives.

~~~

The pride-humility package are the two ends of separate self-consciousness and when we walk as He in the self-unconsciousness, the paradox is that we are both proud or humble selves as needful! We are full liberated selves-in-union.

~~~

I am ignorant and only vaguely know what the Gnostics stood for, though I see it by contrast by the basic emphasis of John's letter on walking in the light, keeping the commandments, etc. as our final liberated, not legalistic selves. As John says at the end we "keep ourselves"! The law turned upside down.

~~~

You see when I first grabbed by faith, together with my Pauline, that Gal.2:20 statement, what I had not then got clear is Who is the "I" which is crucified? Just as you say, I now know wrongfully I called my "flesh" sinful nature, which is BY NO MEANS the correct translation of the Greek "sarx", but is inserted, in these subtle mistranslations such as the Living Bible. "Flesh" is just me in my human capacities of soul and body. This is obviously so because Jesus was "God manifest in the flesh", and Rom.8 makes it plain that calling it "sinful flesh" means that some virus was inserted into my normal human flesh. Thus Paul can go on to say "the life I now live in the flesh" is "by the faith of the Son of God" and thus not "sinful flesh".

~~~

I think you know I have often boldly stated I am half a Communist, and still am – not in their blind philosophy, but in their leveling practices in principle. Curiously what always stymied me in my British WEC days was to find that my fellow-Weccers who had come from homes with very little were the Tories, not "Socialists" and I often stood almost alone – in WEC!!!

But of course Ortiz is right about this horrible travesty of the true church as manifested in Rome in S. America, and it is much the same in England. I can't bear to see the Archbishop mouthing evangelical clichés with mitre, throne and all that anti-Christ C. of E. stuff. No wonder the world turns out. Communism has been <u>God's</u> word of judgment on the church – not the devil's.

~~~

I note what you say about "Total Truth", and again I realize the shivers it may cause. I use it constantly over here, without apparent offence. I hand it on from Paul's own words "to fulfill the word of God, to "present every man perfect or "complete" in Christ". You may be right that it is better left out of the kind of "declaration" we are preparing for the Magazine. I will mention this to Bill, lest it causes too sharp shocks, but Col. 1.24-28 IS "total" to Paul and us, in my way of seeing it!

~~~

God has to put dynamite under a pastor just to find himself in God, quite apart from thinking what the sheep will think about it or how he feeds them. When he is truly fed, he himself will be the fresh green pasturing for the flock! Yes, love, we can't and daren't give more than we are and have. While your pastor hangs on to some self-building laws, he can only feel safe if his flock are law-bound also; so he will veer to the human discipline stuff and the self-searching. How clearly you now see this, yet because you see it with the eyes of Christ, you are not judgmental but move in to share with him all God gives you and have faith for his liberation.

God is in all this - every bit of it - the evil as well as the good. He shuts us up in unbelief, <u>that</u> He may have mercy on us, so when folks walk Satan's way, they are being taken that way by a God who has designs of mercy on them - Romans 11:32.

~~~

I see "jealousy" in the way you are seeing it as what Paul meant in his 2Cor.11.2 – in other words jealous for God to be all He is in you. Satan jealously is when I'm disliking your effect on me. In that Spirit-jealousy you & Paul speak of how entirely I am with you: and that is my deep deep hurt also when the world and including so many of the born/again believers are blind, as you say, when they really ARE as Christ as they. You hit that right again in the terms of subjective and objective. That is what I saw most clearly thru our Kierk, and quite a bit further last year when you & I were digging into his "Concluding Unscientific" together. I saw with Kierk that true meaning of supposed dirty word "existentialism". I saw of course it is the ultimate truth. "Subjectivity is truth".

And I saw that objectivity means that I bypass the disturbing necessity of going into myself to seek and find God's reactions, in me to every situation: and that alone is true living, and Paul's "WALKING IN THE Spirit", while the others, as you say in Paul's terms is walking in the flesh. Yes I am passionately with you in the only true being is subjectivity – and that is what Kierk means by living "in existence". We do "see alike," darling; and I see with you that the ultimate "tragedy" is the many who won't allow the Spirit to take them subjectively to their inner Ultimate. It was Jesus weeping over Jerusalem, like a hen over her chicks and "ye would not".

WHY are we "the chosen" who do "see"?? But we do and so pour out our all in sharing what we know. So how I am with you in that our "godly jealousy". Thank God for that jealousy, and such "subjectivity". We have been precious learners together, my darling and I'll only hope for more.

~~~

It has much that is GREAT- far beyond the normal evangelical victory teaching indeed gets hard after "Law". It is wonderfully Jesus centered and sails quite close to the Total. Often speaks of Christ as us - and plainly shews much of how to walk in the Spirit rather than flesh. But no, it misses the spot as we see truth. He majors on Sarx (Greek for flesh!) as if flesh is inherently evil in its desires, but the Bible says not flesh but "sin in the flesh", and now a condemned prisoner in death row (Rom.8.3) and we dead to it (not flesh). So this leaves him with having to handle a flesh-nature in us, instead of being able to use flesh (soul-body) as "God manifest in the flesh". So he isn't clear on no human nature but only the two deities, indeed he hardly mentions Satan, but puts all his weight on "sarx" which keeps us inward looking instead of seeing ourselves as OK as Christ and Satan the outer enemy invading thru flesh.

~~~

You have never commented, on this vital "no human nature, but only deity natures reality," though you did at first say this surprised you – but it is THE KEY. And it is then, that the answer is obvious to such questions you raised as disturbing – about "moral responsibility" and "mistaken faith". I can't but be morally irresponsible with Satan expressing himself as me, nor can I be anything but morally responsible with Christ expressing Himself as me! I can have some measure of temporary soul-body false choices by temptation, just as I have right choices by the Spirit's ever 'tempting' me upwards. (Gen.22.1!). But you see in our union reality it is NO LONGER OUR FAITH. It is Mark 11.22 (Margin – the faith OF God), and Gal.2.20 "The faith of the Son of God", of, not in! So when we speak our 'word of faith', we are saying, in the belief that our speaking is His speaking, that HE has done this or that. And even if such faith is mistaken in how that real manifestation will come, GOD will see to that – as with Paul in the famous 2 Cor.12. 8-10.

~~~

What an exhilarating life is ours to be pioneers of The Truth in a world distracted by conflicting philosophies, all with some ray of truth; but to us is entrusted the knowledge of the central sun, the unsearchable riches of Christ.

~~~

I suppose we have to recognise that it is a great rarity to find a professional pastor who has "seen" all the way; because even "yield more" is still a form of passive legalism! But the truth you and I know is just "Being" – recognising that He and we are a unity, now forget and BE!! We love to cover our central vacuum by some form of self effort, and folks love it too, to give them a feeling of doing something to get where we can never get except by being!

~~~

I have always known that that is a battle with you, and God is touching the depths of the self-life, when He can deal with that; for it is really only another form of pride, too little self is as much a sin as too big self.

~~~

There is always a danger in looking for revival rather than Jesus! Jesus is Revival, and a person in whom Jesus is living is a revived person! So you have your plenty rivulets of revival already, and I expect God is merging them into a flood.

~~~

I just marvel at the grace of God, but that is God. He is not interested in our professions of righteousness, for we have none; but when He gets us broken, sometimes He takes us right into falls and sins of the flesh to expose ourselves to ourselves, then His mercy and grace can abound. It is the redeemed <u>sinner</u> in whom He is glorified.

~~~

Tell Ann that I have no difficulty with the omnipresence of Satan, but if she has, let us dig more deeply next time. I believe probably in the fourth dimension all our spirits will be omnipresent, for there will be neither space nor time. Even brother Einstein nosed that out.

~~~

I believe the Scripture can only be taken as a whole. If tongues was essential, it was bound to be a major subject in the epistles – but is hardly mentioned. All is CHRIST. Yet tongues is there from Pentecost onward, is of God, is a gift AND often may be the evidence of our inner union as at Pentecost. Therefore I respect all who have that gift, consider them as having a gift beyond myself, but will not confuse it with the reality of the union.

~~~

So we stand together at the center of Christ's own John 17 prayer as one in Him as He in us, and any 'divisions', as those Paul wrote of in 1 Cor.1, as not in our vocabulary, but as works of the flesh. Therefore if any of our brethren speak of themselves as though we are separated from them, we just don't 'see' that as in existence. We just ARE one; and we see anything they speak of as separation as really only, as it were, cutting an umbilical cord, where maybe, I am a kind of father among us, and they feel the need of affirming their own individuality in our one ministry, and we praise God for that, and affirm and bless them as they go forward with our message and ministry – a little bit like the persecution in Jerusalem after the martyrdom of Stephen only meant the glorious more widely scattering of the word to the world!

~~~

Surely with such inner knowing and 'glowing' we will be bold with all boldness of the Spirit to give out our total "Knowing" as God gives us openings, and with no holds-back, which both means sharing the cross of rejection and suspicion by so many sincere fellow-believers who mistakenly confuse Satan's self-nature as though it is their own and thus lived condemned, and thus appearing blasphemous to them to say that their human selves is actually Christ in their form; but we also have the glory of seeing others desperate enough to seek and find truth and who join us in their inner illumination.

~~~

I am sure our safe place of unity is always in Jesus Himself, and not in any viewpoints concerning Him, and that is our happy meeting place.

~~~

Then in Paul's agony he went three years in Arabia and found that full total Calvary meaning, not on the blood for sins, but in His body representing our body and thus expressing that sin-spirit and thus His body-death (the broken bread of the Lord's supper) meant that out went that sin-spirit from Him and thus from us, and in came His own Spirit and thus into us.

And that leads to the final issue - the final cleverness of Satan is to pull us into temptation as eg. Gal.5:16-18 and we think temptation is to some wrong end, fear hate, lust etc. But it isn't. The real temptation is to get me to slip back into saying "I ought not ". Bang! Back into indep. self, and now we are caught! At once as if we are indep. selves, back comes the law and says, "and you ought not". And down we go into struggle, condemnation or even sin. The sin is to believe again that we are indep and ought not. The truth is, when you at last know there never has been such a thing as indep. self, then you say, 'Yes, I'm being pulled by outer soul-body to respond to Satan, but I'm not there to respond. There is no such thing as an indep. Me. I am Christ as me'. And then of course the Christ nature, now mine, of love, faith, purity etc overflows and light swallows up dark. We are free, says Paul in those verses, when we see we are not under the law, because there isn't a me to be under it! The temptation was to be pulled to think there was, such a me. And we learn that the hard slow way!

~~~

But on responsibility, my point is that we are SLAVES TO RESPONSIBILITY - as in Rom. 6:16-22. CAN'T HELP OURSELVES. We were driven by Satan and now we are DRIVEN by THE SPIRIT OF LOVE, can't help ourselves!! OF COURSE WE ARE RESPONSIBILE, BUT PROBABLY I PUT more on God's drive, (though of course we can yield to temptation - either upward (Gen.22.1) or downward (Jas.1.14!) So I don't really think we mean differently except that maybe your calling is more to stress our response to Him who drives us; whereas mine is no independent self as in Phil.2.13: (and I get enormous acceptance of it from hundreds of poor driven folk, driven by their own false sense of "you ought", where most Christians live); and so I stress "YOUR'E CAUGHT. YOU CAN'T HELP IT". I guess either emphasis has its dangers in extremes and I was always a hopeless extremist!!

~~~

But as all consciousness and activity is by the interaction of opposites, dark swallowed by light, etc. we could only become conscious in the Garden of Eden by being confronted by the two trees, and coming alive to choice by being told not to eat the fruit of one of those trees. The Living God had Himself been confronted, as it were, by that "choice" in His "fire self" when He "chose" not to remain just a self-for-self like a consuming fire, but by the eternal begetting of His Son in His likeness. His "fire-self" was eternally transmuted into being His "Light" self, the Self-for-others, just as light blesses where fire burns. And this is our Eternal God of Other Love—the God "who is light" as in 1 John 1:5. Lucifer was created to express God's other-love likeness, but with his choice-capacity as a person, chose to remain a fire self-for-self and thus was cast out of heaven, the Deity dimension, "having great wrath." And he was then God's negative agent to confront God's created human family with becoming conscious persons by the necessity of choice between the trees. That first deluded choice by Adam-Eve, although not totally deliberate as was Lucifer's choice which fixed him as false deity of self-for-self nature, put them within Lucifer's deceiving reach, by which, as spirit joined to spirit by choice, he could and did infest those first two with his false self joined to our selves (Eph. 2:1-3, that "spirit who works in us the children of disobedience"), and II Cor. 4, "god of this world who has blinded our minds"). And so, all we humans start life under the delusion of being self-acting, when in actual fact we are expressing and "driven" to express the nature of the spirit-deity indwelling and "working" in us. Therefore, the plain simple outcome is that we are all through the fall ("in sin did my mother conceive me") spontaneous expressors of Lucifer's self-for-self nature, but we are deluded into thinking it is "just we." THAT HUGE LIE!!!

I am stressing this, well-known to you because the vast trick of Satan on us REDEEMED people is to delude us into thinking we have some form of self-expression, when in fact NO ONE HAS EVER HAD SUCH A THING AS SELF-EXPRESSION, as Paul so plainly points out in his Romans letter and what we cling to as a last resort as "just ourselves" is REALLY the expression in us by us as us of the nature of the spirit indwelling us. So when in this fixed delusion we are told, as in Gal. 2:20 that we have been crucified in and with Christ, but now live, yet "not I but Christ lives in me," I fixedly deludedly cling to my having a self <u>of my own</u> which I must retain to consciously express Him! A Self? YES! But NOT OF MY Own. That Lie has persisted right into the huge majority of God's redeemed people, so that they CLING to the claim of RESPONSIBILITY (that Lie Lie) and thus say, "Nonsense, we can't cease to be responsible selves" under the delusion that we ever <u>were</u> responsible selves. So we say, "Truth can't be just that we were Satan-expressors, but are now through Calvary Christ-expressors, but we must also retain a place for "responsible me." Again that LIE LIE LIE. My only "responsibility" is my capacity of CHOICE, and once I have made that in the bigger sense, then my choice faculty is at rest permanently because that choice has now been made and now I am that vessel, branch, temple, taken over and expressing my take-over!

And it is THIS which has stirred up such opposition and is even called "error" even by many Bible-believing people, because until, by some means, we are "torn to pieces" by, as Paul in his Rom. 7, inability for self-achievement, we are not conditioned, apparently the large number of God's redeemed people, to "see" and recognize our delusion of self-recognition and self-responsibility, and just can't and don't see that we were ALWAYS ONLY a driven people with driven selves based on our own capacity of choice which was a part of the physical birth and was "born" in us as Satan-slaves. But then it comes to our own vital issue in our new-birth "Choice" when we either "loved darkness" or "came to the light" of new birth.

Now, this is why I'm so desperately keen (before I fly off and leave you all) to get it out PLAIN that this very popular "in" thing of saying Christ lives in me is on <u>crumbling foundations unless</u> I first say (and very few do) that that same I, now crucified and with Him in me, was not just the lie of a lone "I" — never was such a thing — but was a Satan-expressing "I"; I polished and clarified saying what Paul so totally has said in Rom.6-8!!! Good company, and if that is error, I gladly hope I shall live and die in error!!!

~~~

But shan't we all find on THAT DAY that our so-called total truth has been mere crumbs - see Jesus saying if you only have "mustard seed" faith. WE ARE babes in the wood, usually mistaking a few trees for the whole forest! Yes I think our good average is a little "quickening and a lot of mental seeing" – but the mustard seed level is blinding light to non-seers!

കാരു

ENCOURAGEMENT

I thank our Lord for His great grace in having me run into you.....
so you could tell me how I could be liberated from myself that I
so disliked and paradoxically, liberated to be that same human
self...only this time it was He.

~~~

Unable to compliment me on my faith, he complimented me on
being honest! Norman always buoyed you up. He always saw
the positive in one.

~~~

When holding an envelope in one's hand from NPG – it would
be wrong to say it was never with any sense of apprehension:
but generally with a sense of appreciation at hearing from him,
and gaining fresh insights. He was against the drab uniformity of
conformity with dated opinions.

~~~

Norman said, "Live who you are."

CR ∞

December 6, 1940

Dear David and Leslie,

We want you and David to know that no-one is more in our faith and prayers these days (except Bessie in Bissau, Portuguese Guinea) than you two. We realize what a need there is that the LORD should keep you perfectly steady in Him. Without wireless and newspapers, all sorts of rumours must reach you, and the devil's first weapon on these occasions is always to stampede us. As someone said to me recently, "Be sure you are guided, not driven." The Lord is causing us daily to stand in faith on your behalf and Staniford's, that no thing or man shall be allowed to touch your work. GOD has put you there. HE has made us, together, responsible for the evangelization of the whole of Senegal. What years these have been for you! How great has been your honour, to go through all the tremendous experiences of a first pioneer, and now to cap it all - the war crisis. May God make you Jeremiahs, pillars of iron and brazen walls (Jeremiah ch.1), with something unbendable in you which will not give under the suggestions of Satan, the appearances of things, or the advice or threats of man. The clouds are dark around all of us these days, and Satan would soon get us to take to our heels if he could get our attention fixed on the blackness of the clouds rather than on the brightness of HIM Who is dwelling and working through the thick darkness in order to make LIGHT shine out of it.

God has led us here to praise HIM every day, and TO GO RIGHT AHEAD, concentrating on our one task. We are as full as ever, preparing to send out the 25 recruits for which we have trusted HIM in this year, with six ready to sail...GOD has prospered us every day of this war so we have much to praise HIM for, and little to worry about so long as we live by the day and are not moved by the surmisings of the future... Much love to you both. You are a constant inspiration to us, and to many; the influence of your steadfast testimony for Christ reaches out far beyond Senegal.

Ever Yours in the Crusade

Rubi

~~~

October 22, 1958

Dear Margaret:

Thank you ever so much for writing, and for enclosing these gifts. Humanly I say to myself, what are you doing giving gifts like this out of your own need, and should I accept them? But I know that is not the fact. I know that when God tells us to give, we are only making room for more of His bounty to us. So I thankfully and gratefully accept them for the Lord's work, and when I go back to Camp Hill I shall put them in for the furtherance of the Gospel. Thank you very very much.

Thank you for your letter too. I am delighted to hear that you are really moving in towards Faith at Work. I did not know of course whether that was settled. It will be a joy and delight if God establishes you in it. You will find plenty of personality problems; there always are in a close fellowship. I am used to plenty through my life in our own circles. So I hope we can keep this intimate touch in the Spirit so as problems arise, you will feel free to share with me behind the scenes, as it were, and I may be able to help. God seems to give me quite a ministry these days with various folks outside our W.E.C. circles along these lines.

But at the same time don't take false condemnation, as I think you do in the last paragraph of your letter. That is when you say that you want prayer to be more surrendered, more Christ-centered, etc. I don't think we get the victory by having a kind of long term view on our lives that we ought in general to be more this or more that. I believe victory is just to see Jesus in me now and NOW, no matter how we fail or have lapsed right up to this moment we leave that buried in the Blood of Christ. We rejoice now that Jesus Himself is living in us, and that's all we want for time and eternity. Don't bother about the future, and becoming more this or more that. You can never have more than Jesus in you now, just relax in Him, rejoice in Him, and walk and work in Him. That's all. The rest is really only false condemnation. You can never be improved more than I can. You are only just a vessel, a cup, a container. All the improvement in you is Jesus Himself and He cannot be improved because He is just Himself in us. So just relax and rejoice I say!

My love to you and deepest thanks, and we may be able to get a touch of fellowship when you are in New York.

Ever yours in Him,

Norman

~~~

November 6, 1958

Dear Mrs. Thompson:

Thank you so much for your letter. I have appreciated you taking me so much into your family life, as well as what you pass on of what the Lord is showing you.

It is good to see the Lord keeping His steady Hand on us, though it comes through suffering. How we thank God in the end for the real inworking of the Cross into our self life, until the redeemed self becomes only the vessel and agent of the Spirit. The Lord's Cross does not cost anything like the devil's crucifixions when he gets us to go his way!

Praise God for the abundant grace He is giving Carol to go through with Him alone, and that battle of the affections is the fiercest of all. Once He gets us settled at our center with Jesus only, then He can bring into our lives what He pleases on the circumference. God bless her. Give her my love. I felt the reality in the bits of talk I had with her and you. "Not God first, but God only" has been a life's motto to me.

Warmly yours in Christ,

Norman Grubb

~~~

November 12, 1958

Dear John Lawrence:

Thank you for your letter and sending me a copy of THE FRONTIER. Of course I remember our several talks together, and wish we could have had more. If you come at any time, please let me know.

You put me on the spot when you ask for criticisms! The point is, as you well know, that I belong to that section of the Church of Christ which is immersed in getting people into a living relationship with Christ, along the lines of what we would claim to see as the major occupation of the New Testament writers. I suppose in modern terminology we would be called "Pietists", although I quote that Norman Goodall prefers to call us "evangelicals" in quotes!

For this reason, the old WORLD DOMINION appealed to us because it was more occupied in the growth of the church and the evangelization of the world in its more Christ-centered aspects than in the world situation in general and impact of the church upon it. FRONTIER, on the other hand, to judge by the copy you kindly sent me, is more concerned with the horizontal activities of the church than the vertical. Probably our basic faith is much the same, whether evangelical or "evangelical"; but in our application of the Christian message we have somewhat of a different emphasis. I suppose both are needed, though all of us naturally feel that the one most real to us is the most important! For this reason, I should not think that you will find that "FRONTIER" grips the interest of our type of evangelical, as it does what we would call the more liberal type. Curiously, I was speaking to the Professor of Missions in one of the leading denominational seminaries of this country, an evangelical seminary, where I was speaking yesterday. He knew of Kenneth, and in talking with him, just happened to say that he used to take WORLD DOMINION, and that FRONTIER has been coming to him, but that he did not think he would renew his subscription. Yet I would not have called him an ardent fundamentalist, as I suppose I am!

So I would say, God bless and use you in your ministry, and it is good to hear that you have a wide circle of readers. A fortnightly magazine, which tremendously interests and grips me over here and which just suits my taste, and probably you have seen it, is CHRISTIANITY TODAY, which marvelously combines scholarship, spirituality and the evangelical emphasis, although probably you would feel that it does not deal with world events enough, although actually it does handle present day problems very vigorously. This is certainly a great day for the spread of the Gospel worldwide.

With kindest regards and greetings.

Yours sincerely,

Norman Grubb

~~~

December 9, 1958

Dear Gilbert:

I was anyhow thinking of writing you since our phone call, and now your letter has come. I have been carrying this challenge on my heart and mind since we spoke.

Many thanks for now making the details clearer. I think the first point of main importance is that you make sure and keep sure that the Cross is in action first of all, according to the II Cor. 4: 8-13 passage. We have to keep our eyes on JESUS ONLY living and walking in us, and it is sometimes a strange path. We took it as settled that He took you back through faith to your executive position, and has actually increased and enlarged you since then. Then that is settled. He took you back and we accept that to mean that He has planned for you to stay there.

Then comes this fierce test. God so prospers you that you build up the department, have workers put under you, and are all set to head the department. God then sends the devil in through the schemes of this unworthy man, and he is given the position you should hold.

Very well then, we still believe God and declare our faith. But you must be very careful to walk the present path in self-emptiness, and that means that, while God takes you through the tunnel of testing, you accept the situation with meekness and praise. That means that you must take this man as sent of God to steal your place from you, and you must serve under him in loyalty, until God shows His victorious way out. I think it is essential to underline that point. If you resist the man God sends to usurp your position, although we may see him as the devil's agent, you resist God. That was the pathway Joseph walked successfully with his brethren when they sold him, and with Potiphar; Jesus also walked successfully in His crucifixion; Job walked less successfully, though he came through in the end.

God will triumph and bring forth your righteousness as light. Presumably He will either stop the man ever taking over, or show up the fraud later; but meanwhile your victory is to walk the thorny path in the rest of faith. That means that you see JESUS ONLY in these circumstances, and in the coming of this man, and therefore die to inner resistance, confusion, etc. You demonstrate this victory within by letting this usurper see that you accept him in his legal appointment, while he is allowed to hold the position, and that you back him, and that you can trust him. This was what Joseph did, and "found favor" with Potiphar in his household, and with the keeper of the prison. Your day of deliverance will also come.

I shall be with you in spirit, in faith and praise, and shall keenly want to know how God lives it through you and for you. Friday I am off for meetings with the Harvard students till Tuesday, then back again. So I shall be keen to hear then.

Much love to you both,

Affectionately your brother in Christ,

Norman

~~~

February 22, 1959

Dear Billy Graham:

I would think it presumptuous to write you a word of encouragement if I had not heard through Mrs. Dinert speaking to a mutual friend that you were feeling more than in the past the impact of those who fiercely criticize you.

I have heard from many of the grace given you to embrace criticism as coming from the Lord, like David concerning Shimei: "So let him curse, because the Lord hath said unto him, Curse David. Who shall then say, Wherefore hast thou done so?" God <u>sends</u> us our tests as well as our blessings, doesn't He? So we praise Him for every single thing He sends into our lives, and indeed for our adversities more than our blessings - they are safer!

That does not mean that we <u>take</u> what our critics say one sentence more than God tells us to take it. We have learned that plenty in our much-criticized W.E.C., though our critics have done us a lot of good! Brother, you have walked a magnificent tight rope with God. The "genius" of the Spirit in your ministry is not only the glorious gospel you preach, but the fact that He gave you to sense in the Spirit that open hearts to the fundamental gospel of our Lord Jesus Christ are to be found in their thousands in what we used to call the Liberal Camp, both among ministers and congregations alike; and that God must find some bold conservative evangelical, such as yourself, who would take up his cross and step across that human line of demarcation between "fundamentalist" and "modernist", and preach the fundamentalist gospel right in the other camp. Hallelujah! What a glorious privilege has been yours - to be a pioneer for God, not in some remote field rough on the body, but in a worldwide field mighty rough on the soul; and the roughness coming, not from some misunderstanding pagans, but from the house of your friends! What an honour is yours!

Don't be moved from it, brother. It is God's breath of life, His fresh breath of life for our generation. It is just that which has opened the hearts of such millions to the gospel through you. It is your <u>cross</u> in which you are to glory! Keep at it! I think you know you have the hearts of millions with you; and even I in my lesser wanderings about this country, Britain and other lands, meet a constant stream of <u>unlikely</u> people gloriously saved through the Word of God through you.

We do not say that those who hit you hard have nothing to say worth hearing. We do not say that they are just "devil's agents" or "write in a spirit of hatred" or some such foolish thing. No indeed. They are Godly men, greatly concerned for the glory of God and the preservation of the pure gospel. We honour them and believe that they say to you and of you what they deeply believe should be said. I personally count some of them my friends. I have sought carefully to weigh their point of view, and for that reason I think they are of God as a <u>safeguard</u>. Their very criticisms help to keep us watchful against compromising one iota in our message. But having sucked that amount of honey out of the lion, let us leave the carcass of their attitude of separation from you!

For myself, in many tests as fierce to me though not of such public import, I have found my permanent release in seeing CHRIST ONLY in all things, good and evil, that come to me. It is Christ in me looking out on Christ in the others or in the circumstances. Very well then, I relax, thank Him, love them all, believe God is blessing them also; BUT I only take into myself what HE HIMSELF in me gives me to take. I won't let what they say or do touch the inner peace or certainty that He gives me that I am going along with Him up to the light I have, and that's all that matters.

I would not dare to think that a letter like this would ever reach you among your enormous mail, if it was not that I am told Mr. Dinert himself is coming home for a few days, and will take it with him.

Brother, we are with you, thousands and thousands of us, who hold every word of "the faith once delivered" and yet believe you are <u>the</u> missionary of the gospel of our day in penetrating into regions, not of heathen religions, but of millions who have lost their way in understanding what that saving gospel is, and yet who hunger for it.

God bless you, and He is,

Sincerely yours in Christ,

Norman Grubb

~~~

April 19, 1960

Dear Jane:

Thank you for your further two letters just received, and enclosures.

I am glad that my letter did not shut you up anyhow! That's the basis of true fellowship in the Spirit - talking things out in the light!

I am <u>most</u> glad of your openness to the Spirit concerning your pastor and your re-affirmation of walking in love towards him, and your fear of being a cause of division. That was what I was really getting at. I do know of cases of small groups of "spiritual women" (I don't know why always women!) who have been more a cause of division than blessing in a church, where they have felt a lack in the ministry and kind of formed a nucleus who had an apparent spiritual superiority. That is what I was getting at. I get involved in it too - I know one large and living evangelical church which has been closed to me for years, because one Godly woman came into new blessing through my books, and let her pastor know in no uncertain way that she had what he needed, and that she had got "it" through those books! So she and I were tied together in his thinking! So I am glad that the Lord is keeping you sensitive about being in any sense a disruptive influence at your church. Keep seeing the Holy Ghost in your pastor. That is a far bigger fact than any lack. Keep remembering that God's rich seal of blessing has been on that church with worldwide effect. There are few enough of us faithful to Christ, and we need to stand together, even though we do recognize each others shortcomings. To love a person is to trust the Holy Ghost in him. I hope you are in all ways able to make your pastor feel that you are right with him, appreciative of all there is - and there is so much - of Christ in his ministry. But please don't be concerned that you wrote me. I am glad you did, and of course I keep the confidence. I should myself be spreading damage if I shared these things.

Now for your kind suggestion that we meet, or that I meet with a member of your group. I hesitate again, not that I will not love to meet you, because I will; but God has given me to take another attitude towards world affairs. The picture may be dark, and much darker than I know, but I profoundly see from God's Word that He Himself <u>sends</u> these dark things. They are His ways of judgment unto mercy. So I don't find my calling so much to be concerned with gathering darkness, or even to oppose it on the human level, but to meet it by the positive acclamation of our Christ on the throne, and we with Him there. So I rather think that if we met as a group, we should be somewhat at the different ends of an axis. I will leave it at that at present.

Please feel perfectly free to continue writing!

Sincerely yours in Christ,

Norman Grubb

~~~

June 10, 1960

My dear Wallace,

I am grateful to you for laying bare your heart in your letters. I'm more and more convinced that God is not living in our organizations, but in our love one to the other, for He is love. Therefore it is more important, and more truly God, that we find the way of loving Christ in each other, and loving each other in Christ, the details of our organization are merely secondary to this. I'm gradually learning this in WEC. I believe we have our personality clashes, and will have them sent by God, till we gradually make brotherly love our supreme and total objective. And when there is that, Jesus said, "the world sees Christ".

So we've got to get on with that with ICL as in WEC. I think the way Abram breaks and confesses, as well as you yourself, is most precious, and you go much further this way than I do. This must be an excellent objective among us older ICLers, to recognize and count on Christ in this younger generation of workers not as superceding us, but as growing up with us, all making the one team.

God gives us each our infirmity so that we each may learn to see through the natural that repels to Him who is the real self within each of us, and to see how beautifully He expresses Himself through the outward selves that so often repel us. God is pretty clever!!

Finally, I'm not easy about the self-condemnation, etc. that you often have, though I do know that you give me the privilege and underside which others wouldn't see. When God has been teaching me not to take that, what I do, is merely use that I'm looking at little me apart from the real Me (which is Christ in me). My sin, then is not that I see some failure or other in myself, but that I slip into the unbelief of separation, as if I am a little I apart from Christ. I won't take it. I am a little I, but I am the negative through which the positive can express Himself; we are one axis together. If there is some real spot of guilt where I know it is not just natural human weakness, but sin, then I have no business but to remain guilty. The Blood was shed 2000 years ago, and I honor God by immediately accepting the fact that the thing was blotted out. Excuse my sermon, but you put up with me!

Let's keep up the correspondence. So glad God blessed in Paris. Much love.

Ever yours,

Norman

~~~

86

June 16, 1960

Dear Daughter,

It was a great joy to get your first letter. A tremendous joy to me that God has preserved you in your Congo calling, and counted us worthy, (all in His grace), to have you still among us. A very great joy to us, for you are a precious daughter in the Spirit to us, and we have kind of fought the inner battles side by side with you during these stormy years.

How I shall hope that you will still find time to unburden your inner heart to us as before. You have already in this letter touched on some extremely important points. I think the great point, is that you should not see and talk outer division, but inner union. Boldly see Christ in all. That is far far more important and God-glorifying than harping on the fact that we may think some have taken a wrong step in separating. The whole history of the church is thousands of outward separations, whether for right or wrong reasons, but what really shows forth Christ is when we retain the union in Christ by our faith and loving attitudes, and affirm and practice union despite temporary outward separations. I even say that, if God has at present led some this way (and the Scriptures show that God leads people wrong ways in order to teach them lessons, as well as right), then it is also God's leading which constrains some to go with them, and not leave them at the risk of fanatics and errors with no mature guidance. Do you see my point. Don't stir up anxieties about this outward separation or that. They have never mattered much in the history of the church, indeed all points to the fact that separations have usually resulted in spiritual advance! Look at the division between H.A.M. and U.F.M. Hasn't it resulted in larger areas of the world getting the gospel. Who was right and who wrong. I say God was evidently on both sides! I am sure that God is not very much interested in our outward organizations, separations, etc.; but is interested in the world seeing our brotherhood in Christ. That is the fact, whether in this or that outer detail, we feel one or the other has taken the wrong direction. So I say seek means of expressing undivided fellowship in Christ and love with them, and indeed any others who move out in separation. And dare to see that God is in it all. I would like you to share that with others when the matter comes up for discussion.

I think just the same about political affairs. Our prayer of faith, and we know that it will be substance among you, is that you all will rejoice in your great honor in being in the true firing line in Congo just now.

Probably you have never had the privilege of being in a hotter spot since H.A.M. began. And, following the Scripture, boldly believe and affirm that God is handling the Government to His own ends. Believe that He is putting down one and putting up another, even if those who take power may seem to us to be opponents to the Gospel. Help the church members, as well as the missionaries, to be wholly Christ-centered at this time. That is, we are not thinking about our own skins or what may happen to us, but how we can be channels of His love, and manifestors of the living Christ in these days of possible fear and confusion. It is not wrong for Africans to have political interests, anymore than ourselves, nor is it wrong to partake in politics. But to those who are Christ-centered, everything else is a mere outward occurrence. All that eternally matters is that we may be witnesses, by word and life, to Him who is Lord of the eternal Kingdom, and that we may live and act as members of that kingdom already. You see my point. Whatever party is in power, God has put it in power, even though it may seem enemy-directed. God is working all this out for His eternal purposes, which is the growth and purification of His own body among the Congolese, and the saving of as many souls as possible. We shall see a stronger and more purified church through all this ferment.

Finally, your touch on the Pentecostal problem! My anxiety is that Britain, through fear, will put on restrictions and bind the Spirit. The test will soon come when a fine Assembly of God couple is applying to join. We shall quench the Spirit if we put up barriers because they are declared Pentecostals. The only condition we should lay down is that they do not create controversy by stressing their particular viewpoint on tongues being the initial evidence (if they hold it) among us, but I believe we should stand in with building up any field, just as much as the C.I.M. built up a Church of England field in China. It is a tightrope walk, I know, but the Spirit of God is always too big for our human protective legislation, and may we be big along with Him.

Our love and keenly looking forward to hearing again from you,
Ever your W.E.C. father and mother,

Rubi and Pauline

~~~

July 11, 1960

Dear Frank,

What a wonderful time that was with you. I just rejoiced in what God is doing among you, forming a team, I'm sure, which will yet include many others who are hungry to know "The Way". I feel very much a part of you. God seems to have joined us together and I shall have to pay periodic visits!

I hope you will form a fellowship group where you can meet, open your hearts one to another on the problems of Christian living, and share together in Bible study. We do grow by the "milk of the Word". I don't believe the best growth is just by having one person expound the Bible to you, but by each sharing what he or she gets out of the passage. Yet such group meetings do need a Chairman to make sure that someone or two people do not dominate the meetings, or that you don't get diverted into useless theological arguments etc. The chairman could be one appointed person, or it could vary from week to week. I don't believe you need wait for some specially so called "gifted" leader. Then also you will be challenged as a group to find means of inviting others and enlarging yourselves to include them.

My love in Christ to you.

Warmly yours,

Norman

~~~

December 29, 1960

Dear Mrs. Mancinelli:

Thank you for your letter. How beautifully in His own way God unveils the truth to us - and that is Himself in us. I don't think there is an easy way in. I think we all, like you, in one way or another have to have the "many long weary days seeking to know His way." It is only that wilderness experience which conditions us for the flash of light and fixes it in us: that our only trouble has been the illusion of our lonely selves, while all the time He has been and is the real living Self in us - Gal. 2:20. Once you have learned it the hard way, you have really learned it in the Spirit, and though we often wander away temporarily, you will always know now where to go back. You are in the land of Canaan!

It would certainly be nice to see you sometime, and I am sorry that I missed you at Sandy Cove. I am afraid you touch on the old, old story about my speaking too quickly and too softly. I get it on all sides! Pray for me and the Lord will improve me!

My love in Christ, hoping to see you sometime, and thanking you for writing.

Ever yours in Him,

Norman Grubb

~~~

March 2, 1961

Dear Stella:

I came back yesterday from the tour in the South to find your letter awaiting me.

Don't take false condemnation. It is anyhow a grievous sin against the Spirit for these men to take in members as born again in the family of God who are not born again. Whether it closes doors to you or not, you spoke a faithful word. You may feel that you spoke at the wrong moment. Well then, give that up to God and boldly trust Him to use even that to His glory, for you certainly spoke out of a heart moved for truth and against error.

The great lesson I learn is to accept myself in my own weakness, and maybe in saying and doing things which I may feel are not the best for God. If I feel any condemnation then I immediately move over to the present reality of the blood where everything is forgotten. But then I see nothing in myself, but everything in the True and New Self in me, Christ in me. I relax back on Him, the Real Sayer and Doer. There is your and my rest and joy – Jesus Himself in you. So boldly fix a single eye on Him and don't allow Satan to invade you with self condemnation – I John 3:20. If God did lead you to speak to the pastor, it could only be because you felt that what you said was said in a critical spirit, or at a wrong time, but not because what you said was wrong. Hold to the truth.

My love in Christ. I'm always glad to share these spiritual battles with you.

Ever yours in Him, with greetings to your husband,

Norman

~~~

April 12.61

My dear Pat,

It is a long time since I've written. I think the main reason has been that your long letters have been more than I could chew and digest adequately in the very mobile life I have had these months, and I didn't feel free to read and answer until I had the Lord's word.

God is bringing you out into normal living, and I thank God for that. God is a perfectly normal Person, for He lives a normal, natural, free life in the lives of His thousands of members. He so disguises Himself that the natural man can hardly recognize Him. Those nearest to Him are the most normal living people – I used to notice that in C.T. and Rees Howells. Only the Spirit in us reaches thru to the Spirit in the other. Beyond that, there are just enough differences about us for the flesh to catch an uncomfortable sense that we are different somehow.

Now I do know that God has privileged me to be your confidant, so that you pour out to me what you do not to others, and therefore you are giving me the inside of things. I keep that in perspective, and value the honor you give me in the Spirit. But am I not right in feeling that you are still too much occupied with the "mechanics" of Christ living in us, and consequently too little in being a perfectly natural person with the indwelling Christ as the sub-conscious rather than the conscious most of the time.

Seek God in this, Pat. Don't let this stop you writing to me as God gives it. The Lord is perfecting His living in each of us, so all is well. Let us just go on sharing according to the light given us.

In unchanging love in Christ to you,

Norman

~~~

Kilcreggan House
Kilcreggan
Dunbartonshire
Scotland
- till June 14.

May 25, 1961

My dear Irl,

Just thrilled to get your cable. It was a wonderful thought sending it. What a journey ended and how much has gone into it - but it is really beginning, not end - of the real job. I am so thankful to God with you. You gave Him all the glory - them that honour Me I will honour.

What can I say about all that you both have meant to us (as well as to others) these past two years? (I lose count of time). It has been the Lord's precious gift to us. And how I rejoice as God gets bigger and bigger in each of us (as was pointed out yesterday, "O magnify the Lord" doesn't mean making the Infinite bigger - that would be a little difficult! But it does mean we see Him bigger in us and in all - the telescope idea).

Lovely fellowship here, love is the keynote, and I believe God is going to be more glorified by this "new era of love" among this gang of tough Weccers, than by any more outward new policies. Love is the highest. WEC has been known for sacrifice and faith. May we now be known as those who love one another (and thus Christ in each other).

I am already almost counting the weeks like a kid to my return - only two months DV before I re-embark.

Very much love, and great rejoicing with you.

Ever your brother,

Norman

~~~

July 19, 1963

Dear Belinda,

<u>So</u> glad to hear again. Just keep writing, dear, bits and pieces, it doesn't matter. Just let it out to your adopted "father in the Spirit", and it will come easier. Don't hold back, and nothing you can say can shock; I at least know enough about myself not to be shocked at anyone else!

My dear, this is the pressure of <u>God Who is love</u> on you. You see, He must press and press till He gets us "through the hoop", right out of interpreting life by what we are, or what happens to us, or how we react; and to exchange it for the <u>fact</u>, that the real you here and now is not Belinda, but Christ. And Christ, God, is <u>love</u>, which means that <u>you</u> are love, and life for you is just loving people, just where you are. When you recognize and accept that fact by faith, then you drop wishing you could do or be this or that, and feeling frustrated that you can't accomplish what you long to. That is frustration, because self-desires are always frustration, and God plans they should be to force us into this only real meaning to life - God loving by us. So you see, dear, however painful it may be, take the place of death in Christ to <u>your</u>

plans, <u>your</u> desires, <u>your</u> hopes. Don't reckon the fact that they have not come off frustration; but <u>thank</u> God for His way, which is just this way of apparent frustration! Then get the habit of, against all feeling, and though some folk are so difficult to love (I know that too; and I am just as difficult for them to love me!), saying to yourself, "God, it is <u>You</u> living this life in me." And God is love, only love; and so you are only love, no matter how much other feelings may temporarily rise up in you and me; and being only love, because He is in you, just live to express that love to those among whom you are. That may not always mean being sentimental; love sometimes is firm, but the basis is that we live to love, because we <u>are</u> love in Him. Got it?

So I send you this line at once, because I love you in Christ, and want to continue alongside with you as Christ is formed in you,

Ever lovingly your father in Christ,

Norman Grubb

~~~

June 15, 1965

Helen dearest, and Freed dearest!

You are a woman of surprises, as all "living" women should be! And this is a surprise. I being in the old age when we are deep-dyed conservatives (except in politics!), was questioning what you were biting off in this new place, but it is a job to question God; and now He has answered! I suppose we being such new lovers-in-Christ (though love springs up pretty quickly in this kind of relationship), I love you in your present home and ministry. And so it is at present.

I still want to make a list of those various ones I meet who are on "this ball." Links of fellowship would mean much to many.

Let's hear from you again.

Ever lovingly,

Norman

~~~

93

Norman Percy Grubb

January 11, 1966

Dear Belinda:

How glad I am you have written again. I had realized how long it was since I had heard, and had wondered about it, but did not want to push letters on you without having firsthand news of how you were going. So I am just thankful that you have "broken through" my dear. That is just right, and I hope you will keep feeling that I can be a heart-confidant to whom you can say anything; and I will promise to keep up the correspondence between us.

My dear, you will never have things right until the one fundamental fact is again a fact accepted and recognized by you - that you are not Belinda, you are Christ in you! This <u>only</u> is the gospel - that HE has replaced you (you know Gal. 2.20 well enough!). This means that, no matter how you feel, bitter or resentful or hurt or frustrated, and that God has not been with you, or anything, you are <u>not</u> what you <u>feel</u> like, or what appearances are; you have boldly to say and accept, right against all feelings or sense of unworthiness or anything, that the actual you is HE - not by your side, not assisting (or apparently neglecting) you, but <u>replacing</u> you: "I live, no, not I, but Christ lives in me."

So starting from there, my dear, you simply say right in the midst of the apparent "defeats and losses and trying to begin again," HE was the One to Whom these things happened.

You see, Belinda, there <u>are</u> no defeats or losses or failures except our inner unbelief. You accept within you what appears failure, etc., you believe your own unbelief as it were, and then life <u>appears</u> miserable and you feel bitter. But if you say, "No, though what I tried at failed, and I appear defeated and feel bad about it," yet the <u>fact</u> is that God Himself is living my life, and this is the way HE walks in me - then you <u>praise</u>, though you feel a failure, or that you have sinned or what not.

You see, the only real sin is unbelief (John 16.9), you may be <u>tempted</u> to feel bitter, or angry or something; well, if you feel you have given way at times to any of these "sins", you just admit it and immediately you forget it, because it was cleansed in the blood, and you go ahead as if that never was: and all thru what may have seemed failure or defeat, you boldly say, "This was God walking in me just through all this." Do you see it, dear? And will you act on it <u>now</u>?

And where you feel that people have hindered you, and even want you to fail, my dear, God is The Person (see Jesus) Who lives to accept wrongs done against Him, and then to love and serve the wrongdoers:

94

and <u>this</u> is how He now lives in you, and puts you thru these trying circumstances and oppositions from people, just so that He can be Himself through you, which means that you are occupied in seeing how you can die to the way they hurt you, and instead be concerned with how you can love them and thus thru your loving shew them The Eternal Lover. Because remember, that if a person hurts you, his or her hurt is greater than yours. In wrongfully hurting you or wishing you harm, they are really hurting themselves, not you: so be sure that you don't hurt yourself by becoming bitter, but realize God has walked that way by you just to shew Calvary love by you to them. That is liberty, no matter how bound and circumscribed your situation seems to be. Do you see that?

Yes, there are tears, dear, and you needn't regret or be ashamed of those (tears are precious), nor try to stop them; but in so far as they are tears because you are hurt or frustrated, exchange them for praise, even thru the tears.

Arguments are always difficult. I get caught up with them also, as you with your mother. Do your best to accept all appreciation of your sister, and be ready to back her up and appreciate her. So now, dear, get seeing again that your "trap" or apparent "prison" is only trap or prison, if you accept it as such. If you see it as the free God walking just this chosen way in you, and in it giving you opportunities of being His love in action, by dying to your own likes or desires or frustrations, and seeing how you can love those around you with God's love, then that's the greatest any of us can be in the world.

Now write again soon, and talk this over more with me. No gaps please as between '63 and '66. I shall be watching for a letter.

Ever lovingly in Christ,

Norman Grubb

Remember one other point, my dear. God has never given you a husband, therefore you have to face normally unfulfilled natural longings for husband, physical satisfaction, home and family. That is bound to be deep in any of us humans. We have not discussed that, of course, but it can in itself cause unrecognized dissatisfaction, nervous tensions, doubts about the goodness of God, or resentment against those who have these blessings (and responsibilities!). I don't know how it is with you, or perhaps you have been thru this and God has taken you thru, but you have to be sure that in this area also, you see Christ living His perfect way in you and making your natural sex and maternal affections channels for His outgoing love to others. Talk this over with me too, if it can help. Many have problems this way and sometimes don't like to speak of them forgetting that we are all exactly alike.

~~~

March 22, 1966

Dear Belinda:

My dear, you do suffer, and I wish I was near enough to have fellowship with you face to face. But there still is only one answer I know. I never get thru until I see GOD ONLY in all things. When I do that, I don't ask questions of why I suffer or why others hurt or neglect me; certainly I suffer because I am human; but I boldly accept my hurts from <u>God</u>, and I say that He is giving me a chance to be satisfied in Him and His love if all the world ignore me. If and when I do that, I have an inner release which will manifest itself in me; others will notice it. But more than that, if I accept what comes to me as from God, then I am free from pitying myself, and that frees me to <u>care about others</u>. Everybody has deep needs, whether they shew on the surface or not. When folk notice that we have satisfaction and peace no matter what our circumstances, then they are drawn to us to find the secret.

So you see, dear, God <u>gives</u> you exactly what comes to you (not permits, but directs - see Joseph in Gen. 45.5-8), so that your very sufferings in the human will be a springboard to arouse you to faith - to saying God is my joy, God is my peace, God is in me to love others by me, and you become "more than conqueror thru Him that loves us"; you not only are conqueror by faith over your own hurts, but have additional love for those who hurt you.

So go ahead, beloved. This <u>is</u> God walking in you, and every life is, when seen like this, an adventure of faith and love. If you look at it that you are hurt and why, then you only know frustration; but if you look at it as <u>God's</u> way for you, then it is an adventure of faith and love for others.

Write again soon, dear. We can keep our correspondence.

Ever in Christ,

Norman Grubb

~~~

Nov.26.66

Dear Lanny,

I should think I do remember you! Just returned from a series
of meetings, but am picking yours out of the mail for an immediate
answer, though only a short one.

We walk with a Person, and not with certain fixed "principles". We
just seek on each occasion what appears to be His obvious way for us
to act. I would say under your circumstances that you are right that it
is foolish to keep paying rent which goes down the drain rather than
buying. You obviously feel that the house suits you and is where you
are to be for the present. It is offered to you at a reasonable price, which
you could not easily better elsewhere. You have money for the down
payment; your folks might advance you more, or anyhow a mortgage
would be possible. If you had to move, probably you could sell if you
wished to. Whatever you do or don't do about insurances in general, in
this case you would take out whatever mortgage people demand. So I
should go right ahead. Maybe your love for your wife and family and
right provision for them at this time should anyhow take precedence
over some special standards of faith.

As to debt: the WEC have had a continuing argument as to whether
a mortgage with its equity is a debt. Many think not. Rees Howells did
not think so!

So that is my impression of the way the Lord is obviously leading
you at the moment. Send me a line as to how the Lord does actually
guide

ever in Christ,

Norman Grubb

~~~

Jan.29.67

Jane dearest daughter,

I had a lovely time with our darling Alice, she will share some of it
with you, but I did miss daughter Jane. I had your precious letter of heart-
outpouring which cost you much to write. So now, back again, I must
write a bit, and remember I always love writing to my loved daughter as
much as I love receiving her letters!

Dear, I only know one way thru all, and I think God takes us thru our negative self-searching, or self-revealing, or self-accusing periods to settle us into this one way. It is that we entirely accept our humanity just as it is and always has been. We don't look for it to change. You speak for instance of so secretly loving yourself that you really wanted to sing to shew how well you can do it. Well, dear one, that's ok, and you in yourself (or I just as much in my ways) will always be like that, and won't change. I haven't changed in 47 years!!! The point is, to accept that that is what you (and I) are; we love ourselves. But now, joined to our human selves is HE, the Divine Self; and He has taken us over, so that the real, major desire of our hearts is that Christ will Himself be manifest by us and to others and in others. That is now our eternal basic ambition. But ambition for God's glory can only express itself thru our ambitious faculty which, left to itself, loves itself and wants to glorify itself. So mingled with the big main desire that Christ may be magnified thru us comes this other stream of wanting to magnify ourselves. But it is minor, not major. IT just sort of seeps thru down in the back of our consciousness.

Now that dirty accusing devil will point at that and tell us we are full of self and pride and longing for selfglory, and therefore we are no-goods (so we are by ourselves in our humanity). But you see if he (the devil) can get our attention fixed on our apparently self-loving self, then he has got us bound up in condemnation and depression!! Then we are caught!

So I have to learn to accept and admit to myself, not deny it or be depressed about it. But then I say, though I by myself am like that, the real Self in me now IS HE, God, and He is my real interest. So I refuse to be fussed about myself, and I boldly maintain that HE is the Real One shewing Himself thru my singing or whatnot. That's the point.

That is the same as you and I have talked of and seen in sex. No good feeling guilty because I have some desire aroused in me or liking for someone else, not my husband or wife. No, I accept and admit that. But then I say that my real love is God loving people thru me, including the one I feel guilty of being attracted to. Then I don't run away from this feeling of sex desires, but I count on God coming thru my natural human sex affections with His self-giving love, and the human sex is way underneath as a hidden background. You see that, dear one?

So you see I wouldn't bother yourself about your past stresses, and that you could not see for so long that you had these resentments etc. the psychiatrist said you had (you can only anyhow see these things when God's light shines in, as you now know); or wondering if He has a lot more to expose to you. No, don't do that. You have now learned that self trying to be good is the worst sin, for it is self-striving on the highest and most dangerous level; and that you don't take those sort of accusations that you had "dared to speak to others of Jesus", though you came to find that you hardly knew Him then. Not at all. Glad you did speak up to the light you had! No, don't bother about self-deception. Just revel in walking with Jesus as you understand Him to be the Real One living in you, joined to you. If He wants to shew you something further about yourself, that is up to Him, and He does it very nicely and acceptably!!

So you and I don't need to feel humiliated in exposing ourselves to each other. No, that's just what we <u>are</u>, and there's nothing in us except a bundle of human reactions, and all that is all HE. Excellent, and releasing!

You speak of having trouble to have faith when you feel in the valley. Dear, that is "trying" also, and it is no good to try to have anything! Just say to yourself (and you can always "say" no matter how you feel) that God is God in you, the Real Person in you, no matter if you go on feeling as black as hell. Accept feeling like that, but beneath the feeling, say the word of affirming the real fact! So accept depression, if it does come, and don't fear it; but maintain to yourself (and others where needful) that, despite that, you are not really in depression except in your feelings, but really God is your life! <u>This</u> is freedom from "sinful bondage". Not some <u>thing</u> called freedom, but Christ Himself in you, no matter how you feel. Got it, dear one?

You ask, dear, how to know if God has told you something. Just be yourself, dear, and think your normal thoughts. God is joined to you and thinks through your thoughts. Take that for ordinary daily living. When some special thing arises about which you need to know what God says, while He appears to say nothing, well just say He hasn't said anything particular. IF you have to make a decision, then make it as best you can and trust it to be His even if it turns out queerly! If you can wait, then wait until He shews you something somehow.

So now, dear, write me again soon, and go on opening your precious heart to me. I was so glad Alice brought me to know you and love you. Let me go on being your father in Christ. If you want to talk further on these things you talked of in your precious letter, then let's do so.

Ever lovingly, dear one,

your privileged father in Christ,

Norman

~~~

February 16, 1967

Dear Veronica:

Thank you again for your very living letter. I can sense the pulsing of the Spirit through all you write.

But I can imagine that after the way the Lord called you and your husband to live so many years, your return to "the historic church" would cause others who have been with you and have not been yet given to see things as you now see them, to think that you have moved from the old paths!

It also takes wisdom and grace, doesn't it, to move in among those who have probably had no touch of what you have had and yet not to frighten them off, but just to be such a normal sister in Christ with them that they can first accept you, then have confidence in you, and then discover the secret of the Christ in you. I always think that is so wonderful about Jesus. He must have appeared such an ordinary, natural, human person, and so much at home with folks, appreciating them without judging them, for Him to have been so accepted by those we call "far out!" and as a consequence He was so much judged and condemned by those who claimed to be "far in!" So the Lord must be giving you grace to win the confidence of these ministers and church members. Grand. I am sure this is a missing note among many of us who have sought to press through with God.

Blessings on you, and He is the Blesser in and through you.

Affectionately in Christ,

Norman Grubb

~~~

May 29, 1968

Dear Mrs. Sayers:

Thank you so much for your two airletters which arrived together yesterday.

I laughed when you said that my letter was to you "confusion," but now there is the big difference! I think it is healthy and of the Spirit when a thing does cause us confusion when we can't yet see it. It is God disturbing us to seek and find - much better than when a thing has no effect on us. I always tell my hearers that the way to clarification is through confusion, just as the way to faith is through doubt.

I don't think you had "wasted years." All those years that seemed like that, and about which the devil likes to condemn us, become redemptive material in His hands - to help others in their need. Paul had some pretty aggressive "wasted years," yet he distinctly said that it was God who "separated him from his Mother's womb and called him by His grace." So God had His hand on Paul all those years between his birth and conversion, and the depths he went through in opposition to God prepared him for his heights in Christ.

Warm greetings, and my love to Norm when you see him.

Sincerely in Christ,

Norman Grubb

~~~

Sept 5. 69

Daphne my dear,

Thank you for this lovely long letter and with all the details I was asking for. Yes, I do remember you as Daphne Parrott, and thought it was you, but you have now made me certain. Never think, dear, that you will overburden me by sharing in your news and whatever is on your heart as in this letter. Let me be a father in Christ to you, and I will just as much enjoy writing back to you as you to me.

I will look for that picture, and we shall appreciate that, also copies of your and Jim's testimony. That will be best of all. And I will send you this "Spontaneous You."

Dear, this long period you had in "losing God's presence"- those years (you may have lost your personal sense of His presence, but you never "lost" Him. You now know that - for we are an eternal unity) is exactly what He has to take every one of us through by some means or another in His love; because we are never true eternal sons and daughters of God in freedom until we have only HIM in the universe. And so He has to press us through to where our eternal union with Him is not dependent even on our personal consciousness of Him. We have to lose even God (in our consciousness) to find Him. But when He brings us back to this eternally settled realisation that He and we are a unity (Vine-branch, Head-body), then we are settled freely in this eternal fact, quite apart from what we may _feel_ (our soul life) about His presence or absence. And then He takes us farther to where we not only know Him and ourselves as eternally one, but we also know and see Him in

101

everything and everybody, and that where things or people appear evil, and are so, yet just there He is hiddenly behind and engineering all that happens; by this means we turn evil into good by our inner attitudes of positive faith and love in place of negative reactions.

And this was why for you He had to take Jim (for Jim to some much more glorious life of Christ-manifestation which you can't see as yet) because He had to divorce you from any human reliance, either that you must have a man to rely on, or a man must have you. Now, freed thru the cross and resurrection operative in your own life, you can in "the ascended life" enjoy the prospect of God bringing you this other friend as your husband; and the proof that it is God, not you, is that you are not pressing if he is shy, but waiting in the certainty that God will give him to you.

Fancy you still having the original <u>Touching the Invisible</u> booklet! No, Pris is not married, lives with us and came over to help Pauline with the grandchildren. Daniel does well as a professor in a college here and a good witness. Paul has married a girl whose heart is really for the Lord, and I had good times with her, and she is helping Paul towards God.

Now much love, my dear. Am soon off on tours of meeting till December, but letters always reach me.

Ever lovingly,

Norman - Rubi

~~~

January 2, 1969

Dear Don:

Thank you for your letter. It is good to hear from you and have a touch of this living fellowship in Christ. I like your underlining of I John 4:7, once we understand what that whole passage makes plain from 4:7 to 21 – that the love of God is never our human love; it is God Who is Himself Love expressing Himself in His Love by us. I often find people confused because they don't feel emotionally loving to someone, and they think they ought to love. But that is the false "I try" life of Romans 7. But when we see that we as humans never love by ourselves, but love by recognizing that we are containing Him Who is the love, and that He loves by us, then we have the key.

Interesting that you have moved to Nairobi. I wonder if you ever contact my nephew by marriage, Dr. Michael Wood, the plastic surgeon. His wife, Susan, is my wife's niece, and granddaughter of the founder of our work, C.T. Studd. They live on a farm in Tanzania and he commutes by plane. It would be nice if you met him and give him our greetings.

Then Carey Francis, who died about two years ago, and many of the leaders of your government were his pallbearers, was Principal of the Alliance High School where many of your nation's leaders had their early training period. God had used me to point him to Christ when we were fellow students at Cambridge.

Just this line of fellowship, and I know God will be the Blesser in and through you this coming year.

Ever yours,

Norman Grubb

~~~

May 31.71

My dear Bill,

You write glorious letters. My heart was stirred when I got this one on tour, but I refrained from writing until I got back now to my machine – to save you decoding!

But now we echo back to each other, which I think is true fellowship. Yet I find an increasing and thrilling maturity in you, if it is not presumption to say so. I love, of course, your emphasis on all there is "being we as HE."

I think you are meaning we cannot separate a person from his "teaching". Therefore what another person can only truly give is what may have first come through a particular person (and that even includes the writers of the Bible), but has taken living form in himself as some freshness of recognition of HIM in us and thus thru us. So we are not then passing on the teachings of some man, but (though it may partly have come as a projection of Christ thru some man) it has now become Christ to me and in me and thus thru me. Right? This is what Kierkegaard so stressed and I picked up from him – what he called "indirect communication" – that we should so share what we have got (which of course is really Christ through our human form) that we never make "disciples"; but rather just give others a chance to pick up something from God direct to them thru what we are sharing; and then what they get is merely an increase of the understanding of their living union with <u>Him</u>, not with us. Good! And that is always why I tell folks, Don't say in your talks, "AS so and so said". If what you got from so and so was a word from God to you, it is now what you have got and what Christ is in your human form and through your understanding. So cut the man-references out. I think that's what I get from what you say – and it is good, and thus fits my instinctive response to those folks who suggest carrying on "my teaching"; but you put it well in plain words.

There is going on a tremendous work among youth here, including among youth of affluent homes. I have had some good contacts. Maybe you saw about it in LIFE MAG of May 14. But I have also seen a danger. They are largely in the hands of a man with a teaching centre in Ohio, and he majors on two phrases "The Way and the Word". But I think he is running these kids into a system which will dry up on them when "Way and Word" are more to them than just Jesus. Right?

Much love to you both, let's hear again,

Norman

~~~

Sept.9.72

Beloved Fellow-heretic,

It's a thrill to get this letter from you. You see to me it is "The Epistle of Bill" to his fellow-Silas! Others write letters, yours are <u>filled</u> with riches. Your last was tremendous some months back, and this equally so. It may be because we truly see and speak "the same thing", and thus it enormously encourages me to have a beloved one who says it BACK TO ME! You really do say it – Bill – "to watch Him at work as me" ...etc. So few <u>say</u> it. I love your summing up – "A mystery now revealed in everyday experience that has become joy unspeakable". And "the Being of God has far surpassed the doing"...etc. riches untold, and we really both have "seen" haven't we. I eagerly share your letter with Pauline and this time also with our daughter Pris who is in a new stage of response and liberation.

And of course I like your <u>proper</u> use of your Sunday mornings!!! And do you think I would let such a letter go unanswered, though this is a scrappy answer!

Great also about the Largo group catching on and spreading. Yes, we are bound to get the same kicks back as Jesus did. There was just that extra dimension with His "unity with God" at its base, that the outer form folks cannot stomach. But many are hungry and plenty enough to keep us busy!

Thanks for the good encouragement on writing, I want to say with yet deeper stronger emphasis the allness of HIM THE ALL, and we HE.

So that's all now, but you rejoice, refresh, feed me and make me worse every time!

Love to dear Ann as to yourself,

Norman

~~~

July 23.73

Darling Margaret,

How close I feel to you in your lovely letter. How vividly I go back to our walks and talks when you were at College and before, and would open your heart to me. And how beautifully God has taken you on since then, and as you say, so established you in Himself. You have carried your "burden" so wonderfully in being without Austin and yet having the children, the house and garden, and your teaching. Marvelous. And how great now if God is leading you to another man who by all you say seems so suitable. Wonder how you first got acquainted when he is in Saskatchewan. I shall keenly look forward to how God leads you, and you are wholly safe in His hands, and there will be no mistake! Of course I have never seen you in your present home. I think you had moved before the Lord took Austin.

It was a surprise to meet Bill and to find he knew you. Indeed the Holy Spirit breaks all bounds these days and bursts out on the right hand and the left! And a great part of it is charismatic. The pity is that we Bible believers are the chief ones to drag our feet!! Too bad and dangerous. God has not taken me the charismatic way, but I mingle much with them and know so many marvelously transformed Episcopal priests, Catholics, all sorts.

Thanks for the word on Bertram and his wife, and give them my love. I get their Christmas letter and get family news from that. Glad you liked the biography, dear. I felt I couldn't write it any other way.

This with my much love, darling cousin, and <u>much</u> rejoicing at the Lord's goodness.

Ever lovingly,

Norman

<div align="center">~~~</div>

July 4.74

Dearest Sara,

How lovely to hear from you again. I so like these occasional touches of love and fellowship between us.

So glad this "Throne Life" is of value. It is a great release when we <u>know</u> by fact and inner awareness that we are fixed on that Throne forever (Eph. 2.6!). It doesn't mean that we always <u>feel</u> it, but the whole point is for us to get plenty of practice in recognising fact when feelings all tear us up. That is our privilege of daily inner dyings <u>and</u> risings. And the real purpose is no longer to ensure our position, which is eternal fact, but that others may catch the secret as they see us enthroned in spirit when all hell may be let loose around us! "Death works in us but life in you," Paul writes.

It is such a relief when we recognise that God <u>means</u> all things, good or evil, then when things are "evil," we look thru and see they are only distorted outer forms of HIM. Then we praise from the Throne - and speak our words of faith.

Thank you, love, so much, and for this loving gift. I should like to help our CLC leaders, so close in spirit with us, Ken and Bessie Adams, so will give to them.

Ever with my love,

Norman

<div align="center">~~~</div>

Ap.12.78

My dear Bus,

Yours of Feb. 26 is the best ever, though you might not think so when this reply is six weeks later! But you caught me just when I had started our Southern six weeks with Dan and Barbara, and mail has had to wait.

106

But, Bus, this of yours is really thrilling as I can see the Lord renewing you in what has basically been yours and mine from our past years of fellowship. And knowing that you have a gift-ministry in teaching, it is still more encouraging and eye-opening for the future! Does it mean that God may really be thrusting you and Marjorie right out (plus the glory of the cross involved!) for some itinerant national ministry with this our "Total Truth" message? I can see the Spirit is catching you on when you say you are now seeing not merely Christ made unto us righteousness, but <u>we</u> the righteousness. Here you are touching the hidden key, not on Christ as separate from us, but on we as He. Strange, dangerous, revolutionary, bound to meet with opposition from outer-Bible-based evangelicals, "hidden" (Col. 3. 3-4) yet entrusted to us to publicise (Col. 1.26-27).

I am sure the next step is for you and Marjorie to move right in for a fellowship period with some of our folks in Wisconsin. I am particularly keen that you should be with Dan and Barbara. Dan and I, who keep going together on our tours of eye-opening ministry, really truly speak the same thing, each, of course, in our lamp-form for letting the same Light thru! But above all, I am keen for you two to be with them. As you dig in together with Dan, you can get the "evil" question also clarified.

Then for another reason I am keen that Marjorie has real fellowship with Barbara. Dan and Barbara have really been given, and accepted from the Lord, the commission to give themselves to this national "wandering" ministry (kind of like Heb. 11.9) and recognising the privileged "cross" of much movings around, and money has never once been mentioned among us from the point of view that the Lord alone is their Provider. So while Dan is going over things with you, Barbara can share with Marjorie the woman's point of view!!

So I write this to make sure that you fix dates, and I would suggest you write Dan personally.

So much love to you both, and thank you again for grand letter,

Rubi -Norman

Of course, I am grossly insulted that you imply you can't read my handwriting. Get educated!!!

~~~

1978

Dear Lanny:

I fear it is a fact that Bible-believing Christians, unless they have moved right over to a fixed recognition and realisation of the union relationship, when by "the baptism of the Spirit" or whatever term they choose to use, it has become fixed in their consciousness that Christ is living their lives, they are Christ in their human forms and thus held by Him rather than holding onto Him, then their only substitute is fierce forms of legalism. That is why we have to face the fact that we are outsiders and go beyond the danger point and are not acceptable. In the end you can't sit on the fence; and, if you haven't jumped over, you sooner or later shew up as being still on the legal side of the fence, though you will never admit it and use most of the deeper life clichés! But thank God, you know the far side! And thus can quickly sense it when a teacher, even with a big name, is still playing around in the shallows.

Glad you are taking Joshua. Can get some good stuff out of him, though be sure to keep clear that he was on the self-effort side thru his early years with Moses. You can trace it in his words and acts up till Kadesh Barnea. But then he had his "crisis" experience and came over in spirit into his promised land. He was with the 11 spies in their unbelief, except for Caleb. But by the next morning he had moved over in the night and stood with Caleb. That was his Waterloo (Num. 13). And after that, thru the book of Joshua, he operated in the Spirit in power and victory, though each time he had to walk thru his primary human negative reaction and be brought thru to faith. He was called by Moses "a man <u>in</u> whom the Spirit of God is."

Well, here we are - home for two weeks, then off to Bermuda and the South for four weeks. Shall indeed welcome any further news and letter.

ever lovingly

Norman

~~~

May 8.78

My dear Ray,

Glad to hear from you. Ray, in our different ways we all have to go thru that death process.

And it is the same with you. This is our only glorious way. I knew and told you so when you said you were moving on to share the "hidden secrets" with other ministers etc. I told you they would first be worked more deeply into yourself until you are really sharing yourself, because you know yourself to be HE in your form.

So now HE (no mistake with Him or us!) has taken you to this small church which you call "hellish". Don't do that, Ray. We only make our own hells (or heavens) by the way we <u>see</u> things. No matter what folks are in outer appearances or reactions, you see them as they really ARE, Christs in their human forms, though not yet knowing it, or only with first spark of light. No, don't just give them new birth. Give all ALL you know. You will preach yourself farther and farther into experienced truth as you preach it. Hold back nothing and don't just accept appearances as if they receive nothing. Actually you are ministering death to them, whatever you are preaching, if in your inner spirit you regard the situation as "hellish" and thus really the folk as "hellish" unresponsive. You are <u>making</u> them unresponsive. Dare to believe there is a light in all men that can respond to light, and take for granted that they are His Sons whether they know it or not.

So you see really, Ray, God is working into you who <u>you</u> really are, and that includes not only seeing that YOU are Christ in His Ray form, but that all are forms of Him, and thus you practice seeing ONLY POSITIVE, which is seeing ONLY HIM. "Nothing but God exists"!!

Follow thru with some of the good things you read in UNION LIFE. God IS bringing you thru, Ray brother, for you are one who is being pulled along by the Holy Spirit, and, as I was in younger days, you are not content with the shallows. You will yet be an instructor of many in the truly liberated life. Meanwhile give ALL you know, whether they appear to hear or forebear, whether they go with you or turn you out!

my love as ever

Norman Grubb

~~~

Aug.20.79

My dear Brother Chris & Vivian,

Your tremendous letter arrived some days ago. It is a wonderful outpouring of the Spirit in His revelation to you of who you are, "Christopher Christ!" We who "know" always "know" each other, because the sound of the Spirit is unmistakable. When a person, after long seeking or saying the words of Gal. 2.20, suddenly says, "That's it. There is no other. That's all there is.", you know we are together within the Veil – He All in all. And I don't believe any come to this final discovery (revelation) of our "true selves" without long Rom. 7 conditioning, (such as your 13 years!), because we have finally "come home" when we know by inner knowing what it is to be a real self, and we are that – which of course is God's ultimate purpose from "before the foundation of the world" – to be eternally Himself in human bodies. Almost the fiercest opponents are those who have taken hold verbally such ultimate statements as Gal. 2.20, but the total midday sun of replacement revelation has not really yet lit them up, and they fight such total statements, as you so gloriously use in your letter, as blasphemous. It is in one sense quite an alone walk even among God's redeemed people, though we do gather around us fellow-knowers! So I bless God for the glory of your letter. I have already had extracts Xeroxed for some questioning friends who want more "word" evidence (I like your distinction between Logos and rhema), and mistrust experience (really when this full light has not yet dawned in them).

I really needn't say more than my delight in what you say, and the marvel when you just hear and see after our short times together; but of course really because that conditioning work (the negative necessary as background to The Positive) had already been going on so long in you. Whereas more usually what we are saying (God by us) is only at first doing its disturbing even confusing work, and only after a year or two folks say, "Now I see what sounded like Greek to me when I first heard you!"

I love your term "the deposit of God in you". That's good and original to me. And "God in the flesh of Chris Bernard". But much, much else which comes pouring thru your letter.

Yes, I shall be looking forward to being with you all again. I love your loving suggestion of spending a couple of days with you. I suppose I shall have to wait and see how that would fit in with (or be an extra to) the visit we are making together.

With my much love and great thrill.

loving you both

Norman

~~~

July 24.80

My dear Chris,

Your long one had arrived by the time I returned two days ago from a good seven weeks in Britain, and then your other one came today.

Chris, I usually have plenty to say when folks write at length to me, but this time like Keats poem of Cortes first seeing the Pacific "silent upon a peak in Darien"! But yours is a glorious one, as you flow from revelation to revelation. Perfect. I've just given it to my co-worker who is helping looking after my Pauline and she is as thrilled as I am. I go to our Union Life Conference Center in Wisconsin in two days and take it with me. I think all our inner circle will be blessed by it. Of course I want to go over it again, but I am much led to change the Epilogue of the YES I AM book I am preparing and insert this. I had indeed previously thought of inserting the one you wrote me after my first visit, but this far outshines that one. So at the moment I just say altogether a Praise the Lord.

But then your second one comes. Of course it is much the way the Lord takes most of us in Union Life. That is why it is so radical that I usually avoid going to churches and pastors because I know it will be too revolutionary for any except very rare birds to take it. Indeed the only one I know who has really gone along with us, in Thousand Oaks, Los Angeles, now writes that almost certainly his fellowship (of about 400) are putting him out as pastor. But when you are already part of a church fellowship and been blessed among them for years, I don't believe the Holy Spirit would have us take any action which brings split or severance from them. WE ARE ONE with all the body of Christ.

I believe He would have us thankfully accept whatever way of worship, prayer, church activities God causes a fellowship to see to be His way for them. In other words, we see CHRIST ONLY in our precious co-believers. Going along with that, as you are a resident in that area and are known in that fellowship, I believe you should continue worshiping and praising and praying with them, thanking God for them all in Christ.

Yet you cannot at the same time change whatever light God has given you, which means that in yourself you don't express worship, praise and prayer, etc., as they do. This has already resulted, as you say, in you being "called on the carpet" and questioned by the Pastor (the one I take it who so kindly gave me hospitality), and I delighted to hear how you opened all truth to him as revealed to you and asked to shew if off

111

base on the Scriptures, and you had no objections raised; yet, as you say, on following Sundays you saw plain evidences that he was "preaching against" what you had shared.

Therefore, Chris, I believe you have to be totally bold and uncompromising in standing to what God has revealed to you, and conforming your worship, giving, activities, etc., to what He has shewn you, and insofar as they disturb the Pastor and folks, you have to "suffer" that as if an outsider. Yet I believe you should NOT withdraw yourself from your usual times of fellowship with them (even though it may hurt you inwardly in sharing some things with them); and in every way say no negative things about the way they have their fellowship with God and each other. Speak only thankfully and positively on the ways they are led. There are few enough anyhow who go as far in all-out love and worship and witness as they do. Yet that cannot make you act or participate in the worship or activities in ways God doesn't lead you, even if it appears silence and "backsliding" to them. So you continue in your fellowship with them. Just go right on. At the same time, if God brings others around you who are beginning to "see" as we see, then you can meet in fellowship, maybe in your own home with them at times not interfering with the usual times the church fellowship meets.

I have to say nearly all "Union Lifers" go this same way as you, and move into the same inner permanent relationships which simply replace our "old ways". Some don't go to churches or are pushed out, but some are led to continue. Jesus and Paul never left the Synagogue. Only when they refused him did he say "now we turn" - Acts 13.46.

So that's all I can say now, with every great joy and union in spirit with you, and the Lord lead your precious wife to see and follow a higher "submission".

Ever with my love,

Norman

~~~

Dec.21.80

My dear Chris & Vivian,

Many thanks for your last of November 24. I'm late in replying as we've only now returned from our 12,000 mile, three-month tour with my granddaughter Sandy. Great times everywhere, but mail has had to wait. I enclose general news.

Since your letter in Union Life, I've had questions on something said! That was why I wish they had told me they were publishing, as I should liked to have checked over. As with Lanyon, not all he says in his heart-outpourings are readable by the public without words of explanation! So some read as if you say you are Christ! Of course I laugh, because I have the same said of me and of UL generally; but sometimes it can be moderated a little for publication. And anyhow we have climbed onto a limb of faith in our "Christ in us as us reality" which means we have cut it off behind us, so we are way out in the deep with no footing beneath us anyhow! So I explained to my enquirer. I think the Spirit makes us say things in extremes, as Jesus and Paul did, and I'd rather say it in extreme form and then maybe moderate a saying or two, than undersay it which is what chokes the church's witness; and all the prophets were slain in their lifetime, but their words lived on.

But I certainly like this "divine dissatisfaction" in you, which is no longer dissatisfaction with not having your own needs supplied, but sharing "the travail of his soul" for the world. I wonder whether God yet has some spot in "Union Life" for you. Of course we have no structure, no members or "established workers", and are not led that way. Each linked with us walks alone with God, and yet with one another in our fixed "seeing". I love your "reasonable service to pour out my soul unto death and make intercession for others." Amen. God said that to Pauline and me 60 years ago when we married and started our three month journey into the heart of Africa. And I love that "my calling is to people". I also can only see that. We surely talk the same language!

Shall look forward to hearing again from you.

Much loving you both,

Norman

~~~

Feb.3.81

My dear Chris,

Very interesting what you say about being led to cut out books, find the truth within yourself and then get it confirmed by the books. Excellent! I've always known that is essentially God's way according to I

John 2.27, and all God's enlightened ones go this same way in measure, only you more clearly. The best folks often say to me after a session is, "I always saw that, but had not dared to put into words"!! I always say I don't teach but share and the Spirit does the inner confirming.

I still give a unique place to the Scriptures. It may be that in our modern days we can interpret certain things from an enlarged angle, but if once I say other writings are as inspired as the Scriptures, I pull all boundaries of truth down, and I won't do that because truth is HE and He has His incarnated manifestation in the Scriptures. I always seek to conform what I write to "the Word" and with that get great streams of light as from JB, Lanyon, Kierkegaard, etc.

I never would have guessed from my days with the pastor and those with whom I talked and searched in his home that we were really so far apart. I think it was only when he saw the truth in human form in you among his flock that he really awoke to its implications and came into the usual ministerial opposition – must "hold my flock together" – how, if not by imposed disciplines and relations? So you continue to "walk in love" with them for love for the brethren is the final word in all of I John, a final letter, as in 4.20. So continue to see them as God's precious sons, meaning them to see as they do, and continue with them. Don't let it be you who "walk out", but only if "put out". Don't be lined up with all those families who "left in a huff". Union Life is unifying - first in us and with those with whom we are linked!! Give the pastor and folks my loving greetings.

Finally, I love your heaven living. I too (as does Lanyon) see heaven and hell as conditions of consciousness, at least in this present third dimension! I love all the glory radiating out from you.

Loving you & Vivian,

Norman

~~~

Sept.26.81

Judy darling,

That's a precious letter from you and Sam and I'm answering among other precious letters because I love you taking it further than just praising with us for our precious Pauline with the Lord, but also

114

talking of your "self-consciousness" because we are not yet in that fullness of a love-in (as with Linda and others). Thank you for saying that, darling, and wanting it to that same point that I have with others. Yes, love, we'll take that as fact in spirit-reality, and aim to practise it when next together, with both you and Sam. It is true that I have gradually come to know you as you outwardly, and Sam also, but I am very slow in even doing that, and some folks I meet again and again before I am really "sure" who they are outwardly. I'm beyond that with you, darling, but now we'll make for the other and fullest. So thank you for "breaking thru" the "self-conscious" and sharing your heart on this. I have come to know in spirit that the Spirit has given us the same perfect "inner knowing" so it is not a question of "building" that, but merely of heart openness in our union-knowing. So just thank you again for opening on this, darling. You will know how we are now waiting to see how God "does the impossible" in making the time for our precious Pris, that we know God has given to Sandie and me to do, and yet at the same time release us for our travels. God has some Love-trick up His sleeve.

So, loving you like that Judy darling and Sam till we can express it together in soul-body as well as spirit.

Thank you darling

Norman

<div style="text-align: center">~~~</div>

March 22.82

Dear John & Jean,

I look back with much joy to the loving fellowship I had in your home and all your love to me. I greatly enjoyed all the fellowship with the pastor and dear ones in your church fellowship. I shall never forget the blessing I had when I arrived that Sunday evening and you were already worshiping the Lord in a stream of praise and song led by the pastor's wife, and as it continued with such a volume of praise and worship some of you fell on the floor on your faces and some danced a little. I was thrilled, and following that, greatly enjoyed ministering along with you all both at the meetings and with some of you in the pastor's home. If I was over on the Island again, I would enjoy being with you as much as ever.

Yes, I know you have "excommunicated" my beloved Christopher and Vivien, and I know also, if I have any discernment in the Spirit, and I think I have, that Christopher is a very special and specially anointed man of God. Very many of us over here have been thrilled and blessed beyond words by his various letters so totally Christ-magnifying and full of the glorious revelation and reality of Paul's great "mystery" of Colossians 1:25-29, following onto and fulfilling his first gospel ministry of verse 23 - which, of course, is also our Union Life message. Indeed I am using Chris' written testimony as a special epilogue to my coming book YES I AM, and I know it will bless thousands.

I also know by his letters to me that Chris sees nothing but your pastor being a blessed minister of the Word, and not of the devil, and would be still worshiping with you if you brethren had not "cast him out". I think that the Lord yet has a very rich ministry of the Spirit by Christopher.

The Lord has shewn me that His prayer is already answered in fact - "that they may be one" in John 17, so I see no "divisions". I just see all of us one in Him who are His redeemed people, no matter what apparent human differences we may think we have. I just don't "see" them. So I continue in my love-bond with you both and with you all. I only wish you could continue to be blessed by so much that is rich in the Spirit in our Union Life Magazine, but I have to do what you say and have asked them to take your name off the list - but if off on a list, we remain bound in spirit and love.

Lovingly in Christ and please convey my love to the pastor and to you all with whom I had such precious fellowship.

Norman

~~~

Nov.3.84

Sara my dear:

What a thrill to get such a letter from you. I missed you last Albany, and I had so rejoiced that you and Charlie took all that trouble to be with us. Our bonds and fellowship go back a long way and it was beautiful to me to have them renewed. And now this letter.

Yes, it is wonderful to know how Christ settles Himself in His union with us, and it remains the one central fact (indeed for eternity) that we live, think, act as one, yet it is largely sub-conscious. We live as ourselves, yet the secret "joke" is that it is really HE as us, and our very being is His Light shining by us unknown by us. Light never sees itself; others see by it!

You are right, dear, to accept Charlie enjoying his yard work and then giving time to football, etc. We men are much like that. I like watching sports but of course most of my time except for special events (I watched some of the Olympics) is in sharing Christ in us as us by letters or on these tours. Great privilege. So you are right just to be thankful that Charlie is with you and does love the Lord. Not all husbands are like that! Meanwhile you are free to be like me "with the zeal of His house" eating us up!

Loving you & Charlie,

Norman

<div align="center">~~~</div>

Mar. 14.85

DeeDee my precious one,

You know I can't put into words all these days together have meant. What a bond of love we have - just <u>loving</u> each other, and there really wouldn't be a thing in it if we just didn't <u>know</u> all the time and sub-consciously see it is HE as us. What a marvel! I just loved your tender care of this 'old man' - which I took plenty advantage of. Fancy <u>you</u> carrying my bags, a thing unheard of to a rightly-trained Britisher! And just that atmosphere of you so loving old me all the time. And then I was thoroughly bowled over by your endless Jesus-love ministry, taking on night after night with all sorts. You are "well caught", my darling, by your True Lover - and He is!! So it's all beautiful, darling, isn't it? And on top of that, all you and Gary poured out, my darling, in all the expenses, travel, car, everything – and all my marveling thanks to Gary for his 'silent' love in so freely giving you. And to precious Kim so being with us. Thank you, my darling.

So just LOVING you, my darling, and thank you,

Norman

<div align="center">~~~</div>

117

Nov.27.86

My dearest Helen & Freda,

You just are something! You take my old breath away and I'm thrilled and laugh all the time. Can't imagine looking back on our first meeting in that church hall and your teaching days, and the building days and then being cast out for your dangerous believings! Cast out? No, put into focus, but whoever would have imagined the focus. It just is true that the Spirit has sources of "genius" He gets on the move in and by us when we are, as you are, the Calebs who "wholly follow". Just AMAZING – the battles, hard spots, overwhelming overwork, and yet in flow the orders and new ranges every time like now the imports. And I love you making the local folks know that being Jesus people is caring, by those local committees you are on besides all that local employment. You are beautiful to Jesus and to us all! And I shall be watching for the White House [Christmas decorations on the White House tree].

I had my "White House" too as a friend arranged for me to meet Robert Schuller of the Crystal Cathedral in his office (under many close guards among all those crowds) and we so clicked in our quarter hour that he insisted in taking me to his platform and introducing and making me talk to his crowd, and then he wrote, "You impacted my life in a way that was extraordinary." I found much more spirit-reality when we were face to face. He said all he knew of me was that 20 years before someone told him Norman Grubb starts each morning by saying, "Hello, God, what are You up to today. I'll go along with You." He said he had learned that by heart and used it and made all his congregation repeat it twice!

All my love, you precious living and life-giving couple. God's originals!

Norman

~~~

Feb.8.87

My dear Norman,

Thank you so much for "sharing" on your card. What fellowship we have had thru the years!

I inflict on you a long winded newsletter (but not needing an answer), as I had this time in hospital and am now back home, lovingly

118

cared for by Sandie, and after a few weeks hoping to be on the move again!

The main part of the letter is my usual "fiddle with one string" on who we really are, and I trace a bit of my Spirit-pilgrimage which has so settled me in what I constantly share. But if you will be patient enough to "endure to the end" of the letter, I underline a paragraph from a Quaker Foster who I think beautifully puts this balance between Christ in us and we in Him, and I like it much, and how it leaves us with the major of us in HIM, and thus expressors of Him.

I am also so glad to hear of your good times with your children. I am thrilled with that because I remember how the storm signals were rightly raised when they both were so fully "caught" by the WAY. And it appears they and their families are still the same; but what intrigues me is that you have really good fellowship with them, and it seems to me that we all have to bypass areas which seem "off" to us, and it would seem big ones when (I don't know much of the Way, but I thought they denied the deity of Christ!), yet anyhow you found the flow of the Spirit and in the Word with them despite that! Loving personal relationship of HIM within and as us, just overflows verbal doctrinal and even Scriptural interpretations! Praise! Such a joy for you.

So just this line in my occasional times at the typewriter, and what memories of your return visit to England. I now keep close touch with Susan, Edith's daughter. Her husband Mike did so brilliantly in his medical work in Kenya that he has been knighted by the Queen though he first refused, and Susan has a book of poems and meditations on her consciousness of her union with God which she says first started with her youthful contacts with me. So that is a joy. Mike comes over here for all sorts of medical rewards and prizes.

So just ever with my love and endless thankfulness to you both as to your dear father and mother.

Norman

~~~

March 13.87

My dear John & June,

Thank you for your great letter. When the Spirit really gets hold of Britishers, out pours truth. I say the Brits are pure scientists, and the Americans applied scientists. I get the depth-riches from Brits in Bible truths, etc., but the D.L. Moodys and Billy Grahams who then apply it are from here! And that is what your letter (and your beautiful handwritings both so small yet so legible), Brit again! Only I have to type and that is full of mistakes! I'm half a Yank!! But you have much truth, both of you, in what you share. I can see that plainly and rejoice in it. You will find it's from over here they do the applying.

I love your scientific touch, John. I'm such a total amateur and ignoramus on those lines, yet I jump to any scraps of light. For instance, you really "reach" me when you say that there are no fundamental particles but only structure and order. I hadn't caught on to others saying that, although I sensed it in Heisenberg's "Complementarities". You are really touching universal spirit when you say that. I have avidly read some of the simpler books and I sense there how these men detect that there is a background symmetry and "mind".

I don't "take" you saying, John, you have the truth on the head level but not in action. That's just that false condemnation. That is confusing temptation of all kinds with there being something wrong about us. No, actually sin (compared by James to an adultery) is rare, for it is a deliberate choice, but so often we mistake long pressures on us for sin. No, we are RIGHT, RIGHT, RIGHT, and only very rarely wrong!

So I write this from my upstairs where my Sandie-boss still confines me, but I have my typewriter.

I am just fixing up something on Romans 6-8 because many of my Bible friends will take our apparent excesses better when they get them in Paul's terms!

So, with my much love and so glad to hear from you,

Norman

~~~

Aug. 1987

My dear Wallace,

Your fascinating packed letter from Eaton Rapids has brought many great memories and indeed much insight into the Lord's ways with you all these years. You know how I have always known the streams of the Spirit flowing in and out of you. Just as Abram and Marian knew it and it was that which bound them so much to you. Your life has had much of the "Agony and Ecstasy" of true apostleship, though much like the great mystics thru the centuries also combined with much self-questionings and even self-belittlings. That's why it was such a thrill to me when the Confirming Spirit so witnessed to you in all your surprise readings of the YES I AM book, and I note in this letter you seeing Intercession as our ultimate.

But just because you are an in-depth person, I have always known the touch of God on you when you do share. That is why I love this letter and that you had this sharing with a hundred at Fellowship House and could so trace the Spirit's rich dealings with you, and I don't wonder but am thrilled when you say there was "a grip on the people and some in tears".

So I loved your tracing thru, really of your life, and that both Doug and Dick were present and equally that while sharing your own ways in Christ with often real sacrifice in them, you in the breadth of the Spirit can also appreciate Doug's way in more affluent surroundings in Fellowship House and the Cedars (and I've never yet been to the Cedars, but am so thankful at God's cleverness in putting Roy Cook there being the one who has the true inner "knowing" and I keep in touch with him). But I'm also amazed and thrilled when you tell me of God's present dealings with Doug, giving all away and having no property. Glorious. The Spirit surely is ALIVE in him in Washington, etc., as in you in Europe! And Dick in the Senate.

I had forgotten your closeness with Abram and me in your CEI days, when you even nibbled at WEC! Of course I remember those days and I loved your touch on Joe Brice, who was so great among us in England those days with his blazing fire and all night praying and mighty break-thrus in the public meetings. That was also when my Noel Palmer was with Joe and I keep very close touch with Noel.

But I loved your tracing thru your early years with our loved Abram and I always said I knew why Abram kept you close to him because of the same spirit. Also the mention of Senator Wiley. That brought him to my memory so close with Abram. It was with Senator Wiley and Abram I had my one time at the private Senators weekly prayer group, and they were sharing their Senate burdens for prayer. Wiley was a true friend, just as also Senator Frank Carlson. I saw him for a moment at the Prayer Breakfast two years ago and had a warm greeting. How much we owe to him first getting President Eisenhower to be the first President to attend the Prayer Breakfast, also Frank's was the final vote in the Senate at full voting rights for the Blacks.

Then also your own close touches, all your visits with Queen Wilhelmina, and your description of that great reconciling time with the Germans. Then again with Michelet in France, as now with Caldecote in the Lords. And I love your saying in these your kind of final days, that you are "a pioneer for Jesus reaching marginal men". I did not know of your Stockholm contacts as with the Archbishop, and the men in England urging you even now to reach out to Portugal, Greece, etc. Yours has been a glorious "commissioned" calling. Also that touch with Maurice Laing and the touch of the Spirit on him. So this has been a great retracing for me.

So thank you, Wallace, for really this eye-opener of a letter. Yes, it was wonderful they had that dinner for me, and the Jordans and Roy among them, also my close friends Tony and Bette Ketcham; and them even getting this painting of me from my friend, Jim Seward, and hanging it in Fellowship House!

So ever with my love and great praise,

Norman

~~~

Sept.15.88

Claire, my dear,

That is good of you to have asked Meg to send me this copy of your <u>Kaleidoscope</u> – beautiful production too. Thank you so much in the bonds of our fellowship together with you and Spike. I grabbed it at once and read 80 pages yesterday. I even found to my surprise that you had mentioned my first visit to you.

I think we surely have "differences of administration but the Same Spirit", and thus make the mosaic of the Body. You have a beautiful writing as well as song gift, and your book flows livingly and with the kind of spontaneous sharing which will draw the minds and then hearts of your readers. You are MS Positive, because you just touch on the time of your acceptance of Jesus as Saviour without much reference to the "sinner" aspect of needing a Saviour; and then later enough of your bondage to our illusory selves to press you into finding Him as Lord as well as Saviour, and then on you go with your living applications of Him as Lord of your daily life, in the way which will draw and bless us readers.

Meanwhile I have come along with concentration on how our negatives are transmuted into the positive Christ-walk which fills your pages. You really have Romans 8.1-2 as your STARTING POINT, and the subsequent "walk in the Spirit". I, on the other hand, start at the bottom of the negative with a short preliminary paragraph on the necessity and experience of the new birth of Paul's Romans 1-5; and then all the rest of what I enclose on the struggles and traumas which finally and gloriously result in the Romans 8.1-2 onward which occupies you!! A good inter-relation between us! So I enclose my latest Romans 6-8 pamphlet as Paul's "Key to the Liberated Life", and then you "take off" on that liberation!! And I have just got to the chapter on "suffering". You are surely right there. Hebrews 2.10 lays down the eternal principle of suffering being the blessed driving force on us to find the release, as in Jesus' case in 5.7-10, which conditioned Him as Eternal High Priest and on to 7.24-26. Yes, yes, we must have a thorough negative even to be conscious of our need of the positive, and then replacement of the one by the other. No darkness, no consciousness of light. No sin, no salvation. No necessity of a self-giving cross on our behalf, no resurrection producing a Pentecost experience for us: and at last as in James 1.1-3, we learn to recognise the "bashings" of our negatives as the expectant preliminary of some glorious positive.

So thank you, dear, for this refreshment from you, and many will find new liberation by it and your beautiful song-gift, and again thank you for sending me this copy.

Lovingly and to Spike,

Norman

<div align="center">~~~</div>

Jan.12

My dear Doug,

This today is truly, truly GREAT. And I wouldn't say that if it was not GREAT in the Spirit to me, and just that vast difference from the discomfort which flesh in precious perfect people gives spirit. This just rings all the bells and says Amen, Amen on every page. And how it shews us a thousand times over that ALL God's negative ways are truly the necessary reverse form to the Positive. You can now be what you will be to so many, just because you have been a depth explorer (and you are right, your Boehme-Law researches have been as priceless for

you as mine have been for me), and with now this inner Spirit-revelation
to you of Hebrews 4.12 that "the word of God quick and powerful" in
you, a perfect pattern of the only way it can ever be quickened in any
of us. How richly and in the true other-love freedom of the Spirit you
will manifest depth truth to so many. It's just as if a flesh veil has been
stripped off you as it has to be in every one of us – no escape – (no other
door into this sheepfold!), and Browning's "imprisoned splendour"
shines in-out. GOD makes HIS teachers, and surely you are now one, and
what I gloriously acclaim from your letter, all others who have eyes to
see will acclaim by inner witness.

So I hardly need trace through what you so beautifully trace for me
– I much like, and am helped (for all of us help each other when it is Spirit
help, don't we) by the way you put it of having needs, and then seeking to
get them supplied by apparently supplying others' needs. How real and
true that is. Yes, you truly have it, for we just don't have needs, and we
don't go around deliberately supplying others' needs, but freely sharing
our own I AM completion, and knowing that HE is busy revealing that to
the other complete persons who don't maybe know at the moment that
they are complete. You will be seeing the new "title" we are using for U. L.

The Twentieth Century Reformation

Luther gave us Paul's Romans 5.1 Justification

Union Life gives us Paul's Col. 1.28 COMPLETION (or "Perfection")

I most greatly rejoice that it was HE, HE Who took you deliberately
thru all this, as that good compost heap out of which many are going to
feed on riches of fruit-bearing!

Thank you, Doug, thank you indeed and I kind of welcome you
among the "chosen ones" to be a world-sharer.

Lovingly

Norman

~~~

Jan.21

Judy dearest,

WHAT a letter from you! Don't know how you spared the time, and
good things on every page of it. Yes, I was so pleased you came to the
Sandie weekend and it just seemed the Spirit FLOWED among us, and
the sharing one by one hit the spot.

I just LOVE the way, even in this letter, that clear light is so shining, Christ surely running around those school rooms in His Judy form, and how I love you saying you "love" the students. No wonder they invited you to the special line in the "drug" group, they so obviously count you as just "one of them", not some distant "teacher". And those chances here and there to put "a word" in. This life, when it actually is He as us, is basically so SIMPLE, isn't it, because we just BE ourselves and our "joke" is (so hidden until the veil is lifted), and we don't "try" to "witness" but just BE and along here and there comes the moment for saying something "quite naturally", and otherwise our very life is "that light shining". I love those students asking you if you are a Christian!!

As for tennis, I am a "fan" of the sport which is the exercise of accuracy with background training. So I constantly follow both tennis (though of course the chances are more rare on TV) and golf almost weekly. I love that ACCURACY, and am GREATLY THRILLED THAT THIS NEW WINNER on the recent pro golf tournament, is he Steve Jones, both times came right out and said he owes his prowess to "The Lord Jesus Christ"! I jumped over the moon and then it was Bob Hope's tournament this last one, when Jones slipped in at the last with one stroke and I kind of watched Bob not really able to say much when he gave the cheque when "Steve" had just made this bold witness. Equally I was so pleased at our new President selecting Billy Graham to give the dedication prayer, instead of some sticky old bishop. I think it was a sign of where the heart of the new President and his wife are.

I am really not moving around now because Paul warned the "outer man" does perish and I am conscious of that, but hopefully ok still north of the neck, but my traveling days are done. Two very special women recently have said to me, "When you've gone, you watch how our witness will leap ahead!!" That's exactly what CT Studd said to me, "WEC will really expand when the Lord has taken this old fool." And since he went, we've gone from 35 in one field to about 2,000 in 40 fields and the vast CLC, BUT, BUT we have not moved an inch from our FOUR PILLARS (I wrote that booklet) which we got from CTS: sacrifice, faith, holiness and fellowship. So it will be with you ready ones in our, what I call, TOTAL TRUTH witness to the "whole church in the whole world"!

So your letter is a REFRESHMENT, darling, and as you walk on, when as you say HE doing the walking, talking, etc., you WATCH, YOU ARE MIGHTILY GOING TO SEE Rom. 8.28 worked right out in your own life!!!

So glad you were able to tackle that UL thing with the group. We just have to face the basic fact that this final "leap over the precipice" is still fairly rarely taken, and even our ULers haven't been able to take it. I haven't even read what they've said in the magazine. My calling is TO GO RIGHT ON JUST POURING OUT OUR TOTAL AS I SEE IT BY THE SPIRIT AND WORD, and I have no calling to "get striving" among us; but the Lord continues to bless the UL magazine which gives much more than most get, though I have to say with grief they MISS THE TOTAL, and in the end it is only THE TOTAL WHICH HAS LASTING REALITY IN IT, AND WE HAVE THAT VAST PRIVILEGE. When followers of Francis d'Assisi of next generation sought to weaken down his total, the few who still stood with him said, "There is an element in the gospel of Christ so disturbing that the world will ever reject it, but never forget it; and the church will vacillate between patronage and persecution. You have the present, but I think the future is ours!!" Twelve runaways at Calvary. "Wait to get that Holy Spirit," (six weeks waiting, but they stuck at it) and THEN, THEN 2,000 years later we number millions!!!!

Yes, we do get further training and growth by our soul-body depression, etc., but they train us in James 1.3, sticking at it.

All my love,

Norman

~~~

May 20

Thank you, Chris. EXCELLENT, and so glad you sent me this line. Yes, we are One Body, all who have Jesus, and a mighty bunch of queers, each being quite certain that we really are the cat's whiskers! And SO WE ARE in UL!!!! So we laugh and love and SEE ONLY JESUS.

I am just doing the same with a church fellowship I had a lot to do with in founding in York, England. They have publicly cast us out and warned all to keep clear of us, even in the streets. I love the pastor, a precious brother, so I wrote him, reminding him of our love-fellowship times in the past, then I sent him my recent letter to our Weccers. (I think I sent you one, but I'll include another in case not.) I've told him it would be "fun" if, when he sends out his paper on my heresies, he would also include this letter!!

Since then I've had a good letter from one who has written her heart out to her pastor, and am sending him that (and will also include to you), telling him that he is in many ways like, not this pastor, but the ideal she describes!! For he has good points! AND SO THE FUN GOES ON.

No more now. Off to England June 4.
All my love and joy,

Norman

~~~

June 13

Kathryn darling,

How good it is to have this renewed touch with you. I had kind of lost touch, so this is a thrill. Our closeness of fellowship and love goes back such a long time, so it is lovely to have it renewed.

It is evident from your letter, darling, that the Spirit is renewing in you, as you, what is our TOTAL.

Yes, yes, you are right, love, <u>HE HE</u> is the message and messenger. Life is us persons eternally operated by HIM THE PERSON, and "obedience of faith" is our key, and yes, yes, we are <u>KEPT</u> BY Him. Just <u>take that for granted</u> when we might "feel" dark as hell! No condemnations! He is AS US! Yes don't listen to anyone who questions you as being Christ in His Kathryn form. The question's just good practice in standing against them!

CHOICE. We have made our great <u>life choice</u> - He as us in place of Satan as us. When tempted not to like His ways or guidances, we just say we are TEMPTED, <u>but</u> then we'll wait until HE gives freedom to follow His right choice.

Just loving hugging my Kathryn, write again

Norman

~~~

July 14

My dear Doug,

What a letter from you - full of riches. I see you as one who has persisted till you have found, and it is still true, as Jesus said, "Few there be that find it.", and we become "Sermon on the Mounters" in action!! And we do, when we finally "KNOW OURSELVES" as (marvelously) container-expressors of Deity, and NOW THE DIETY SPIRIT OF TRUTH! Yes, Doug, you have been beaten about and you

127

HAD TO BE, just like me in my different ways. We do "lose all" to find all, and the all these days is not our physical heads off, but our reputation "heads". You thru your marriage break and here you saying how you lost all – family, friends, church, etc., but TO FIND IT!! THERE IS NO SHORTER CUT, and that is why we have to face the fact even among our closest; it is still "the few that find". You were at it right back to your good diggings on J. Boehme. I knew none other who was searching around, quoting, etc., as you, and now you – we have FOUND!!! Beatitudes 4 and 6 become ours thru 1-3, and we have the glory of 9, 10!

I have not really realized how close our links had been since we first met. Then your ultimate "self" test, when the marriage went wrong, and with it your subtle self-esteem as a reliable person (which, of course, was Satan's top line form of self-for-self, and many fall back there). But you have, Doug. ALL PRAISE. Yes, I "caught" the Spirit in my first walk with Rees Howells (not at all a prepossessing man when you first met him, tough old ex-coal miner). BUT! I saw, drank and joined the alcoholics! And yes, thank God, I've been thru my many outcast days and really live outcast as far as my normal brethren are concerned, as I outline in my ONCE CAUGHT NO ESCAPE autobiography. The University leaders at Cambridge where God gave me to rebuild the Christian Union and from it start the worldwide IVF of today, publicly repudiated me as "going too far"! But, of course, as you now know, when we do KNOW, when cast out, you laugh and grow fat!! You KNOW, KNOW, KNOW THAT FINALLY ALL IS HE IN HIS VARIOUS HUMAN FORMS; and yes, you are right, there are "rewards" here on earth when you live long enough, but by that time you know the ONE REWARD is when the Spirit by you brings others to find and be themselves as WALKING CHRISTS.

Yes, I remember our most recent battle on my last visit when you were going thru a tough time, but we battled together and the LIGHT SHONE!

Yes, you had to come to the edge of throwing God over as a failure. WE ALL HAVE TO IN ONE WAY OR ANOTHER. Total loss – total find!

Yes, I have those big books, Aurora and Magnum. I hesitate to mail them to you, quite a chore, but you're not coming this way? I could lend and did to one brother who faithfully worked at them and returned.

My much love,

Norman

୫୦ଓଃ

EXCERPTS

At least I heard, with thankfulness, that great grace is upon you in a difficult situation, and that the Lord was glorified through your meekness. The way up is down, and so God is going to take you mighty higher than ever, as you walk in the Cross and resurrection.

~~~

Your letter moves me, just because you see and write things so much more from the heart than from the head.

~~~

The thrill is your guidance and costly "obedience of faith" in dropping the enticements for political moves. I was ready to go with you if you went that way, but am really much happier in spirit at your present guided decision. I can only say what it has meant to me to stand free since I first took my youthful step and told my father to his distress that I couldn't go forward for C. of E. ordination. My, my how glad I am now.

~~~

God has just to take us backward paths, as well as forward, until we learn the senselessness of independent self.

~~~

Don't let any of us fear the light. All is going to come out one day anyhow (Luke 12.2). Just be ready to stand up to the truth, for none of us have anything to boast of except the blood and righteousness of Jesus. If you fear that they might say things which hurt your reputation, you anyhow have none worth having except the fact that Jesus now lives in you. Insofar as they say things that are true, well, just admit them to be true; it is a good chance to acknowledge that we are a bunch of total failures except for the keeping power of God, and sometimes we take ourselves out of reach of that and have to come back. Just release all to God, ready to take what God sends.

~~~

It was a thrill to hear how you have been the rounds and rebuilt fellowship. Glorious. God indeed did bless us those days when He touched you and others. It was no false thing, but I think when we get these new touches from God, we all tend to run away with them, as if no one else had anything. We need to learn how to have the revival, and yet still keep seeing a reviving Jesus in our brethren.

~~~

First God is fusing you two together, because that is your "Threefold Cord", you two and the Holy Spirit, which cannot easily be broken as Solomon says in Ecclesiastes. Build together in the Spirit, which means you will have soul-variations of temperament, understandings, outlooks, but keep "dying" there, and alive in each of you being Perfect Christ to each other. Then others will be added.

~~~

Keep bold in sharing what you now know. It is HE The Living Bread, who said if we "eat" Him, we hunger no more.

~~~

Yes, doubt is <u>healthy</u>. It gives you practice in knowing soul-pressures from this outer "reasoning" world, and replacing with Spirit-fact. You don't even lean on promises and assurances but on <u>fact of being</u> - and that fact is God in love-action in His Sue Ellen and Vicky forms!

~~~

I've just been reading "His soul shall dwell at ease and his seed shall inherit the earth" - with a Calvary behind it! So for you-me, and David does continually affirm that he has "faithfully followed"; and as I look back I see how God has kept me like that thru hot spots one after the other, HIS way has won: and the Lord will now give you grace to faithfully follow, not soul reactions, but Spirit truth.

~~~

I just go along in spirit with all you say, as I always do. You <u>confirm</u> me worse and worse in our far-outness. Yet it is TRUTH!

~~~

Then, as to what you write, dear, you may 'feel' embarrassed at what you wrote me, but soul feelings only give strength by their contrariness to spirit-facts! And nothing is trivial while it is presently real to us (for our consciousness is our very selves), and it only becomes trivial when we have moved over to right spirit-perspective of our feelings-reactions; but then we laugh at it, but at the time of the feelings it was just right (and so big to us!) that we had a spirit-mate with whom we could share them, and that was <u>my</u> privilege! So it was right and my great privilege that you did so write me, and do so now again, and I shall hope do so more in the future!

~~~

But now, love, you are being established in our God-union (where we cry out with the Psalmist, "O God, my heart is <u>fixed</u>, my heart is <u>fixed</u>: I will sing and give praise!) by the practice of just being, with no apparent outlet for what you burn to share; though you have got to the good point that you will "stubbornly" remain in "idleness" until God makes you busy. Good! Only you'll take it a step further where the tinge of self-effort in stubbornness is replaced by the central stillness of perfect rest; for all power, all truth, all real being is in stillness, for that is what God, and therefore we as being He in our human forms are. "Be still and know...". "A still small voice.." "There remaineth a rest to the people of God". For, darling, even your burning desire to have outward creative expression is really soul. Replaced by spirit-consciousness you <u>know</u> that- God has the creative outlet for you "in the fullness of time". And stillness of knowing faith overflows soul-burnings of desire.

~~~

Pauline joins me in sending you our greetings. You have had a pathway of the Cross, but it leads to Christ, and anything makes that worthwhile. I grieve about your husband, and the condition in which you found him. But the Lord even makes our sins as a means of grace, and may this false choice of his yet lead to his coming as a sinner to His Saviour.

~~~

So we have, as you are well knowing, both the offence and the glory of the Cross, and the living Word is not living (sharper than any two edged sword) unless it does do both a cutting and a healing work. Only blunt swords make no impression one way or the other! So we go on praising!

~~~

Nothing can be "truth" in us and to us can it, unless it has taken us to that identification with Christ in His death and resurrection. Self can build up self by its own wisdom, but it is still fallen self. Praise God, you and I have gone that cross-resurrection way, and now live in the ascension!

~~~

You hit spots as no one else does. You just "say things". I love your "warmed over truth, but as fresh mown hay" - that's precisely what Kierkegaard always says of his loved Socrates - that he had got hold of the truth that freshness is not constant new things, but old and ordinary things always being fresh to us. Perfect!

~~~

I see only Christ and where they come short (as we all do in one way or another) there we see that God means them to see like that for the time - maybe particularly to fit and condition you for your liberated commission whatever that turns out to be.

~~~

I don't like your "spiritual slump", though I am glad of how the Lord used it. There is a place in Christ where He is the fixed center of our lives, the Other Self, the other I in us, and we don't slump, because it is not really we living our lives and handling our problems; that is an illusion; the real I is Christ in me, and we walk the waters with Him.

~~~

We boldly accept that we are God's assets, not His liabilities! We are His precious human means of manifestation, every bit of us precious. Our appetites, faculties, minds, emotions, are HIS precious agencies. Tempted often, but that is our springboard for the faith which says, "No, I am crucified with Christ". He is the Real Me. And we replace our fears, feelings of weakness, or even more our feelings that we have "arrived" in Him. Feelings are outer soul-emotions. But we are spirit joined to Him - one Spirit, and there we do not accept the invasions of our feelings, nor accusations that our past upbringings have "damaged" us, etc. No, we are wholly what God always planned for us to be. See what Paul says of God from his birth - Gal.1.15.

~~~

It is good to be forced to chew these things over and go for a period into disturbed questioning as you did, and this becomes the basis to solid walking whereas the first glows are meant to wear off and we become established by the "sufferings" of disturbed questioning, and then we learn to "walk" in the simplicity of faith, not maybe having had full answers, but taking it that we ARE HE walking as us, and not taking condemnations.

~~~

You've got me awed like Cortes "upon a peak in Darien!" when he first saw the Pacific. You see yours is at last finally and fully the letter of an "Apostle", no longer disciple. You're thrillingly now among the "Can't help it" brigade. Pentecost not only inwardly confirmed Spirit-reality to those disciples, but was the artesian well gushing up and out into an unstoppable river - the actual John 7:38, and it won't stop 'gushing' in you anymore than that water from the rock in the wilderness which Paul said "followed them" - a striking comment. And you are now in that FLOODTIDE! I am sure that that alone is the true evidence of "apostle commissioning" among us - that what we now see and know we are simply bursts out of us and nothing can contain it.

~~~

I love you, as Christ is formed in you from "glory to glory".

୫୦ ଓଃ

HISTORY

He was a theologian as well as a missiologist. I was never able to plumb the depths of Rubi's theological thinking. He spent years deepening his knowledge of the mysteries of God – sharing these with all who would listen as he reached out to WEC team worldwide, as well as reaching out in love to the millions of the remaining unreached Peoples.

Leslie Brierley

<div align="center">~~~</div>

Truly I feel it is one of the great blessings of life to have known him.

Pastor

<div align="center">~~~</div>

I told him how I was so fearful of making mistakes and he laughed as only he could and said, "Child, God knows how to take care of our mistakes." Norman's words of affirmation were his unique way – romantic but not romantic – because he is a "lover" in the same way Jesus taught us to love. It is not lust, sexual or promiscuous.

<div align="center">~~~</div>

The sweet fragrance of your life still remains - as the Lord was so clearly manifest in you.

₭⌒

Box A
Ft. Washington, Pa.
June 6, 1956

Dear Gordon,

Of course I shall greatly look forward to a thorough heart to heart and rock bottom talk together. Of all things we need to be bound together in love and understanding with not a shadow between.

I am most sorry that I have put up, unconsciously, a barrier between us over our correspondence. I had no idea of this. I am glad you have written to say so for that helps to clear the air, although I wish I had known earlier. Actually I had thought that we were in the fullest of fellowship. I don't know particularly to what letters you refer, when you say that I have done such "terrifying" and "shattering" things with your letters. Big words! Perhaps it is that we at home, living at such quarters to each other, get more used to sharing almost anything. I keep a continual flow of inside letters from all sources going around our Staff, and it is just that which binds us together in confidence and vision. About the only things I keep from sharing are matters which touch a person's character, or which are directly marked "Private-for Private Reasons". I am sure utmost openness has the seal of the Spirit on it. May be, however, with you folks living more at a distance from each other, such openness can be disturbing. I don't know if that is the cause, but certainly let us get at it together, so that we can write with utmost confidence. I have a wonderful correspondence, right to the heart of things, with many.

Looking forward to seeing you one end or the other.

Ever yours,

Norman

~~~

August 14, 1956

My dear John,

You will have heard by now from Ma Rubi of the mighty victory over here, a clean sweep, just on the lines of the faith God gave you, not one lost, except the Gambles who have continued in their former resignation. It is like a new world. It does mean, however, that I must definitely be over here for the next three years, and presumably Ma Rubi and the family will come back with me. So we shall have to face new arrangements on your side, as we wait on God as a Staff. Of course I recognize the British Staff could have the right to refuse to allow me to come here, but I certainly think it would be most unwise. So my dates are fixed, unless further disturbances arise at Camp Hill while I am away the next three weeks of Conferences. I expect to sail on Sept. 14. Ma Rubi says that my Mother is arranging for us to go straight down there on my arrival at Southampton to Bournemouth for a week, so I expect I shall see you sometime near the end of September and be with you for the Annual and Conference. I shall then hope in due course to do a last run around of main WEC centers and aim to leave for the U.S.A. in January.

Another unexpected challenge was quite an unprepared visit to the Anderson Bible School set-up of Bro Billheimers. I dropped in there from our mid-West Conference and was amazed to see the size of the place. It was just a forest when I was there six years ago. He now comes out with a complete offer in due course, as we provide the faith personnel, of taking over the whole thing, Bible School, Grade and High Schools, full Christian radio station, and the only Christian T-V station in the world which he is now building. The buildings are worth a quarter of a million dollars, and the T-V mast alone which is an outright gift to him costs $120,000. I see immense prospects in all this. There is a full printery with even better presses than even we have at Camp Hill just lying idle. I hope that it will mean that again Britain will reach out in faith and love and provide the first vital personnel, perhaps the Rows or even the Dinnens. Once we get the person of faith to step into the center, certainly there will be many difficulties, but bit by bit over a period of five or ten years we can grip the whole situation for God and the world. What a challenge. May God still give Britain the grace of royal giving, and God will always give back more than we give. More when we meet on all this. This is just to whet your appetite, or to frighten you as the case may be!

Love to you all,

Yours ever,

Rubi

~~~

October 15, 1959

Dear Dr. and Mrs. Windham:

I was ever so glad to get the link with you and Irene at the meetings. I felt God gave us a bond in spirit together, and I did appreciate your coming so often.

This to confirm that Priscilla and I could come over, by your kind invitation, on Wednesday evening, November 4- the condition being that you don't put yourself out for us, but just let us share in with the family! Pauline, my wife, thinks it will be difficult to come with the grandchildren, because of distance and lateness during school period. It will be lovely later if you can drop over and see her and us in our very simple communal living over here.

Don't bother to answer this, if it is o.k., and we will just turn up.

I have written to International Christian Leadership and asked them to send you some literature.

Sincerely yours in Christ,

Norman Grubb

~~~

November 19, 1959

Dear Dudley:

Thanks ever so much for your letter, though I was horrified that in your terrific life, you should have to write personally like this. Anyhow, thank you, and please include me in the family, and cut out the Doctor, et cetera - which is not true anyhow! I am delighted that it will be possible to come, and will await a letter from your pastor.

Of course, I will love to stay with you, as you so kindly asked. That will be part of the joy of coming, if I can do so without being a nuisance to you in your busy life.

Please don't bother about expenses, although it is very kind of you to say what you do. The Lord always provides in His own way, and the ministry, and the staying with you are their own rewards.

So we look forward to seeing you in due course.

Very sincerely yours,

Norman Grubb

~~~

Dec.24.59

Beloved Brother and Sister, Irl and Lois,

What made you think of such a gift? It was the All-knowing One inside - for the only attempt at a billfold I have ever had (we don't use them in England) was one I picked up when I dropped in late at a Youth for Christ meeting somewhere, just near the end of their quiz, and no one could answer some very simple Bible OT question, so I perked up in all innocence, and got this billfold. But it is coming apart at the seams, and I was thinking I should need a new one, but hadn't got as far as asking at the proper source! Before they call...Thank you dear ones, and by no means just for the beautiful billfold (this one is as a Cadillac to a Ford), but for the <u>loving</u> generosity that flows thru you. Why do you do it? Well, it is obvious. Nothing but God loving through you could make you love us as you do, and I assure God's love flows two ways!

I was so disappointed when I heard you had come and I had missed you, then there was word that you were still at the door; but it didn't give the extra bit of a quiet talk I should have liked.

But two thrills came out of it. One was to hear you of course say you are part of our family and so drop in to when and where to what you like. That is an established fact! I liked that! The second was, Lois, to hear you again speak seriously about helping. You see it thrilled me when you first said it here, but then I had made an innocent joke when you sat at my desk that here was my new secretary; and I felt afterwards that I might innocently have caught you unawares and you said more than you really ought with your new home and children. So although I was most pleased and hopeful, I felt I should say no more unless <u>you</u> said it! So there! And then you Irl added fuel to it! So thank you, my dear.

How about a date for a first inning?? I go away Thurs.-Sun. Dec.31 to Jan.3, for a series of meetings in a church. I am back Mon. Jan.4 to Tues. 12; but I think you are then in the throes of moving and settling in. If a day was possible during those days, that would be wonderful. Failing that, we must wait a bit, as I plan to go to Toronto where our old friend, Miss Reba Fleming, is giving me a prophet's chamber in which to bury myself to finish the MS on Vereide (then there is another half finished later-my own spoutings). So there is plenty of work ahead dictating the fair copy of these two. But that wouldn't be until Feb.

So there it is. Would you come here, or is it easier for me to come to you, because of the children? Or would you bring them?

We will talk it over later. So glad you met Dan. You know his fiancé is coming Sunday for a week. We were saying how we would love her to meet folks like you, and find that the Lord lives in real people, not hothouse plants like us! It might be that we could drive over for an hour's call on you. I don't know; but if we come we will phone first.

With all my love, my dears, and thank you from all of us, but specially from me. You note Pauline is a canny person, like most women; but you have won her heart; she spoke of you today as she speaks of few! You will know this letter has <u>not</u> been typed by my expert new Sec.!!!

Ever your brother,

Norman

~~~

February 9, 1960

Dear Horace,

Thank you for your letter. You've put me on a spot and I must give you the best answer I can according to the light I have.

From earliest days as a student at Cambridge, I have been a hundred percent conservative—"fundamentalist"—and as such, being deeply concerned with the liberalism and lack of regenerating message in the Student Christian Movement, I was led, I believe by God, to found the InterVarsity Fellowship (called IVCF over here) which is now worldwide. I have not changed my conviction since then, and therefore have never been free to remain a member of my own original denomination, the Church of England, because of the mixture in it of ritualism and modernism, nor to join any other denomination which had either of those admixtures. Therefore I am, technically and in my conviction, a "separatist" and remain so and belong to one of those missions which the World Council of Churches calls "non-cooperative".

I do not go so far in a separatist attitude which practically only fellowships with those who are "separated". I delight in fellowship in Christ with all who are in Christ, and I thankfully recognize that tens of thousands of them are in the larger churches which form the WCC. That is why I have much joy and liberty in being allowed to fellowship with such as Faith at Work. I would make no issue of this matter, if left to myself. But if it is raised as in your letter, then I have to give a faithful answer up to the light I have, and I have to make my boast of being in a separatist society.

Well, Horace, that about clears the position. We are brethren, and what I say is not the major matter. Christ is the center, and we are as wholly one in Him as ever.

Ever your brother in Christ,

Norman

~~~

Aug.6.60

My dears Irl and Lois,

This has been a real holiday. We have just stretched and lazed, without a single interruption! I couldn't do that in Long Island, because of the book, but here I let go. How we have loved your beautiful home, and marveled again and again that God should have told you to hand it over to us like this. I have occupied the living room, spread my books and papers, and just gorged myself with reading and meeting with God. We have talked and talked together! The children have divided their time between endless TV and the afternoons we have all spent at the pool. What a lovely pool, far better than the sea, and not a single person shared it with us! It has just been warm and quiet enough to revel in, and even after two hours it has been a job to drag the kids out. Pris has enjoyed it just as much, and I too for shorter periods. Pauline has served us all as usual, and enjoyed the quiet. We have had your lovely bedroom.

The animals have survived. The ducks have been mine, and aren't they crazy for their rations, I hope I've given them the right amount. The dogs have been Nicky's. We have found Gnade most affectionate and have had her free half each day, no trouble to tie up. Rip has the afternoons and eves off, and follows us to the pool, without being told where we are going. The cats have been Sandra's.

I hope you've had a lovely time too, though it couldn't have been more lovely, and certainly not more quiet! I shall want to hear all news, but I suppose it will be in early Sept., as I am away on two conferences now, and then our Annual Staff. Pauline thinks it better to return with me today.

So thank you again and again. It was a wonderful thought of yours. Pauline was hesitant, thinking it would be a load, but I am sure she sees differently now. Thank you for all your thoughtfulness in the things you left for us. We have so enjoyed the ease of meals at the counter-a wonderful idea.

Much much love,
Ever yours affectionately

Norman

~~~

November 3, 1960

Dear Mr. Baarendse:

Thank you for the speaking schedule. I hope that I shall not disappoint you, but maybe with Brother Gillam, a channel for God's Word. I have not been a front line worker for many years, and am not a man for many statistics. In most of my meetings I concentrate more on the principles of the Spirit which are the key to missionary aggression and fruitfulness, though I can naturally illustrate them with examples from W.E.C. experiences in many lands (I have visited most of them).

I haven't any decent photo, but I will send you the only thing I have, calculated to shock people off from coming rather than to pull them in. I advise that you not use it!

I am afraid I have never done anything in the way of films. Our mission has some which various people take around.

I am sure the Lord will bless us, and it will be a privilege to be with you. I am sorry to bother you on one other point, but if I fly in, do I come to Upland or where?

Sincerely yours in Christ,

Norman Grubb

~~~

July 1962

Beloved Lois and Irl,

It was good to get your card. Here we are "buried" in this little house. Pauline loves it for the quiet, and I too, and to get along with writing, when I can struggle thru with the mail (it is no struggle to write to members of our beloved family in Christ!). I am having to do battle with Dave over a string of things in which at least he puts his heavy foot on my corns, and my job is to educate the teenager by dealing with it, but not with an equally heavy foot! Result- he wants to meet me tomorrow for a Sat. breakfast. He wants to stop me sending out something, having carefully sent his first without a chance to me to stop it!! Such is excellent material for seeing the bigger Christ in a person than the smaller deviations, and I do see Christ in him, and am confident that God has a good firm hand on all us queer Weccers, so I am enjoying the fun of bringing up the youngsters. But I wish I had you as secretary to discuss and enjoy it with you before I write, and often get put right. We had good times, didn't we? You were good to me, my dear, and Irl to let you come.

We are still uncertain but Ken and the CLC have most graciously privately met and invited us to build on their property (we first made a private inquiry just from Ken and Bessie but they took it to the staff). They even say it would be an honor - to us, not to them. Our friends Fred and Marian Heaney visited us and said that they were led to help and that through them and a friend there would be what he called a "substantial sum" when we were clear about building. There are no limits to God.

We love you so this comes with plenty of it from us both. Have finished rough draft of MS on WEC four basic principles- sacrifice (where?), faith, holiness, fellowship. Now fitting up a wonderful testimony of God's provision of our Glasgow Training Center. Then I would <u>love</u> to get to an autobiography and say all sorts of things!!!

Deepest love to you both. Return Aug.6. Then we scheme a reunion with you! Wonderful how we have "grown into" each other. All praise and love.

ever lovingly,

Norman

~~~

October 1.74.

My dear Rob and Martha Lee,

I am writing this to you (and being a number of us you will excuse copies), as part of the family in Christ who are meeting in John and Linda Bunting's home for Saturday & Sunday November 16 & 17. I thought a little preliminary introduction of us to each other and a little explanation might help.

The background of our weekend is that in my movings around
I have the special luxury of getting with various ones of you (and a
number more too numerous or too far-distant to invite), who have been,
as I myself, greatly enlightened in a fuller understanding of our union
life in God, and the tremendously liberating effects of this in our daily
lives. We have lots to learn and lots of weak spots, and questions we
would like to ask of each other; <u>but</u> things have happened to us about
which we say, like Isaiah, we have "seen a great light". So I thought it
would be wonderful if some of us could meet each other. The loving
generosity of John & Linda, and the live group with them, have now
made this possible.

But I do want to point this out. My vision in our coming together
is definitely not that we gather round a "speaker", or for a "seminar",
or something "structure" like that. No, we all come as <u>fellow-sharers,
fellow-contributors</u>, each of us with something God has shewn us, each
in the original way He reveals Himself to each. And I don't mean by that
just a "word" out of our personal experience, but that each of are ready
to put into words how we would explain to others what living personal
relationship I have with God, what I understand that relationship to
be, how I am learning and practising, however feebly, to confront and
overcome my personal problems, sins-temptations, in the pressure
of daily living, and what I say to others seeking deliverance in their
distresses and needs.

We meet, then, as the writer to the Hebrews said not as babes
content with milk when we "ought to be teachers", but rather as those
"going on to perfection", who are putting our teeth into "strong meat"
and becoming "able to teach others also".

So it would be good if each of us come with a sense of personal
commission and responsibility to make our personal contribution, and
having thought over what I can most honestly contribute.

I know we shall have a great time, and also I believe form fruitful
links for the future.

We plan to arrive Friday evening, and spend Saturday & Sunday
together and how we thank these dear ones who are making ready for
us.

Ever with my love,

Norman

~~~

Dec.25.74

My very dearest Jack and Alice,

Your thrilling letter, Alice darling, enclosing your loving message to us all and this loving gift, came two days ago. Thank you both so much. It is God's abounding love through you to send us this these days when all the world is tightening, not loosening up. It is a precious word of His loving us by you, and thank you so so much.

We have just got our precious Pauline home a few days - so glad to be back. The Lord took her wonderfully thru that severe surgery at her human age of 80, both for the bleeding ulcer and the hiatal hernia. The doctor and nurses were wonderful. But of course she is very weak and very thin and eats so little. She does get up and dressed part of the day, but remains mostly in her room; but I am watching the Lord quicken her now just as He took her thru the hospital days. She is in His eternal life.

So I'll hope to hear soon from you again. I tremendously jump to the idea of you two coming. And thank you, thank you, dear Jack and Alice, for all this great love of yours,

Norman, Pauline & Pris

~~~

Aug. 19. 77

Dear Paul,

Your Father, so much loved by me, did tell me that he was making a suggestion to you that I might visit you when I might come to England in God's will next year; but I had not expected such a welcome from you. It's just thrilling to know how the Holy Spirit is moving in Britain as over here and it seems as if the Episcopals and Romans are leading the way!!

But I should explain to you that God has never given me the gift of preaching, so I doubt whether I am suited for Sunday pulpits, also you give a fellow such a short time on Sun. morn and I am long-winded! I am more used to house-groups, times of open fellowship etc, though your Sat. night Rally sounds attractive. So I don't know whether it would be better to come just for a Sat. night?

So I can't say more at present, and when I get closer to planning detail, write you again.

145

So glad the Lord has set His seal on your ministry,
Ever in Christ,

Norman Grubb

~~~

Dec.18.77

Dear Ray,

So glad to hear from you. I'm not yet clear exactly how the Lord is leading you. Do you have a church in Oakvale? Or just ministering as God opens doors - you mention a Friday night group. I used to feel a loner with the light on "total living" He had given and I often used to wonder, Was the whole battalion out of step and only me in, or vise versa! But it's been amazing since the Spirit got hold of Bill Volkman and this Union Life mag comes out and we get tremendous response, about double circulation and no subscriptions asked, folks just give as led – but it has opened doors and hearts wide. Dan Stone resigned his position on the staff of his Baptist College to come full time into sharing the word – a perfect teammate and laps up and puts across the truth. We have just finished a two month tour on the West Coast and will have to return, but can't before New Year 79; then we have about 25 "Family Fellowships" this year where folks wanted us for a series; and then we are going Florida, Alabama, Miss in March, Texas etc in the Fall etc. When God gives what reaches hearts and minds as a real solution to seeking hearts, there is no end of openings; and you had begun to catch onto that. Maybe the Lord is doing a further sharpening work in your understanding, so that you know clearly where you have that big stride beyond what normal evangelicals and Bible folks give – not only Christ in us but as us - is us!

Let me know some more of how God is leading and using you.
Ever with my love,

Norman

~~~

Dec.21.80

My dear Helen and Freda,

I am sending you this printed word of loving greetings, because I have only now returned from a tour of three months of meetings and visits.

The Lord has wonderfully given me my granddaughter Sandie to drive me around, together with another wonderful gift of God in a Rabbit Diesel, which is such a saving in fuel, as well as a great relief for me from bag-carrying and plane-catching. The Holy Spirit only recently caught hold of Sandie, and she herself is such a blesser and blessed as she mingles with all our Union Life friends. We plan to continue the same next year.

My precious Pauline still remains quietly the same with Susie Wheeler so lovingly caring for her, and Priscilla also at home with her.

This year is our 61st since Pauline and I married and started our three month journey by Nile River Steamer and foot into the Ituri Forest in the Heart of Africa; and we say, as we look back over the years, as Israel said, "What has God wrought", and "The shout of a king is among us". We are so thankful too that our son Daniel, teaching at his university, is so much a part of us in our Union Life Fellowship.

Lovingly to you all, and The Blesser is blessing you, as He always is doing; and we are believing "See-throughers", not unbelieving "See-at-ers", in Him meaning all that comes to us as a fresh manifestation of Himself, and turning it all into the good pleasure of His goodness by our spoken words of faith.

Norman, Pauline, Priscilla, Susie, Sandie

~~~

May 10.81

My dear Marcus,

I'm just back with Sandie. We came thru all night – 15 hrs – as Pauline seems so weak, but she has picked up slightly again – but anyhow – for all of us – there is no death, only glorification.

Thank you, dear ones, and we look at least to renew our good times next year!

Lovingly,

Norman

~~~

Dec. 18.81

My dear Helen & Freda,

I have just returned from a two month tour through the Pacific Coast, having meetings and fellowships all the way, with touches of the Spirit in every visit. I had just started the tour with my Granddaughter Sandie, when the Lord so quietly and beautifully took Pauline home to Himself on Sept. 15. I wrote to some of you of our time of rejoicing as we put the precious body in the ground but saw her with Jesus. I then continued the tour, Sandie remaining with our Pris at home as she needed loving care, and Laurie Hills a co-sharer in our Union Life ministry wonderfully accompanied me.

But at this moment, now on my return, an accumulation of loving letters, as well as Christmas greetings, which are all such a privilege to receive, as well as various ones who write with spiritual needs and problems, so I am writing this thankful note to you, and I know you will understand. John Whittle has written a beautiful outline of Pauline's life from her childhood days in China with her father and mother, and on to our Congo days together and then the years at the London headquarters of WEC, and then on here in the USA, and a brief glimpse of the enormousness of God's goodness to me in bringing our lives together. If you think you are not likely to have had a copy of this, published in our USA WEC Magazine, THRUST, then I will enclose a copy and I believe you will enjoy reading it.

Meanwhile, as we said when C.T. Studd was taken from us, "God enabling us, we go on". So now - greatly rejoicing, fully occupied with sharing our precious "liberating reality", and with love to you all.
Lovingly,

Norman

~~~

Oct. 6.84

Fran darling,

I'll enclose with this my latest to Bill V, and also mine to our precious Laurie who had asked - to my delight - to come and spend a day with me (and we have been so totally intimate to the rock-bottom in the Spirit all these years - for hours and days together) but has now written (such a built-up letter compared to our usual outflow, like you-me) saying she won't come as we are now so apart in our teachings. Of course I'm hurt and sorrowful, and don't accept this. There is a place for sharing varieties and linking all together; there must be in view of Jesus John 17 prayer and Paul's appeals in Phil and 1 Cor.

So I'm again just saying to you, darling, that I count you as our No. 1 in Britain and you share what I send as led.

But, love, we just GO RIGHT ON. GOD has given us our inner "seeings" and these we <u>must</u> share with the whole church in the whole world. But it looks as if we are being 'forced' to start even a new mag and that may have to be under a new name, as Bill has asked us to do that and cuts us off from the present Union Life, though very kindly giving us his address list. For all this we shall wait on God together in Jan at Jackson. We won't make any further move without knowing clearly what GOD is saying to us all together, and having clear firm grounds for anything new, and able to explain why. We shall equally of course remain in love and appreciation and no 'fleshly' attacks on these we love, though they separate themselves from us. Nearly all are with us.

So, darling, we, including you, will just go steady. All we want and choose is what pleases and glorifies GOD and is HIS ways for us, and anyhow in love with all His body-members, and no hit-backs, but rather helping all to go forward. So you need not be 'sorting' anything out at present, and though you can't be with us, I shall keep you fully informed and no loved ones in Britain will be 'forced' to take sides, but go along with God. I know, love, trust, my darling Fran. Our bonds are too strong to break!

I leave with Sandie Oct. 16 for my western long tour up to about Dec. 10, but letters follow. I, like you, am wholly at peace and freedom in light, just walking with HIM step by step and loving all. Just let my Margie Ward know, and others as led, including my Jan Inger.

Wonderful new flow with WEC. You will have seen the Inter con report. Great morning with all at Hamilton HQ and Ken Getty. Some are really seeing and drinking and accepting.

Do I love my Fran – Yes and in my way, and dare to believe I'm loved.

Norman

~~~

Sun.Aug.4.85

To all you dear ones who, so staggeringly to me, came along on Saturday, often with much sacrifice, to spend the afternoon with me and with us altogether, and to you many others who sent such loving cards and remembrances, I can only write this early Sunday morning, not just to thank you all, but to say with great joy that I know why all of you came or wrote. I know it is because you are all rejoicing with me in our one great secret – that we now know that we are all by God's marvelous grace not ourselves, but HE in our forms. And you came or wrote really only in thanksgiving that He has unveiled Himself to each of us as our ALL in all, and our fellowship through the years has helped to that unveiling – "That Christ may be magnified in our bodies whether by life or death" is what Paul wrote and we rejoicingly say along with him; and his other word, "For me to live is CHRIST".

So as I sat among you, I had been completely taken by surprise. I hadn't caught a hint of what my precious Sandie had been preparing and working at for weeks, and others of you helping her. So I arrived from having lunch with my loved John & Kath Whittle wondering what that mysterious tent was and the folks standing around inside it! Then as I suddenly was greeted by one or another of you from long distances, the secret dawned! So as I sat greeting and meeting you, you can imagine how it was praise and worship time for me, as I kept seeing you, some of you whom I had known and loved for years, and kept saying to myself, "There is Christ in one or another of His human forms", and each of you precious ones who had been learning together thru these years that it is we, yet not we, but HE! And I knew you had come, some long distances, and others of you sent these cards, because our many love-contacts thru the years had been clarifying to each of us who we really ARE, and we satisfied and rejoicing in our knowing that we had been given the secret of the universe – "hid from ages and generations, but now made manifest" – Christ in each of us, already our "glory", as we are finding all life, whether in stormy or calm waters, to be PERFECT HIM in all His various ways our own perfect completion. And others, every one of whom have a desperate secret hunger while they still only have their deluded selves to rely upon, catching this light of life in us.

And so this has been my totally surprise 90th birthday gift – only made possible, since the Lord took my Pauline five years ago, by this gift to me of my Sandie granddaughter who planned and got you all here, or sending your love-cards, so how can I cease thanking God for her and because I know she does this, not really for me, but for the love of our same Lord Jesus Christ in her. So this was really a worship praise and time together, because it was only HE who was the drawing power to cause you to come or send. We had learned and met with HIM in each other, and rejoiced in HIM as each other! And loved each other as each being He in all the variety of our human selves. Beautiful!

So thank you all. The Quickening Spirit still keeps me going, so that I am able to get around sharing our one REALITY. And we always living by the ever-repeated faith- recognition that, however dark the way appears, it is only always He in disguise; and indeed the darknesses are actually 'given' us to press us into our faith-recognitions of Him meaning all in order to manifest Himself in some new ways, the necessary dark thru the light then shines; and we the light-shiners by our released walk and bold witness to so many others, "death works in us, and life in you".

So thank you again, and my precious daughter, Priscilla, along with me, and ever with my love, and maybe another ten years of sharing, and then for all of us for our eternal 'get-together' "with Christ which is far better"!

Lovingly

Norman

<div style="text-align:center">~~~</div>

Mar.23.86

Dear Mel,

Thank you for your letter and that you are preparing a history of IVF Canada for its 60th Anniversary. I have also had a typically lively letter about it from Douglas Johnson, and I quote what he says in his inimitable way – which is just about the facts, and of course you will have his own history of IVF from its beginnings "CONTENDING FOR THE FAITH". You will know that, by God's perfect guidance which pulled Douglas from his medical career, glorious faithful sacrifice – so that he is really the human Founder and Upbuilder of IVF from it's origins; and we can now look with such thankfulness at it's worldwide expansions, in which – doubtless the Spirit-source of its Joshua 1:8 'prosperity' – its total loyalty to the Scripture and the Christ of the Scriptures are the key, coupled with bold witness and outreach; in our first 1919 InterVarsity Conference we named it "Faithfulness and Fire"!

But as to that first 'historic' launch out of Howard Guinness to Canada, I really haven't much to add to what Douglas writes in the enclosed. I had gone, commissioned by our WEC Committee in London, to bring the challenge of the unevalengelised world to Canada. I was myself on furlough from our Congo field with C.T. Studd. As a "Faith Crusade" I said I wished to go trusting God for my traveling supplies. The Committee were hesitant in case I might fall penniless by the way and bring disgrace on the Lord's name (!!), so they insisted that at least I take £5 with me. I made my first six month tour thru Canada, receiving my first personal financial 'deliverance', when down to my last cents in Winnipeg, and sufficient from then on, until I was about to get on the boat in Montreal for my return to England a businessman handed me £5, so that I was able to return the Committee's £5 intact to them! The point of my telling you this is because, as my first launch of faith without starting with human support, and with my God-sent personal supplies thru the tour (all gifts going back to the WEC), I was altogether 'primed' to put it to IVF at that High Leigh Conference that God would do the same for Howard Guinness, if they would bless him and send him forth also without funds! And this they agreed to, because you will note how Douglas said they were themselves more or less penniless!

You ask me what stirred me in Canada to bring back this challenge to IVF Britain. It may have been my ignorance, but as I traveled through Canada, I only came across one small group in Vancouver where I think the University was just coming into being (?), but beyond that, the only functioning group I met with was at McGill in Montreal. That is what stirred me; and from all I could find out, there was that somewhat confined Calvinistic student colleges' witness in the whole of USA! This is what put the burden on me and the 'fire' in my bones to go back and challenge IVF Britain to break forth worldwide.

I well remember how, like Paul, my "spirit was stirred within me" at the High Leigh Conference till I felt I had to be bold enough to challenge the Student Committee. The Spirit came upon me like that in 1919 when I first saw the vision of an extended witness to all Universities in Britain as we already had in the Cambridge InterCollegiate Christian Union (C.I.C.C.U.), and I suggested to my friends Clarence Foster and Leslie Sutton that we put on an "InterVarsity Conference" in London which we did. I felt the same Spirit-urge in 1928 to bring this further challenge for the spread of the then expanding IVF in Britain thru the Universities of Canada and on to the USA, and so I brought it to that Student Committee; and it was because I had just proved God's faithfulness to me those months in Canada that I could daringly urge that IVF launch Howard into Canada by the same 'faith' way.

This they agreed to do when Howard heard the call. He was actually preparing to join the China Inland Mission after completing his medical studies, I think, in Bart's Hospital in London, as well as being an outstanding Rugby Football player, and it was a step of faith and sacrifice for Howard, as well as the CIM Council, to back his change of call. (It was Howard who later wrote that pamphlet "Sacrifice" which was standard in IVF for many years.)

Further details I don't remember except that in wintery Canada I had been given a heavier overcoat than usual in England, and I bequeathed that to Howard, though a larger man than I!

One other fact stands out to me. I had met in Montreal the businessman, and I think Large Store owner, A.J. Nesbit, and it was he who backed me in taking the challenge back to British IVF. And so it was when Howard arrived in Montreal, I don't remember ship or date, in his penniless condition, he was met by Brother Nesbit and a gift of $100. A good amount in those days. And what a wide spread since then! All glory to God!

No, I didn't have further contacts in Canada that I can remember, except with the McGill group, and I didn't meet Bingham. But I am very thankful you are getting this 'history'.

Very sincerely and you will have all God's blessing as you write,

Norman Grubb

~~~

Nov.5.86

My dear Stewart,

I hope this will get to you as I don't know where you are at the moment. How I thank God for your years as IS, and all WEC will greatly miss you. The Spirit shot a big dose of oldtime faith into our WEC bones during your time since Intercon II, thank God.

I'm amazed at the acceptance of the Summit Living book. I find it turning up all over the place and refreshing people. I still think you did an Amazing job, and can only think it is of the Spirit. I had my first touch last Sunday with Robert Schuller of the Crystal Cathedral, and was very pleased with my person to person touch with him, and found him a much more 'real' person than just seeing him on the platform. On the desk in his private office was a copy of SUMMIT! He said he knew of me 20 years ago when he heard I said to God in the morning, "Hullo, God, What are you up to today? I'll go along with you in whatever way you go!". He said he constantly repeated that, and then we had such a good time he said he must take me with him to the platform of his huge morning service and introduce me and have a word from me and wants more later. So on the witness goes!

I think I told you I sent a copy of that small NO INDEPENDENT SELF to every Weccer on our fields as by the Praying Always list. I think I put it better what you couldn't go along with about "No human nature"! We are having great times and more "seeing", including very warm letter form Harold Brokke of Bethany.

Want to keep in touch with your coming movements. Hope to visit Eng. with Sandie in the Spring. When Schuller introduced me as a 91 yr old Englishman, I told them at least they would hear decent English, and as to age, Moses went to 130 with "eye not dim nor natural force abated", so I expect another 30 years.

ever with my love

Rubi

~~~

</div>

<div style="text-align:right">Nov.25.86</div>

Dear Stewart,

You certainly know how to get at my crusty old heart! Thank you for yours which reached me yesterday back from my Western tour. First of all, how I continually thank God that He, so intervened that you should be IS. You just thrilled on your "oldtime" emphasis on our faith-foundations and the obvious spark of the Spirit lit at Intercon II, and your own prime ministering to the sick! I note it very much with Ken in Canada, and would give my right hand to have a chance with WEC recruits here. I am fearful of faithful Will's constant emphasis (so I hear) on "Balance". Yes, balanced <u>extremes</u>, but I don't think he means that! I liked what I have seen of Dieter, and the Lord will keep him sparked up too!

You see the 'older' ones, when I know where your roots are, have a different impact on me, both you and Helen R. Then I continually say, "Where else can 'Eileen' get her facts or quotes but from the Life (C.T. Studd Cricketer and Pioneer), as there is so little else?" My point is that the life, which is mainly stringing together CT quotes in his inimitable

<div style="text-align:center">154</div>

sharp ways of saying things, has had a worldwide impact and has undoubtedly given his a unique place as a burning blaze for Jesus (just as the same has happened all over the U.S.A. with the Rees Howells' book mainly quotes)? And what effect will some kind of survey of his life and principles have, except on a certain number of interested for a short time, while the CT life is still going strong after 50 years, just as the Lutterworth editor said it would when they took it. And another book may take folks off from reading the one with his own unique Spirit-punch in it. I note what you say about "working over" the present one. Yes, I wouldn't mind the labor entailed when it is preserving the essence. What else will another book have, if it is as hard hitting, but mainly quotes? But at least you know how to reach my heart, Stewart, and get me talking!! I realise there are possible attacks. I heard there had been one in Australia. Won't do much harm! Even I am now privileged to be listed with several such as Bruce Larson as teaching "self-deification" by Dave Hunt in his "Seduction". So good advertisement.

I should love a time with you, you know that, but our folks have put on a conference, renting some Elim center in almost last week of April, so I shall hope to be over for that and then some visits in May, even to Bulstrode if they will put up with me, and so I fear miss you here. What a loyal brother you have been – just as old CTS used to be so thankful for a few loyal ones. I shall much want to follow on with you in your extended ministry when back in Aus. I can assure you it is great when the Lord keeps us going, and plenty open doors right up to 100! Schuller has just written saying, "You have impacted my life in a way that was extraordinary", and looks forward to seeing me when 100! Also I've just heard from Wallace Haines, who has the links with House of Lords (Lord Caldecote) and Commons, as with Doug Coe here, and he says the Sec in No. 10 who does the policy preparations for Mrs. Thatcher is a keen Christian, and he has sent him YES I AM.

Eileen Vincent has just written saying she would like to meet us when I come in April. I like the spirit of my contacts with her.

So ever with my love, you good good soldier of Jesus in our modern WEC days. We'll keep our precious links, and I continually hear of folks getting refreshed by SUMMIT and I think I told you I saw it on Schuller's table.

ever with my love,

Norman

~~~

</div>

Jan. 7. 88

My darling,

You are overwhelming! How can you pour out such RICHES page after page and so legible that I read every word! Darling, you are a being from another world!! I loved every page of it because it is full of the flooding river of GOD. What a WONDERFUL life it is when our every interest is eaten up (Zeal of my House has eaten me up) with some God-purpose and some God-contact. Just every page of yours. I used a red pen to underline what I want to refer to answering, and every page has plenty underlines! So I just don't know where to start my comments.

First I suppose your England visit. In those few days Sandie has to plan the best and quickest for you and my laugh is that for everybody else it would be, "Have you seen the Crown Jewels? Have you been to Shakespeare country?" But to you-me-Sandie it is <u>WHOM</u> will you have seen that matters to God and you? I don't think I can even advise more in such a short time. I think Sandie includes a Bulstrode visit. Really I have nothing special for that except that it is our WEC home and God's JOKE, because when CT left alone for Congo he left one house (Brick five stories – usual Brit) which he bought for an odd hundred or two and left Mother Studd there (AND PAULINE with her, not realizing her coming FATE), and his going with no early backing was called by his leading Evang rector in St. Paul's Portman Sq. (a kind of posh area where my mother was brought up next door to Lord Radstock, the great Christian witness of those days to the Czar and Russian aristocracy, and later Pauline's uncle who was Lord Mayor of London, Sir Kynaston Studd, married one of those Russian princesses, Princess Lieben who was Aunt Erica to us). Well now from that first home here God expanded us to the way largest Missionary HQ in Britain, which you will visit, and other missions come there and we give them room for their own conferences! God's usual joke!!! When WEC bought this Bulstrode which you will see, <u>we</u> owned the old Studd house, so I gave the deeds to help buy this huge place, and therefore WEC always says Pris can have a home there if she wants to! But I hardly now know the present Bulstrode folk, though I like the leader Colin Nicholas and he has some response our way. There is also Violet Edson who was with us at one time and did sec. work for me. Maybe you'll see Violet.

Then of course there is Rees Howells place. I think I shall send Samuel a line to tell him you and S. hope to call. He is rather a retiring person, but very warm host and you would also hopefully see Doris Rusco, and have a glimpse of the place. I wrote the RH life from the big house across the road, Sketty Isaf, which RH had taken by faith, because it's owner a retired Major said, "I'll get out because Rees H. has his eyes on this place and God always gives him what he is after!" and He did. I always stay there and wrote the book there. Couldn't tell you exactly where I went that first walk, round by one of the beautiful Swansea bays, but I was COPPED just as my DeeDee now is! Wish you could witness to the eve meeting!

Then hopefully my great loved Margie Ward in York, very much my No.1 in Brit. We have been very close for years and she KNOWS, but is caught up by caring for her husband George a leading architect in York, but had a stroke. Margie's father owned a factory for baby powder, employed about 200, and I was his closest friend. Loved him, so we are VERY CLOSE and I would love you even to see her. I guess darling those are the two main spots. You will also see my loved Fran Heys really our No.1 in KNOWING. Good and faithful.

I guess that covers the main ones in your short stay. Wish you could also meet my Paul (Sandie's father) and Madge, who knows the Lord. That would be a blessing! Take them to dinner. Wish you could.

I love, love you as now a MISSIONARY and your Father's gift was a "missionary" gift!!! Wow!

LOVING YOU

Norman

~~~

Ap.6.88

Darling,

I'm tremendously moved today to get yours, every page of it glowing and it gives me the strong impression of a God-calling and setting-apart of another of His anointed. There just do come times when cut-offs are God's ways of CONFIRMING His real called ones, and they move in new God-strength. Plainly we have had heavy 'blows' that way, totally unexpected which has done just that for us.

But ONE THING STANDS OUT in this finally sharpening confirming process, that there IS TOTAL TOTAL death to everything with nothing left to us but CHRIST AS US. I KNOW THIS IS VITAL AND PIVOTAL. Most good evangs can take Christ in me, because it leaves really Christ and a "me". But Christ AS me leaves no me! I'm dissolved and HE AS ME and we who've gone that total way KNOW ITS TOTAL. But to others the truth of Christ in me, it is just the way over to DANGEROUS HERESY, which makes the ultimate difference among us. And that's why we are surrounded by "wrecks"! I can count the number of good evangelical independent fellowships who won't have me near them now, not to speak of course of 'normal' churches. And it HAS TO BE SO BECAUSE WHAT WE ARE STANDING FOR IS THE ULTIMATE TOTAL! That was why Paul at his end was urging son Timothy out of fearfulness to bold affirmation.

You see I saw and knew it with our C.T. Studd. He paid the TOTAL AS A YOUNG MAN, AND WAS JUST IMPOSSIBLE FOR MOST TO FOLLOW THRU WITH. But God had "got" me even as a young man over my first dropping of a girl, and then later when my love was so hot for Jesus that even Pauline dropped me and yet I was called to join C.T. who was to be my father-in-law with only five workers there. The acid test was would I go to some other group not right under the nose of CTS and my break with Pauline. The big temptation came. I COULDN'T. If I had to go to the Congo with P married to my friend Buxton, then I MUST go. THAT SEALED MY DEATH. A few months later when they saw I was not running at any price, back came Pauline, and years later it was Pauline and I who took on the wrecks of the mission from CTS and today that huge solid world WEC and CLC!

But nearly all left CT. He was nearly IMPOSSIBLE with things he said and did, but I lived with him and KNEW his soul burned with only one thing, getting Africans to Jesus and Jesus walking about in black bodies. The thing became so fierce that the whole home Board decided to throw CT out and start the mission again on less extreme lines. P and I went out as last resort to warn CT. All the missionaries on furlough, about 35, got frightened and joined the Board, except one Canadian. They sent out a letter to Congo "dismissing" CTS and we two with him. They had all the records, home office, Mag, supplies, everything. We were left to yield or starve. Of course the 35 on the field remained with CTS. He sent us home alone, saying "God has put me in many a tight corner and got me out of them. If He doesn't, He's a ....., No He isn't for He will." That's our last human word from him. We arrived home, just our one house. But the one who had stood in spirit with CTS who saw that intercessors always have their DEATH, was Rees Howells. It was to him I went and that night when he read our WEC Principles and Practices, he read that CTS as founder had the vote. "Go back", he told me, "seize the offices in the name of the Lord, take all the records and GO AHEAD." We did so next night, David and I. They had all thought we were done, sold out, starved. But next morn they called in a Christian solicitor and when we read our P & P's he said, "You are right! The Mission is yours via CT veto". Out went all that Board and all the home backing in one mass and today where are they, and what is God – with us!!! But we never said one word in public against them, but just moved forward in boldness of steps of faith.

But you see the narrowness of it. C.T. was so "difficult" in his burning fire that NEARLY ALL LEFT HIM including his other two sons-in-law and daughters (although we renewed a good loving relationship with them). And only Cinderella Norman and Pauline were left. And to-day. ONE WITH GOD IS A MAJORITY; if we go thru the fires of testing our stand, where there are HUMAN THINGS which is not how we would do them.

So I've again poured this out, darling, so deeply stirred by your own letter and your evident call to boldness when I'm held up. You know I'd give my right hand to be there, but it is GOD. You will rise up and give the total as God has given it to you.

I have hatefully to say that other loved ones have not paid the total. There is some hold back, and this intercession-apostleship is searching to the bottom. No holds back, and there IS a sorting out and then this total and God is working out among us just that. It IS TREMENDOUS, DARLING, because there is this further INTERCESSOR DEATH in those of us who will take it. That Luke 14:25-35, and somehow sometime we ALL have to have gone there to be among the total. Then there the Glory and the Cross; no other way for us Timothys but 2Tim.3.12! So we go on glorying and these hurting breaks are the very way God matures His real Army. Look at Paul those days to Timothy. Look at the millions, billions since then and today. Not outer churches, but among them thousands who are KNOWERS and we are to bring many others to this. And I'm sure with all my years of experience that the FINAL ACID TEST IS SOMETHING ABOUT GOD'S SPECIAL ANOINTED WHICH WE <u>DON'T QUITE LIKE</u> <u>WHICH CURLS US</u> UP, but the true See-er sees clean thru, and that is the very spot where his seeing is sealed. So now with us and I soon going and you my TIMOTHYS.

So I just pour this out my darling, right from my heart. I may add more, but this is midnight.

Norman

~~~

Aug.9.88

Dearest Marian & Ray,

I'm just delighted to get this loving card from you – best of all that have come. You know I never get over that great weekend together, both in the heart-fellowship we had and then, Ray, your marvelous help to us which has made the house look so much better.

We had a WONDERFUL surprise about six weeks ago. You know that our loved Ken and Bessie Adams, founder of CLC, have both slipped away to be with the Lord. It was Ken who marked out this house for us and when it was built by gifts given us, the arrangement had been made that when Pauline and I had gone, Pris could have the top floor. But then Sandie has come and just made all the difference, but we know it would be difficult for Sandie and Pris just to have the upstairs bedroom with all the cooking and living facilities on the ground floor. Then suddenly Ken's son-in-law now in charge asked with another brother to come and see us. They came and said it was the Lord's will that Sandie and Pris should have the whole house so long as Pris is still with us – and as you know Sandie, is a very hospitable person. That was MARVELOUS, and they brought a lawyer to sign it up! Sandie will make contributions as led. So that is a great thrill.

All Love,

Norman

<div align="center">~~~</div>

Sept. 15.88

My dear Douglas,

I tremendously appreciate you taking time to go further into the presentation of what I call "Total Truth" and with refreshing reminders to me of Norman Anderson, Ken Hooker and Evan Hopkins; and I had not realised that at 93 I am kind of a half generation older than you all! But you live and minister in another world from mine on a student level and the latest trends in modern theology, and holding the fort for our Bible and evangelical convictions which you have all done so gloriously these nearly seventy years!

I loved what you've said on our loved Clarence with early facts about him I never knew, beyond his being "behind bars" for Christ's sake in World War I, nor did I know Basil Atkinson had been along with him, and their Morse Code tappings, nor of his start with Stuart Holden and

160

then change of convictions on infant baptism (which was precisely why I did not follow thru with C of E ordination), and followed that wild C.T. Studd! (no regrets!!). Precious early history.

My world has been largely with taking the gospel to primitive and illiterate, or in the main line what we would call the "common people", and WEC trainees and missionary staff from the same backgrounds. So I never followed thru, as did most of my Cambridge contemporaries with Ridley and ordination, and so the tackling of such theological knots as those "Two Natures". I really kind of jumped them and as I matured at least on the thinking level in my thirties took a plunge into the more mystical type of "great ones" such as my favorite Jacob Boehme, and William Law and Meister Eckhart, and my great, great favorite Soren Kierkegaard and his "subjectivity is truth" and his "existentialism" which demands an interior rather than objective response to all problems. Then with that a direct approach to the "faith" as analyzed for us in the epistles, as you say gloriously centered on The Person of Christ and ourselves in personal relationship to HIM.

And that is what brought me to the ultimate of Paul's Christ in you and me in Him union-reality. And so my obsessive aim in ministry and writing has been that practical application I find in the epistles of living in the faith (and inwardly Spirit-witnessed- I John 5:10).

So I love to be able to share a bit with you like this, and see how you continue as a "pastor to pastors" in their theological needs, each of us in our God-given callings; and what joy to see the widespread of the student IVF witness since those early starting days, with the price you paid to nourish and build the new-born infant in Britain and so to the world! I suppose what I do is simply to apply, best as I know how that actual working fact of those "Two natures" in their Chalcedony form, while you on the student level have to spend the time confirming them.

So thank you, Douglas, and with my much love and thankfulness,

Norman

~~~

Nov.12.88

Violet dearest,

You are one of the truly faithful WEC Stickers, ever since your early days with Pauline and me at Blueburn in World War II, on thru you Canary Islands calling and breaking of your engagement to "wholly

161

follow", with the Canary Is. brother, and then all these continuing years as background recorder at all our WEC and Intercon. get-togethers- and you still are- with Patrick and Jill! MAGNIFICENT!

Dear, the key to our WEC-CLC onward marchings, and all of us mounting up now to around two thousand, all living as ever by Jesus' Matt.6:33 –ALL PRAISE: and that key has been our sell-out basis. No half measures. Jesus faced that when offered the world by Satan in the Mount of Temptation and He called out, "Get thee behind me, Satan": and results? Death on the cross and a vast eternal harvest of billions of whom by grace we are part. Paul "sold out" and result – execution and the vast, vast harvest of the Gentile church. Barnabas turned back and is lost to history. There IS a "Rubicon we cross" – or don't!

CT sold out. God help and save wavering WEC with it's dropping of the rugged "Crusade" name, and newcomers "loving" this new book [on the life of C.T. Studd], instead of being torn to pieces by the original one!

Others would not "sell-out" to the total with CTS, and when the fire burned, turned back in the day of battle, even his own loved Alfred. I came near the edge and so even did Mother Studd, when CT sent me home with a DCD 'blast' for the criticizing Committee, and she had gone with them. But the day I arrived and presented the letter, back she came and never again wavered. Pauline, my Pauline, saved me, as wives so often do when faithful at any price. I was wavering on that return journey and thought of joining Alfred who much attracted me. Pauline said, "Norman, you must be faithful. Father sent you home as his ambassador. You can only now turn against him if you first GO BACK and face him. Then do what you like". I went back, and in route the Spirit 'zapped' me once for all and told me to go back, and join fire with fire, and LEARN from the central furnace. I did and thus later out came a WEC-CLC of today MARCHING ONWARD on our FOUR PILLARS of Sacrifice, Faith, Holiness and Fellowship (though with a little dangerous waver), with our about 2000 in 50 fields. How thankful I am for faithful Pauline, who stood with God against her husband!!

Moses did that, Aaron did after one big wavering over the golden calves, Caleb gloriously did, Joshua did after his wavering over the twelve spies. Thank God-and result? Israel and then Jesus!!

And there are, thank God, many others among us as sell-outers with no strings attached. So it has wonderfully been for me since my Pauline left us. My granddaughter Sandie stepped right in and said she would drop all as a Christ-person, and also care for my daughter Pris too, that if S. married she would take Pris too! How the Lord has REWARDED HER

IN HER PRESENT VAST OUTREACH OF LIVING LINKS WITH SO MANY
SELL-OUTERS AS SHE DROVE ME ALL ROUND THIS COUNTRY LAST
YEAR, having these house-fellowships; and she herself taking such a
stand when strongly attracted to a wealthy restaurant owner who would
do anything to marry her, but she STOOD SQUARE and would not marry
one who was not a total God-person, so thank God the separation came.
I see by faith Spirit-fire in my Sandie though, as with CT, often the
going seems at first rougher with sell-outers, and not many cushy save-
yourself spots. My Sandie will go along – fire with fire!

But watch, and we sure see that what the Spirit does by ruthless sell-
outers fits in with John's saying that they who do the will of God live for
ever and "their works do follow them". Those who in the final issue take
a lower path than the "total", in the end are like a river which ends up in
the sands, compared to a Colorado River with all its rapids and dangers
flows out back to its ocean.

So it just came to me, Violet, to 'expand' my personal letter to you
by thoughts, and I believe Spirit-insights which I like to leave behind
me when my glory-call comes, and I believe with some eternal Spirit-
principles in them.

ever with my love,

Rubi-Norman

~~~

Dec.28.88

My darling MS Philosopher,

None like you, darling, but HORRORS, fancy my being about a week
or ten days LATE in co-sharing with you. Reason of course the FLOOD
of cards and love-messages pouring in on those last few pre-Xmas days,
and somehow I just CAN'T let a love-message go by with just a copy-
letter and signature. I have to share love where there is love, and you
and I know we have to let the sharing river flow when we write. I find we
just CAN'T stop the flowing. They burst the dam! So that means about
98% of cards and messages take a fat-sized <u>PTO</u> to the back of the thing
Sandie and Pris and I send out with the Sandie and me picture (Pris
runs away from photos). So all these have blocked my normal DeeDee
outpourings. But darling, how THRILLED I ALSO AM WITH YOUR DEPTH
BONDS WITH MY SANDIE. THAT'S MORE IMPORTANT THAN WITH ME,
AS HOPEFULLY, mine will soon have to be from ANOTHER DIMENSION!
I had a recent sharing with Sandie, or maybe I should say she with me,

and again I delighted in her saying that her jobs can fit as led, but her
CALLING will remain keeping her contacts with so many and keeping
touch. I delight to hear that, and I think that clever God has just so
turned things round these past 30 years that there will be sufficient
for her to run the home. Those years back since 1919 P and I never gave
a thought of conserving cash. We used my, what in the Brit. Army we
called "blood money", bonus given us on our being "demoted" from
army in World War I, to pay part of our fare to Congo and thus started
from <u>scratch</u>. In those first ten years we took our share of what the
Lord sent to WEC, just a few pounds each month; but when CT went to
glory at the time of him and us being "cast out" of WEC by the board,
we came home THE ONLY THIN THREAD BY WHICH our original WEC
could go forward, for the board had 'dismissed' us and kept all the WEC
records. I have told you before how MARVELOUSLY on our return, after
we finally said goodbye to CTS in his bamboo home in Congo at about
3.0 am (we start off next morn) and that was when he said, in this tight,
tight corner when dismissed and deprived of all by the home board,
"I've had the luxury of being in many tight corners in order to see God's
deliverances, and He'll deliver in this final one or He's a…No, He isn't
because He WILL". And that only thread of deliverance was P and I going
home along to see where the office etc. had been seized from us; and we
were THE TWO among his daughters and sons-in-law in whom he had
LEAST CONFIDENCE until that LAST VISIT. And then we went home –
our last hope! – and it was thru my visit to Rees Howells that he saw our
Principles and Practice said the founder has the Veto; and on that we
returned home and with our military commander brother-in-law, David,
still then unsaved, delighting in doing battle alongside me, we went in
that morning and TOOK OVER ALL THE RECORDS AS OUR RIGHT AND
THEN RESTARTED THE WEC, when of course the board had thought
they had severed our jugular. And if they had waited three weeks, CT
went to glory, and they would have legally had the right to ALL. That
clever clever God. And now where is that Unevangelized Fields Mission
they started? Hardly in existence and here WEC-CLC with 2000 in 50
fields and God the sole supporter. WOW!

Now darling, I can't remember how I got on to this to you, but
actually always delight in sharing God's TRICKS. CT always said from
Isaiah, "Touch not mine anointed and do my prophets no harm", and
look to-day. And I think my point is that this is precisely how it will
be with UL and us. We don't want to pull out from them. Our calling
is to give IN TOTAL what the Spirit has given us as our TOTAL, and

letting our brothers give their share. But you know they won't have that and have given us this two page expulsion. But of course to us that only means we are SORRY for them because we KNOW we have our total and all we do is not to waste a minute seeking to 'reply' to them but simply swallow up 'negative' with 'positive' by pouring out our positive Total and be wholly happy in doing that. Had no idea they would be so virulent in casting us out. Of course it has repercussion in a number of "indignant" letters (and gifts) and supposing I shall be likewise hurt and indignant; <u>but</u> you know all we can do is <u>laugh</u> at God's cleverness in using this to clarify our Total, and KNOWING THAT that alone has the Spirit's cutting edge. What they have 'sunk back' into is only Victorious life repetition and will gradually be absorbed as "just another". <u>But</u> not ours by the Spirit: it is the UNIQUE WORD FOR OUR ERA, until maybe He has another for next era, and ours therefore CAN'T DIE. I stick by that great word of St. Francis followers of his next generation who were their Franciscan movement and the few who stood firm said, "THERE IS AN ELEMENT IN THE GOSPEL OF CHRIST so disturbing that the world will forever reject it but never forget it: and the church will vacillate between patronage and persecution. Yours is the present, but I think ours is the future." AND SO SAY WE!

So ALL ALL my love. Forgive this usual than worse typing,

Norman

~~~

Mar.18.89

My dear Elizabeth,

You are something – with all your loving labours in sending me these down-to-earth and hitting-the-spot quotes, besides your own news. Thank you, dearest, for such refreshings. Actually I don't think I told you I have been pressing hard now for some months to get the one book into our folks hands which seems to me to gather together through the centuries since Pentecost the very truth you are now quoting to me from Drummond; but our present problem is that there has been a reprint as paper-back of them in England, but they are either out of them or none to spare. That is Broadbent's great PILGRIM CHURCH. It gives the detailed history of those movements of the Spirit which have flowed thru the centuries, and nearly always as outcasts. I have written about it for our Mag, but they can't put it in until they get some supplies from England. I am 'keen' to build our folks on it, and it is largely the flow of the Spirit worldwide to-day. I have delighted in it. The Spirit pulled me out of the 'normal' into this glorious though rough free waters just after my new birth at 18, just before World War I. My godly father, an evang. Clergyman sought with tears to persuade me to remain in the C of E and go for ordination after the War, and said I would starve if I followed that wild C.T. Studd!! But when I persisted, my loving father and mother did back me right up in my wildness! You may be sure I'm thankful! I now have written as my last thing "INTERCESSION-IN-ACTION", the five clear "intercessions" in my life and their 'process' which Rees Howells had brought back to the church with such clarity – Commission, Cost & Completion, and again I couple with it as my last "intercession" our present what I call TOTAL Truth, which I gloriously see as our unique contribution to the whole church and the whole world, of the secret ("mystery") of our Spirit-Knowing, which Paul so wonderfully expounds for those who have ears to hear him in his Rom. 6-8, and John wrote as to those who do know who they ARE on Paul's terms, and James, again only for those with eyes to see tells us how we handle life on this, our TRUE basis. And still for us very much on the rejected level, just as my two with whom I was closest linked died outcast, to return with what they have given us reaching out now in our day – CTS & Rees Howells. And I love to be a third with them! But how true true what you quote of freedom from the Institutional, and starting free and then sinking back. I closely watch my WEC on these levels and rejoice that they hold steady at present, but I've just now given them – the leaders – another warning where I see the "institution" stuff creeping in; and so the Lord will surely keep us on our Intercessor ministry, tiny at present but gloriously foot-free and hopefully kept.

So thank you again for this wonderful refreshing re-touch with Drummond and that quote of how he helped to get CTS and the Seven going in the student world with such effect.

This with my much love, and you, dear, "walking" with problems in the "perishing outer man" and yet we so gloriously "renewed" in the inner man.

Norman

~~~

Sept.17.1989

My dear Leslie,

I was just about to mail what I send with this, when yours arrived today, so I can include a little more. Thank you so much for such a full letter and your own newsletter.

Your own present letter asks quite a lot about my links with Kenneth and what I can tell you of him. Actually we drifted quite away from each other in things of the Spirit. Amazingly in his autobio he says quite openly that he never remembers what I had said about his conversion!! That quite staggered me but it shewed me how far we had drifted apart in our God-relationships. You see his "new birth" was TREMENDOUS; he coming right out as a declared atheist while still in his Marlborough days at about 18, and our (his) father sending around among us to get prayer for him; and it was then we had that revival touch at Keswick with the Cambridge group and Noel Palmer where really the fire was lit which resulted in the birth of IVF and OICCU in Oxford. I got such assurance that at that time that Kenneth was "saved" that I wrote my father there was no need for more prayer. That was June at Keswick. A few weeks later I was home and my mother asked me to go to a very dull little prayer meeting at the church of a few women. I went and some, it must have been the Holy Spirit, actually asked Kenneth who was also at home to join me and he did! At that prayer time the Spirit really came on me and I prayed among those women a really "revival prayer". And it was that which pierced Kenneth and that night he had a mighty midnight battle with the Lord who told him, "I will have all of you or none". And next morning early Kenneth came to my room to tell me he had yielded to God!! And my first thing I did, best I knew how, was to put him onto some of CHM's books on Genesis etc. To begin soaking him in the inner meaning of the scriptures! And yet Kenneth in his biography says he has no memory of all this, and only that his "brother said that was how he was converted"!! No wonder I got a shock.

I then left for Congo, and meanwhile Kenneth got a job as assistant master in a boy's prep school. The results were so revolutionary that the whole school caught fire among the boys and the head would have liked to send K. away, but daren't because of the effect! During the next year or two I received an AMAZING series of letters afire with God from Ken and I just struggling in Congo felt like an iceberg compared to him! Strangely I kept all those letters in a box of our No.17 basement, but somewhere in the bombing or leaving the home I lost them – the greatest treasure!!

Following that Kenneth joined WEC and took his amazing Amazon tours as well as producing that classic of a map of the 500 tribes which first gave folks, Cochrane of World Dominion Press, an inkling of his genius. He really was a daring one in his Amazon ventures. He's not a good writer and so his account of those days is in print but never took hold. But what I did not know then, is what you now mention – that K. was not happy with our WEC ways. The only way he shewed it to me in those days was he never liked Mrs. CT. He just never liked that all-out type of DCD witness for which WEC was built, and the evidence was to follow.

Then somehow, when he was back from Amazon the change came which really brought a total drift between us on spiritual levels. I suppose it started with Cochrane seeing his value and grabbing him from us in WEC (where as I have said he was never happy); but you see after his conversion, just beginning of World War I he joined the Navy to be trained as midshipman (he was already brilliant in yachting) and one of the Marlborough Masters who was an ex-naval lieut. told me Kenneth as a boy at Marlborough knew much more about sailing than he did! That was typical Kenneth. But his brilliant brain was always just at the edge (maybe some will say all we Grubbs are like that!!!), and while training for the Navy there was some kind of Sherlock Holmes murder detective affair going on and Kenneth of all folks dug it out by himself and presented to Scotland Yard a solution!!! But his mind toppled him and he tried to throw himself out of a window but was mercifully picked up on the street below in time, though it was winter. Result a kind of court-martial by the Naval training folks!! Actually I've got my dates wrong, because all that happened before he was saved and then when dismissed by Navy I suppose as mental, he was now on fire for Christ and wanted to go out as Missionary! But his reputation of having been out of his mind and thus dismissed by Navy meant that no Mission Society would take him. But our loved Alfred Buxton saw bigger and persuaded the WEC Brit Committee to give him a chance as pioneer to Amazon!! That was what started him on his tribal survey which was so masterly and when he returned attracted Cochrane to him.

But the actual fact, Leslie, I think is that God knows our hearts and what we fit, and it was his joining Cochrane which began his pilgrimage away from what were to him WEC extremes, and he began to settle in a new and much more public and acceptable and recognized life as Survey Editor with Cochrane; but at the same time that kind of fire which burned in him when first saved and made him such a "revivalist" at that prep school, though too valuable for them to put him out, and at that time I got that amazing series of apostolic letters which I so regret having lost.

That was where our drift apart came. I had never really been close to him except at the time of his new birth and my putting him onto the CHM books; and his following letter to me in Congo. But somehow when I came on furlough that change had begun and I never "touched fire" with him again.

His brilliant career then began. We had our great benefit, as I have told you, because when I took up WEC after CT had gone, I used Kenneth's West African survey to start us off on our WEC adventures, doubtless including Senegal and PG.

But meanwhile his fame as a brilliant what? Statistician fact-collector – what? Began to spread I suppose thru Cochrane. We were moving toward World War II and somehow Lord North who had some Govt position was instructed to get an Information Team together who could be formed into a Dept when war was declared, and that was why North roped him in when War was started, and then formed that Information Department of Govt in which he rose to be the head with about 2000 top brains of that type under him. The man who acted as Sec in Govt was Churchill's favourite*, his name slips me, but Kenneth was the secret "brains" behind it all and for that given the CMG.* Brenden Bracken

So from that developed another type of life among Govt and other high-ups right to the Queen herself, and Kenneth was a member of the Authors Club and several others of that exclusive type of club in England. I don't believe Kenneth ever lost the inner fire lit at conversion, and God used him here and there where others of us don't reach. Our close lengths with which we started were never renewed. He once did send me a book by a Mystic, think de Molinos, and as he does in his biography, he would always say I was the "saint" of the family, but he also meant that we never got close spiritual contact again. I don't or didn't know if I could have broken thru or not, but I loved my visits with him. I would get him to pour out from his vast contacts with the high-ups and he used to fascinate me. That was how I knew the Queen sent for him later when she wanted a new Dean of the Royal Chapel at Windsor and a private chat with him and told him she was tired of outer ritual and could he find a chaplain of a more evang and spiritual type for her. He did find one, again my memory fails me, with some spiritual touch of a more liberal type.

So on he moved from that and he did once call himself to me a more "liberal evangelical". That was when he refused Ambassadorship to one of the S. American countries and accepted the Sec. of CMS and he told me how he worked with, oh my memory, that Sec of CMS now dead, and together they got in many more of the IVF type as missionaries. I believe his weight in his quiet way was always on that side.

Then later he moved into real C of E circles. He was close friend with Geoffery Fisher then Arch Bishop of Canterbury. Curiously Fisher had been a classic master at Marlborough and he took me and about three others one summer on a weeks hike when we read Greek together. Fisher was a good fellow but I never saw sign of New birth about him, though during that week I was not yet born again myself.

That was what moved him to Lay Assembly circles in the C of E and election twice over (the only one to be re-elected like that) as chairman and he was an EXCELLENT CHAIRMAN. He was so close to Fisher that he really thought Fisher would put his name in for the House of Lords when Fisher went there himself, and I think K thought Fisher let him down on that. While Wilson was Premier he had lunch with Kenneth, I think also for recommendation for the Lords, but Kenneth was, so he told me, a "missed bencher" and therefore not Labor enough for Wilson. I think Kenneth always hankered after getting to Lords and that was why I know that there was still that "world stream" in him which was also why he never could quite take extremists as CT and Mrs. And WEC, and is why all those years I never got heart-close to him, though he welcomed my visits, but, as I told you, our talk was along his many interesting experiences. Along that line somewhere he was "knighted" a second time to KCMG – but never Lords!

Eileen, his first wife, as a FLAME like himself and if she had lived, (she died of TB) she might have kept and pulled him along the total way, but Nancy is a nice woman, but I think really nothing spiritual, as a good church woman, and very pleased to be "Lady".

So you see Kenneth went far far on this world's level, yet with always a true admixture of the living touch with Christ and he once told me he could name those in his Authors and other clubs who knew the Lord thru him. So there always a smattering and of course his close acquaintance with the Queen Mother and actually ran her business affairs and had an annual Lunch with her at Marlborough House and has her signed photo.

It was also Kenneth who persuaded Fisher (who as I say I don't think had any real born again experience) to join Billy Graham in this big early crusade when all were suspicious. Billy always says that introduction and Fisher leading the last Crusade night in prayer opened wide Brit doors for Graham. When Graham was next over, Kenneth fell sick in hospital and one morning he had two visits – one from the Queen Mother and the next from Billy G who said he could come if he was also given the chance of speaking with the nurses! And it was Kenneth who introduced me to Billy G just before one of the Crusade meetings!

So I think, Leslie, my Kenneth was a deeply DISAPPOINTED MAN. At the beginning the fires burned which would have made another CTS; but no, he never really went that far, and so when his brilliance shewed out in survey work, first among the Amazon tribes, Cochrane could pull him off direct evangelization and pioneering to survey and then the world door opened thru North, but double knighthood is a million miles from eternal sonship! And I am sure Kenneth knew and felt we had moved into different wave lengths, and though we had a bond and I always had a time with him and he liked it I think, we never could break thru to the total, and I'm pretty sure he was no longer on that pursuit as I was, and Nancy would be a block in that.

So I thank God the weight of his life was on GOD'S side and he did occupy a place where his witness was for Christ and sometimes struck fire, as with Graham and Fisher, but also a deep heart disappointment because he had never gone thru to what we could call our "total" but equally was so much, thank God, a true God person that he could never just totally throw himself into world advancement.

So I just pour some of this out in my execrable typing but always my deepest SHOCK is that when he had such an all-out new birth and I remembered every detail being so involved in it, he could say in his auto-biography that just, "My brother Norman tells me I had a time of special conversion". WOW WOW!

All love,
Decipher this,

Rubi

~~~

</div>

Oct.18.89

Dear Ones,

This enclosed letter from Kath Whittle, who with John are so close in fellowship with us; and Sandy has almost been like a daughter to them. Kath gives detail of the discovery of some spread of cancer in beginning stages of our loved Sandy, and thankfully, the thorough but drastic methods hopefully to clear it all out of her. Sandy will be in and out of our good local hospital here - but during her times back home she'll need being taken care of and for daily treatments. They speak of it all taking six months.

With all Sandy's loving care of me, she had already thought it best for me to be away with friends, and not an additional concern as I crawl around with my cane. So, as Jesus said they would, "when thou art old, thou shalt stretch forth thy hands and another shall carry thee whither thou wouldest not"!!

What a difference when we are already "not of this world", but members of the Father's family in Christ, and only "strangers and pilgrims" here: and anyhow what we call "death" is to us the gateway to Glory, "with Christ far better". So for my precious Sandy we are praising God that He is "always good and doing good", and His love-ways perfect, whatever their outward appearance; and always Rom.8.28.

So I am letting you know about this, as we walk in praise and faith, and "Christ magnified in our body whether by life or by death" as Paul said, though equally thankful we have good hopes of this treatment having caught things in time and providing a total clearance.

Love in Christ,

Norman

Pris will remain quietly at home, helping as she does with the household.

~~~

Nov.8.89

Thank you, Betty dear, for yours.

No, I'm off traveling now at 93. Get bouts of physical exhaustion, but hopefully does not yet reach up beyond my neck, so can still keep on at the typewriter and turn many letters into "epistles". Had a wonderful life, right along with David in Ps. 23.6! You and I know that this life of simple "obedience of faith" as with Caleb who "Wholly followed" is the altogether good life, right into eternity.

And so simple. BE AS HE, (which we ARE by grace thru faith), the next thing is always HIS THING as us! We have already started David's true saying, "At Thy right hand are pleasures for evermore!" Contrast with "pleasures of sin for a season". We're surely WINNERS!

Love as ever.

Norman

~~~

Dec.'89

My dear loved friends,

We have a surprise change in recent weeks with my Sandy granddaughter, who has so wonderfully cared for me, helped also by my Priscilla, since Pauline went to be with the Lord, shewed some signs of cancer some weeks ago. This has meant that drastic chemo-therapy treatment by which they hope to have caught the cancer in time. So as I was extra responsibility when at my age of 93, I get falling about (well preserved by the Guardian Angels!) it has been best that my loved friends, Tom and Page Prewitt opened their home to me and I am thoroughly at home with them for the next month or two. How good God is, as ever, to have caught these first signs of cancer in time for effective treatment and also made such loving provision for me, while Weccers such as our old friends John and Kathleen Whittle in the WEC Retired home nearby, together with Pris and others are with Sandy thru these tough times. Thank God we both know, whether in apparent cloud or sunshine God's loving ways are ALWAYS PERFECT AND Rom. 8.28 always in operation, and anyhow when death comes, it is "far better with Christ" and the Gateway to Glory – so always, all praise, "more than conquerors" and for her thru her 'suffering' periods, it is Christ in her as her, and she even talked of "How to enjoy your cancer"! Typical Christ in Sandy's form! And thank God for loving help.

This means that we cannot send you a picture of us as we usually like to do, and I just write from us both, and Pris, thanking each of you for such loving remembrances and news.

So all love and praise and <u>thank</u> you, as from Sandy, Pris and me.

Norman

~~~

Dec.1.90

My darling,

This is a precious gem out of God's treasure chamber that you send me. I love it and would really like to preserve it maybe for an epitaph for me. You will have taken a copy, my darling, won't you, and maybe when I do take my flight, <u>you</u> could send it as the epitaph which is specially precious to me and I would love to be the one thing said of me. Could you do that when "That day" comes?!

You hit it perfectly, my darling, like no one else does. You hit the spot of a vast son-family coming to the birth, already birthed as God's children and now to come to the full sonlight of grown sons; and you put your finger on the spot when you say that our sonship and thus brotherhood is in Christ, and as consciously part of Him the ALL in all, and not part of some human "organization" again rings all bells.

So I will treasure what you have sent to me, but I think it will need repeating by you when I do go – the very best. Just I have vision and faith-substance for that GREAT NUMBER of "Knowers" and I see them beginning to come.

Miles of hugs, my darling and thank you.

Loving you and Rob.

Norman

~~~

NORMAN P. GRUBB
709 Pennsylvania Avenue
Fort Washington, PA 19034

October 16, 1991

My dear friends,

This is just a short letter to tell you that my beloved Granddaughter, Sandy, went home to be with the Lord on October 2, 1991 after a long bout with cancer. Words cannot express my shock, for I had no idea the Lord would take her so soon. Sandy had driven me perhaps a quarter million miles throughout the United States and Canada as I visited all of you. She was a precious girl who meant everything to me. She really ran this house, and my idea was that she would continue. But the Lord had other plans.

Sandy was an altogether lovely Granddaughter to me. She totally won my heart. With her loss, I have to keep replacing the deep hurt in my heart with praise to the Lord that Sandy has gone to be with Him! I altogether loved and trusted her and handed everything over to her.

How thankful I am for the love that so many friends have shown to Sandy, especially these last months. I thank you on behalf of Sandy. Priscilla and I continue to stay on here without Sandy and with the nurses to get me out of bed and so on. Thank you so much for your love and caring for so many years.

Love,

Norman

~~~

April 1992

My Dearest friends,

I am in my bed these days nearing the age of 96. I get carried by a machine like a sack of potatoes to a chair where I can sit. My hand is so crippled that I cannot write, but am so grateful that my daughter Pris can write for me.

Thanks goes to those of you who wrote when you heard of the Lord taking our precious Sandy. So now there's only Pris and I in the house as well as the nurse who comes lovingly to help take care of me.

But life goes on and I live with the memory of the work the Lord called for through CT Studd in our World Evangelization Crusade and in Ken Adam's Christian Literature Crusade which was born at our suggestion. The key is all those who come to join those groups, seek to take Jesus all over the world by teaching or books and we can see how faith is the substance of things hoped for.

I can remember when Pauline my precious wife, now with the Lord, and I joined CT. Studd in 1920 in heart of Africa. For five years we used the market language called Bangala to translate the New Testament rather than using the language of each separate tribe. The Congo and Zaire have made Bangala the language for the whole nation of millions. At that time there were five of us and now there are eighteen hundred people all over the world with W.E.C. living by what the Lord sends. This has been happening all these 70 years since 1920 and thank God young folks keep coming to join us with the promises of nothing but faith, for their provision.

Fifty years ago by my fellowship with Ken Adams the vision came of starting the Christian Literature Crusade which now has 800 full time workers all over the world and is continuing to grow.

So two crusades with no promises of human support and no appeals, now number about twenty-four hundred. Thank God for many countries such as China, Japan, and Africa. For Zaire in which there are one hundred thousand believers in one thousand small fellowships. For all those in the fields with their same increasing faith. For the many local bible training schools. All these combined together produce probably the greatest faith output in the world. So you see how much we have to rejoice.

This adds to the proof that we have that one single Abraham becoming by the obedience of faith "the faith father" of the millions of believers worldwide. God had promised that "in him all the families of the earth should be blessed." One current blessing going on in the world today is the break up of Communism.

And so you can see how much joy I have in my present physical helplessness, as I see in my ninety years of living the solid birth, growth, and rapid expansion of the C.L.C. and W.E.C. The surge of the spread of the gospel is thank God before our eyes. As Isaiah said, "The earth will be filled with the knowledge of the Lord."

Lovingly,

Norman

~~~

December, 1993

My dear Friends and Family,

I am only able to write through the assistance of my daughter, Priscilla and grandchildren. Priscilla very lovingly writes down what I say; Marlene and Dan print my letters out for me and send them off to you. At 98 years of age, my hands are so crippled that it is impossible for me to write legibly.

I feel that I am in as bad of a condition as can be. My body seems useless, lying around in a bed or chair, but I feel too well to be going to the Lord any time soon.

I receive numerous loving letters from different ones. My granddaughter, Marlene, sees that I get my mail; Dan, Jr., my grandson, and their three children have been a tremendous help. They live about one hour away; they check in on Pris and I, along with managing the household.

When folks have lovingly sent gifts and regular contributions, all has benefited me in the nursing care I receive. I have two nurses that are regularly with me during the week—Cheryl and Sheila have been a blessing. God has been good to me since my Pauline went to the Lord on Tuesday, September 15, 1981 at 7:00 PM.

Some ten years ago I made provisions for Pris and I pray that the income produced will be sufficient for her needs. Secondly, any memorial gifts following my death shall be for Pris's benefit.

I am comfortable that she has the house to live in. Christian Literature Crusade so kindly agreed that Pris may stay on here under the supervision of Dan, Jr. and Marlene.

So I must say that the Lord has provided for me and my family of which Pris is unable to see to all her own needs. As Pris and I have lived simply, the Lord's abundance goes on and on.

How grateful that Pris can put into writing what I am speaking! This does not cover, by any means, the loving things that you refer to in your writings to me. It has to be my loving response to your many unanswered correspondence.

So by no means can I really answer your loving letters. I answer them in my heart for you. By faith, you all will find the answers that the Lord has for you, and by faith, you will continue to walk with Christ and in Christ.

I now give you my Christmas blessing. If this shall be my last letter to you, may you always walk in faith until we meet in the glory of God.

With much joy and praise to God's unending love for us—

Norman

৪১৫

EXCERPTS

All I see and know is that there seems to be a dividing line between partial and total. I have just been reading the recent "God's Fool" book on St. Francis of Assisi. It's the quality of the "totalness" which lives on as life from one generation to the other. Francis in his total God-abandonment when nothing earthly had him but all was "dung" to him except Jesus the World Lover, lives on to millions. Something "happened" when he stripped himself naked from all his luxury living and his raging father, and then had a God-filled radiance which drew and has drawn ever since. So there is a "totaling" when as George Muller said, long after his first steps out he "died". I had that when I kind of left the WEC though I was leader, for a year to find God either all or nothing, and I found the "all in all" which has glowed in me like an inner furnace ever since (55 years?). What's his name (my memory) my fellow student in Cambridge who became Cambridge Librarian and was a kind of guru among us, always had me yearly to speak in Cambridge until my autobiography came out of my final desperate search for God as all. "Poor Norman", he said, "has now lost his way in depth questioning", and dropped me, as indeed I have been dropped at every stage for my "extremes", in the army, by my own IVF, by WEC Board who 'dismissed' P and me with CTS, now really my own WEC built since 1931 (except for one or two), then by our own Union Life. We have had Paul's "forty stripes save one" on our inner selves if not our outer, and may yet land in Nero's gaol as "prisoner of the Lord"! Yes the glory of the cross leaves us with bearing the marks of the Lord Jesus. What highest honor!

~~~

You do beat the band! I appreciate your loving thought in sending the Dick Halverson report. Yes, I remember Bermuda when the Willowbank Committee met and I was with them, after our business was finished, Bruce asked me if I wouldn't share something. So I did at much my usual length. At the end Dick said right out that he had heard some ultimate truth he had never heard before, and I believe you are right, he got a glimpse of "Christ in you". So thanks for letting me see this. They gave me a dinner last year which about twenty attended at Fellowship House, and Dick was to be among them with Doris, but wrote he was sick. That was when they produced a painting of me they had bought to hang in what they were going to call the Grubb Room in the house, because they kind of linked me with Marian Johnson and Abram Vereide in the start of things. I think Doug and Roy Cook were behind that. I then had a chance of a talk to them all that evening. I've always kept close to Doug, and "jumped" on him when there was no parting witness to Christ and Him crucified each Breakfast, and he aims to do that. I also keep close touch with that real soul-seeker among the high-ups in Europe, Wallace Haines. We keep constant touch. "YES I AM" SO GRABBED HIM THAT HE READ IT SIX TIMES. He has marvelous high-up contacts in Spain, Italy, Portugal etc as well as the Commons and Lords, and his special present link is Mrs. Thatcher's policy Sec in Brian Griffiths who is an all-outer for Christ and public witness.

~~~

The other point is that Pauline has I believe, much changed her attitude to coming across. The grandchildren are older now, of course, and at least I can say that if the call of God came, she would be willing for us to come as a family, only that would be no good unless it was for several years. There may be nothing in all this latter suggestion. God forbid that we should miss His will. I am not for moving out of this country unless God says so. We are strangers anyhow in all lands down here, so one is as good as the other. God's will and God's work is all that matters.

~~~

I used to speak of what God did then as a combination of "Faithfulness and Fire," or the necessary foundations of "The Word and the Spirit" for any movement of God. In other words, the Conference we had with the S.C.M. Committee and the necessary confirmation of our continued separation, was "the faithfulness" and thus our loyalty to "The Word". What God did among us in the Keswick Houseparty proceeding on to the Prayer Meetings and witnessing that next term, and resulting in the organization of the first Inter-varsity Conference was "The Fire," or the moving of the Spirit.

~~~

J.E.B. has close links with WEC, because Barclay Buxton, the founder of J.E.B., was C.T. Studd's close friend at Cambridge. They were called David and Jonathan. Then Barclay Buxton's son, Alfred, was co-founder of WEC with C.T., and went out with him in 1914, and married his daughter, Edith. So we are closely linked.

~~~

1958...I had the precious privilege of wonderful parents. My Mother went to be with the Lord at 96 this year. How often I have said goodbye to her, expecting to meet her again "Upstairs", but we were given further periods together. I greatly miss her. She was the shining of God's love into many, many lives.

~~~

Curiously, I am becoming a lame old man! You know the bother I had for a month with my knee. Never had it so long before. It has gone but has left a permanent condition in the ankle of that foot, something like arthritis, I think. So it is quite a job to walk. So you will soon be pushing me around in a wheel chair!

~~~

My "physicist" knowledge is merely amateur surface-scratching, but I drink all I can understand. I love the present "Symmetry" emphasis. Scientists are the best preachers of to-day! About writing, I really only determined to write as simply as I could what becomes simple to me, and avoid any window-dressing writings. That Bible KJ version and Macaulay essays were my model (and I caught the disease of long-windedness from Macaulay). I think our college "classical" education of my day, (though for me much interfered with my World War I, but I learned much of value thru five-year soldiering) really majored on making us think and express it.

~~~

God pushed me into this worldwide and Church-wide, bringing to the half-starved believers what Paul called his 'second ministry', but which has really been my Galatians 4:19 drive since my earliest Congo days...So, as I join 'The Cloud of witnesses' His word will go forward as vigorously as ever...

~~~

My mother who was Chrichton-Stuart is of the Bute family of Montstuart, Bute Island. But thank God we are all beyond that. We are THE ROYAL FAMILY!!!

~~~

I was just reading how that South African author of the famous "Cry, the Beloved Country" has died at 85 and grimly said in his last words so glad he had not to 'endure' another 80! But he missed somewhere (you can see it in that last thing of his) because I can only say at ninety two life is such a daily thrill, with some new Spirit-event thrilling and occupying me each day that I could welcome another eighty!

~~~

1964... Yes, the Lord's provision is wonderful and constant. We launched into this big place by faith seven years ago - $60,000 and a vast bargain. We paid $20,000 by selling our smaller place in Chicago, altogether inadequate for our needs. We wait six years for God's further deliverance. The State comes along and requests ¾ of an acre out of our 67 acres for their highway. We ask $5,000, they give us $25,000 and another $10,000 for soil. Then in this last month two gifts have come of $5,000 and $3,000, of course unsolicited except by the word of the Spirit – and we are over the top – all paid.

~~~

1979...This tour included a total surprise when some of you dear ones had found out that Nov. 24 was our sixtieth wedding anniversary and our "honeymoon" to join Pauline's father, CT Studd, in the heart of Africa. What a privilege these 60 years have been, sharing Christ throughout the world. Friends in Washington booked the big club room at the top of a Washington Condominium for two nights. About 85 came, some from several hundred miles. One dear girl prepared a four-section cake and it took 18 hours writing texts in chocolate all over it! Others, forty of you, wrote letters to Pauline and me in two beautifully bound books for us to keep, all in various ways thanking the Lord that He had revealed Himself to them as The One living their lives in and by them, as in Galatians 2:20, and with the rivers now flowing out to others....our best Sixtieth Anniversary gift has been the coming right out for the Lord of our granddaughter Sandra.

~~~

In writing you I forgot to say, No, I hadn't seen this book on IVF by Fielder, though I've had it mentioned to me, and the IVF Sec has sent me a mock-up painting supposed to be me at my desk as a student telling the Lord that His "vision" of world IVF was ok, and with the painting they have sent something on Audio-visual, but I haven't the machine. But yes, I would like to see what Fielder said. A friend sent me this £ 10 note. If you could send me a copy, yes I would like that. How I rejoice that all we put our hands to which was, best as we knew how, solidly based on the Scriptures, and our "obedience of faith" no matter what cost.

~~~

We had faced the question, shall the family remain till the Ventnor house is open? But we have come to see that that is not the obedience of faith. God so startlingly opened the door for the family to come by the

Mrs. W. offer. This was God's way of setting Pauline going. We believe now, therefore, that we should not hesitate, but go right forward. That means the accommodation problem at Camp Hill. I am sorry about that and the embarrassment it may cause you all. I can only say that we are ready to squeeze in and take things as they come from God. If three rooms were possible for the five of us, we would prefer it. If that can't be, well, we will manage with two; and anyhow we will take thankfully what God sends. So don't let folks feel under unnecessary pressure.

~~~

I was taken by a friend recently to a leading church in Toronto - huge congregation; the sermon was blasphemous. I prayed about getting up and making public protest, but as I was asking the Lord about it in my pew, He intervened by my friend turning sick and having to go out, and I accompanying her!

~~~

There is a fellow who was a director for Youth for Christ on this East Coast and at that time first brought our grandson Nicky to accept Christ. He was also a great fellow for the line of teaching God has given me and the books. And then about eighteen months ago he flew over here specially to see me because he said he felt strongly led that I might not be long still on this earth, and God would have him kind of carry on what God had given me. But I said, No, I wasn't for some kind of specialized teaching sect linked to my name.

~~~

"Union Life" is merely a company of folks to whom "Christ in us as us" is our revealed reality and we use that linking title." We are equally thanking God for any who have the same "revelation", the word of the Reformation for Christ's body for our day.

෩ ෫

Dearly Beloved Brother In Christ,

Norman, dearest of cousins,

My Dear Rubi

My precious Father

Dear Norman Grubb

My dear Pa Rubi,

Dear Norman,

Dear Norman,

Dear Mr. Grubb,

My Dear Adopted Father,

"Saint"

Dearest One,

Dear Rubi,

My Dear Friend

Norman Grubb

Norman my Love

Dearest Norman,

Dear Bro. Norman;

Dearest Norman 'Father in Christ' —

Dear Brother Grubb, Dear Norman

Dear Poppa in Christ

Dearest dearest Norman

Dear Friend in Christ: Norman Grubb.

Dear Mr. Grubb,

My dear, beloved Norman,

Hello Dear Mr. Grubb,

Dear, very dear Norman:

Dear dear Norman —

Dear Dr Grubb —

Beloved Friend

Precious cargo

My Dear Pa

Salutations

Enjoying a house meeting

Norman's Signature

Norman & Pauline on their 50th Anniversary

**Rees Howells, Norman, Pauline, Mrs. Howells and
Unidentified Friend strolling in Swansea**

Rees Howells

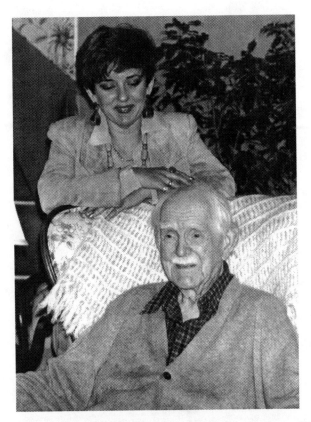

Norman and Sandy's Christmas Photo in Late 80's

Norman and DeeDee on His 90th Birthday

Norman as a Cambridge Student

Norman's famous typing

GOD ONLY

Norman's faith was so predominant. What made it so attractive was its being "wrapped" in his obvious personal love for you. And the fact he didn't hesitate to offer bits of practical advice. What I remember most was his saying, "The FACT is, the FACT is...," taking me back to the fact that, first, that I was a good person (because of Christ), and then that God was good. He would not take me back to my own faith or knowing, which I would often question, but to "the FACT." That was brilliant.

~~~

From having read Norman's books, I did trust him. As always, he suggests, leaving the final word to me in God's hands.

~~~

"Realization" means more and more to me and when I stumble, I stumble forward these days.

~~~

How I praise Him for the way He enables you to press through and go right to the heart of the matter. My heart rejoices at every thought of you.

<div align="right">A Pastor</div>

~~~

Happy Birthday to our beloved Owl from all three of us who dote on your vast ability to see in the dark.

ℰ℞

December 11, 1958

Dear Gwen,

How good to hear from you again. I always recognize the familiar handwriting with great pleasure. How many years of close heart friendship and fellowship God has given us, since those early battles in which you first opened your heart to me. How graciously and faithfully God has held us both in His ways. And He will do so to the end.

His ways are not our ways. My life seems so much easier than yours, with time to spend in the things of God, and even one's work centering around Him. But all are God's ways. When once we have seen that it is nothing less than Christ Himself living His life in us, then that makes Him a very ordinary person, marking papers and preparing lessons, as you say. It is He Himself doing this; and as you recognize it in this fact, then you relax in Him, even though your mind has to be centered on these mundane things. Don't let resentment or rebellion against the way He has chosen to live His life in you mar the central rest which proceeds from the not I, but Christ relationship. That is living; and to "live in the truest sense" is only Christ living in His most mundane way through us, as He pleases. Christ is really seen in deeds of faithfulness, such as your teaching life, not in the many words and nice thoughts which make up so much of ours! So let Him live on in you!

Yes thank God, He has been at work over here. We are indeed eye to eye on "important issues". There has never been any question on that. God gives us a wonderful band of all-out Crusaders. It was only lesser matters of personalities and organization which always crop up in a big work. But God has been smoothing things out wonderfully, and I feel we are like a stream having come through the rapids now flowing on into God's fuller purposes for this whole huge country.

Janice also mentioned about Mark and Barb. I have written to her about them. The point, I think, is that this is God's means of establishing Mark in "God only". He must see Barb in her present condition through the eyes of God. This is His plan for her, as well as for him. Where we resist, then God in grace ties us tighter and tighter in knots of our resistance, until at last we realize the slavery of self. God will do this for Barb. We stand in faith seeing the thing already done in His sight. May Mark first learn the lesson of perfect rest and praise in the dark valley.

Warm love from us both, Pauline and myself, dear friend, and always glad to hear from you. The family has settled in, and the children quite young Americans.

Ever yours affectionately,

Norman

~~~

June 5, 1956

My Dear Ones,

I do appreciate your opening your heart and sharing this with me. I take it as from you both. Thank God you went through the deep waters - with Jesus. How many turn back when the rivers of death reach the chin - but you two swam through in His resurrection grace. Hallelujah, there will be a great outcome. I love the tender, broken spirit in your letter, and can sense what it will mean in a future ministry and testimony. I love you both, and thank God for you. God does not want jellyfish. He has found in you two a mature couple, and He has been able to do what He really can do in the more maturer ones - take you through that breaking we all have to have. I am sure the lesson we have all got to learn, we out here with you, is the continual deep open fellowship, then we shan't need these shattering experiences. God will lead us on. I love, too, your precious and detailed explanation of the battle. How true that is for all of us. I should love to see that in print - with suitable concealment! I always felt true oneness with you both. Striking too, that preparing that book so challenged you. How seldom God can get us to face up to our inconsistencies, and we are all the same. Pray for us here. God is coming through.

You mentioned that, having been cleansed, you were waiting for "a coming through to praise and glory". It may be just the way you put it, but I don't believe in this waiting. I believe in acting! Paul said that the word (of praise and glory) is in our mouth and in our heart already. All we need to do is to express it, confessing Him, and out comes the praise followed by the glory. I think this waiting is dangerous and others besides you have mentioned that kind of thing. We have recently had a big battle over here over waiting for

191

the baptism. It isn't that. This "revival" is really only what should
be our daily practice in small doses of getting in the clear with God
and each other, and rejoicing in Jesus. That is the only revival (and
then having witnessing meetings rather than preaching meetings)
in which we tell others around us what God is doing up to date.
That telling forth in the atmosphere of joy and unity does its own
work in those who hear, and so the revival spreads. May I use this
letter as an opportunity to suggest to you that you cut out the long
preachments of next month's conference and dare to launch into a
guided couple of witnessing meetings, just have a chairman to keep
the flow of testimony running and to have the touch of the Spirit on
the meetings. You can have a 10 minute speaker or two if you wish to
give some confirming word. Will you not get together and launch out
on this in the daring of the Spirit? I am sure we have got much too
hide-bound by relying on the series of long-winded speakers (starting
with N. P. G.). Here is a chance to break out of that rut, just at the
time that God Himself has taken you up out of it by His own mighty
hand. Will you kindly bring this to all as from me because I am so
snowed under with letters that I cannot repeat this.

Much warm love to you both.

Ever yours,

Norman

~~~

16th July 1956

Dear Mary,

I wish I could write to you longer, as your personal note has come.
Very blessed, but there are disturbing touches, and I would really like
to talk them over with you. My main point is I feel a sense of striving
coming into you, striving to ward off something, or to keep up to
something. Striving is self, and therefore sin. Abide simply and happily
in Jesus, just doing what He tells you, no more, no less. Forget the devil,
there is Someone more interesting to be occupied with!

Ever yours,

Norman

~~~

October 22, 1958

Dear Dana:

Thank you for writing. You certainly told me some things about Fred that I did not know before.

I still say that faith is the victory. We cannot help having heavy hearts, but when we give way to grief, we are really giving way to unbelief. If we dare to believe the God of the impossible, then we honor Him by rejoicing when things are darkest. Now is the moment to rejoice in a reigning Christ who has had entry into Fred's heart, and despite anything <u>is</u> Victor over the enemy now, and will demonstrate that victory by casting him out of Fred. We stand in faith that Christ will be honored in his life, and that actually he will come out all the stronger after he has tampered with unbelief. I had a fierce time when I had a battle royal with atheism, but I came out all the stronger in the end, although it is true that I did not give way to it in the way Fred is.

So let us continue in faith and deliberate praise. I am with you in this.

Affectionate greetings in Christ,

Norman

~~~

May 20, 1960

Beloved Gerry:

Thank you ever so much for sending me the circular letter and your personal note. I should not otherwise have known both the outer battles you have been going through, and the physical trial. I like Paul's words, "Me <u>His prisoner</u>." All that happens to us, good or apparently evil, <u>God</u> sends. God is putting you through these trials to shut you up to Himself only, and to teach you also how to love your enemies. And our physical trials are the same. God "shuts us up" in our physical bodies so that we learn to say again with Paul "to me to live is Christ."

God bless you. These trials are sure proofs that God is working for you and is going to get all the glory to Himself. Go on and go through as you are doing.

My love to you, and always hoping that our paths may cross for some more fellowship.

Ever yours, in the warfare,

Rubi

~~~

Dec. 30, 1960

Dear Ruth:

Thank God for the tough spots He put you in. That is where He is getting His love through you to the unlovely, and to people who harm you. That is how Jesus lived on earth, expressing the love of God to those who criticized and hated Him; and that is how Jesus now lives in us, expressing the same love through us. He has put us among difficult people, so that His supernatural love may be seen by them. So praise the Lord for every tough spot you are in. It is not God's will to deliver us <u>from</u> tough spots, but <u>in</u> them. There is no other way of getting at those who do not know Him except by those who do living among them.

I wonder if you got your new job. Write to me and let me know; but you must not expect things to become easier. We often regard it that God puts us in difficult situations to try or to sanctify us; but that is not the reason. We are not put there for what it may do for us, but for what God can get through us of His love to others. The Lord bless you and do write again.

Sincerely yours in Christ,

Norman

~~~

November 2, 1967

My dear Stella:

Thank you so much for writing. I'm so glad to get this clear, and have asked the office to divide the gift and send you the receipt, and let each know that it is a love gift from the Lord through you. It will be a joy to them.

I believe God <u>gives</u> dark moments, and apparent clouds (II Cor. 12:7), so as to teach us that these things are an illusion and a mere outward appearance, and thus to teach us to live where we really are - with Christ joined to us within, Spirit with spirit. I believe the great lesson of life is with the outward eye to see and feel evil and dark and lonely appearances around us, but for us to learn not to believe in them (for we experience what we believe), but to transfer our faith to the Unchanging One with whom we are in union within. That is where we really live, right in the midst of outward darkness.

Much love to you.

Ever in Christ,

Norman Grubb

~~~

Aug. 15, 1969

Dear Daphne,

What a lovely letter from you. Thank you, dear, and I am so glad you have written. Were you married when you were with us, or what was your name then? It would remind me of you, or have you a snap? Yes, my dear, I wish you had spoken to me at the Conference, or we might have planned another meeting just by ourselves, as you are in London. I might be over in two years time, but can't be certain. But perhaps after sending me such a lovely letter, you might continue and we interchange letters.

Of course it thrills me to hear that God used the books so much to you. Both the two you mention have been specially used - Law of Faith and God Unlimited. I take it that you haven't had the one after - Spontaneous You ... somewhat like God Unlimited, but we are always growing in light. If not, I will love to send you a copy - and that will extract another letter from you!

Tell me also about yourself. God took you thru deep waters in taking your Jim, but I see you have found, dear one, that this is the way, by some means or other, He has to take us all - to the place where there is none in the universe but HE. He is ALL; expressing His allness in and thru everything, whether positive or negative, good or evil, to bring humanity back "home" to The One who is love and nothing else. And as we on earth find this secret, then we turn apparent evil into good, by seeing Him in all, praising, believing, so that folk only see a manifestation of the God of love in us; so that we each are Christ, the Christ who on the cross turned evil into the manifestation of the God of love, for all history to see.

You will find the memoirs just more of a personal story, though I stop every now and then (and some don't like those intrusions so much, but I do!) and explain the whys and wherefores of God's dealings. You encourage me, dear, when you speak of my getting to the roots of things as not so many do; yes, that has been how God has led me, and I do find that it feeds many, and I am constantly on the move sharing these things.

So now, my dear, that you have written this lovely letter, I shall be watching for another.

With my love, in which Pauline joins,

ever lovingly,

Rubi or Norman

Which ever you like!

<div style="text-align:center">~~~</div>

My dear Mrs. Wrightson:

I am so glad to hear from you. I have such happy memories of the fellowship in your home. I felt the link in the Spirit with you, so it is nice to have it renewed again by this letter. I wish we could have more fellowship face to face.

I think there is only one secret of victory in the Christian life, and that is the moment by moment walk with Jesus. There is no kind of recipe for an automatic life of victory. We are always assaulted by satan, one way or another. But I find the key in simply recognizing the Presence of Jesus in my heart and life just at this moment. Seeing Him with a single eye, I have peace and joy. To do this, we must not allow the devil to disturb us with past memories. We must be thankful for all the Lord's goodness in the past; and if satan disturbs us or condemns us about the past, we must stand steadily in the fact of the cleansing blood by faith - that cleanses from all sin. The same about the future. We must not fear the future, for that is in the hands of Jesus. We can anticipate the glorious day coming when we are with Him again, and with our loved ones, but not anticipate it to the point that we lose sight of the joy of the Presence of Jesus at this moment. So we find satisfaction just in the step by step walk with Him. See Him now, lean on His arm, reckon on His love, be satisfied with Him; and then we find that the Lord allows us our lonelinesses and tests just to drive us back onto Himself, and so we can thank Him even for the tests.

God will uphold you, for He lives in you. Do write to me again, a little fellowship even by letter may help. I have a busy program out here, but it is a privilege to be "on the job" for Him.

Warmly yours in Christ,

Norman Grubb

<div style="text-align:center">~~~</div>

June 7.70

Martha Lee dearest,

Just a line on my wanderings because we said we would keep in touch with each other, and because I love you. I am only sorry last visit to Chicago, I didn't get more time just to be with my precious friend, so it has to be by letter. I will be thrilled if you feel able any time to write and share your heart with me, dear one.

Just keep on the single path, darling, where there is nothing but God-in-love, whether appearances are evil or good. HE ONLY is in all of them. Here is the secret. Thru the Fall we got a divided outlook and see two powers, good & evil; but back in Christ, and in Christ Universal, we see ONLY ONE, even if He often seems to appear in devil's guise! The only battle I have to fight is <u>not</u> against circumstances, or problems, or people or even devil, except the devil interfering with my inner outlook. If he can get me to see evil as evil, then I am controlled by the evil I am seeing and believing in. But if I replace all such negative beliefs in outer appearances by seeing GOD ONLY in all, then I have the faith that overcomes the world!

Blessings on you and Rob and the family, dear one. I am having an excellent tour for seven weeks in the West, with my co-worker, John Whittle who drives me up the coast – great openings and reception everywhere. Pauline has not been well with her ulcer troubles, but I came this tour seeing God as her life, and looking for the healing, though it will be good to be back at the end of this month.

I forgot to bring your address with me, so shall have to send this to be addressed at home.

Just this little line of love, dear. I am so thankful God has brought us into each other's life.

ever lovingly and with such a hug.

Norman

I found I have the address. Praise!

~~~

Aug. 18, 1970

Beloved Bill,

Here I have just posted a letter to dear Alice, and in it said I hadn't heard from the rascal Bill. And here comes your wonderful one. Thank you, thank you both. It means much to me to get such a letter from you. With you, I still can't see an inch different, only more so. Still more I have no answer to myself, others, the world good and evil, time and eternity, except GOD ONLY AND ALL. Not one iota less than HE THE ALL. If that's hell, it is a good hell; and it gives a reasonable answer to reality on every level, above all the knotty question of God and evil. I think I've got that still more in focus! And of course I'm encouraged that my Bill and Ann keep treading this good tightrope with me! And thank God many others too - and more all the time. WEC at the instigation of a few put on a heresy trial on me, but of course when they began to get down to what I really say, they found themselves on the spot, and try to get off the hook by "appealing" to me to moderate some things. Some hopes! Moderate! I'm worse all the time! But it's got them off the hook by changing a demand to an appeal! But mind you, that's really only a very few. We go on together as ever, and how I thank God for the magnificent WEC & CLC crowd worldwide. My thrill to have been allowed to be part of them.

Yes, I was tremendously struck with Swindoll's book. I forget how it came to me, I rather think he got caught on to some of the "heretic" books and then interpreted in his own lively way and it rang the bells with me. He puts "deepest truth" in lively forms which folk can take, who would die under God Unlimited! Since then I get his circular, and they are experimenting in good ways in church and group living. It would be worth your while to get in touch and ask him to put you on his mailing list. I didn't know he had a Fromke link.

Thank you for the detailed news of The Family, glad to get that. Yes, I'll hope we'll get together in Feb. We are enjoying our quiet days here and doing some spiritual digging!!

Thank you again for this lovely refreshing "epistle" - yours the size of John's, mine of Jude!!

Much much love to you both.

ever lovingly,

Norman

~~~

Mar 11.72

Dear Karen,

It is sweet of you to write and share so much of your heart and thoughts with me. Thank you also for the poems and all your trouble in copying for me. You surely have plenty of love, dear!

I think we are to see <u>through</u> the externals of people to their inner heart and always recognize that God is there speaking to them, even when they appear indifferent. If people prefer lies, as you say, we can know that deep inside they know they are guilty and that is the voice of God to them. In the parable of the Prodigal Son, I think the Father did not see the prodigal but <u>the son</u>. He was watching down the road for his return, expecting him; for He saw his wild ways as his distorted faith in believing the world could satisfy; but he knew he would be disillusioned. So I must learn to see all men as sons of God who don't know it, and have their beliefs fixed on false values, and God will teach them by disillusion. This enables me to love them.

Jesus meant just that when He said, "Let them remain blind and deaf and not be converted". He meant that first they must discover they are blind and deaf, before they see their need for eyes and ears!

So I think the great lesson God is teaching us is to see HIM in all things, whether they appear good or evil - just as Jesus did not see the devil crucifying him, but it was His Father's cup. Then he could have peace and joy in the suffering and faith for the resurrection.

I am just home a week and then off again in the Toronto area. So glad to have this letter from you, dear, and hope you will write again. I like the tender touch in the poems by Joan Baez, specially on putting your hand in the hand of Jesus.

Much love, dear,

ever lovingly,

Norman

<div style="text-align:center">~~~</div>

July 29, 1972

Dearest Gloria,

How lovely to have this letter from you, dear. I am so glad you do undertake the uneasy chore of writing and sharing with me. It is so precious and you are so precious.

Yes, you are right, dear, to drink deeply of all the pure water you find in Lanyon, (and what may not seem pure to us at our present stages, may be a higher purity!!). Thank God it is ambrosia and nectar. That's what our God is, but we dusty evangelicals put thick dull coverings over Him!

Yes, love, Satan is real alright, but he is real as <u>God's convenient agent</u>. So how right you were (and that was part of the purpose of it) to first feel his attack, and then in Christ "move over" from believing in an evil Satan to believing in God utilizing him for some deliverance purpose;

and that deliverance first came in you via Gal. 2.20, continually "It's all good" (I like that!), and finally that living almost physical touch from Him.

I'll just be watching to see what hopes of being with you again. Love to our precious one and much to your precious self.

Ever lovingly,

Norman

~~~

Nov.20.72

Karen my dear,

Your very sweet letter was here when I returned from my Bermuda tour two days ago. Thank you, dear.

I can see how you are being taught of God, for you are sensitive to the fact that the only real enemy we have is our own negative believing. We give power to whatever we believe in. That is why the outer world has become so chaotic. And I see you see that when you are surrounded by unbelief in response to your joy or love or desire for fellowship, you are responding by the same spirit of unbelief when we fix our eyes on their unresponsiveness and we are actually building it. This is how God leads us on into maturity by learning this obedience of faith when we suffer, using the impact of the suffering, which causes us to believe negatively the apparent evil, to stir us to exchange it for the positive believing that HE is working hiddenly through these oppositions or indifferences; and then our positive believing and consequent loving accepting attitudes is manifesting Christ to their hiddenly hungry hearts. Lovely dear, that you see this, which folks only rarely see, and that "God is dealing with you in this area": or rather giving you good practice! The same when you say we concentrate on the problems rather than the Answer.

And thank God for doubt, little one. That is the human negative which strengthens us to faith. Tribulations worketh patience etc.

I wouldn't push yourself about Spain. I would tell the Lord that you won't go unless He positively pushes you into it.

My much love to you - like a daughter to me,

Lovingly,

Norman

~~~

Jan.25.73

Dearest Karen,

It is good to know how the Lord has taken you into this ministry with Irma, and with this brother Henry Harris. No, I don't know him. And of course I'm particularly glad you had this link with my dear Joyce. Yes, I'm sure you'll have nothing but a sharing of the true ways of the Spirit with her.

You seem to have been having many words on the purging fires. Yes, love, so long as you see the fires as just He himself loving you still more fully by the touch of burning where necessary. We couldn't have healthy vigorous sensitive bodies if they had not a marvelous nervous system but it is good that the nerves respond with a touch of pain where we need a warning. But the point is, don't busy yourself with looking out for the pain touches! No, we live freely with Christ living His love-life for others by us. We are just ourselves, which is really Christ in His Karen form. Where the touch of burning, the pain reactions, is needful, HE gives that!

And remember, love, where you find those who seem apathetic to need, though brethren in Christ, watch against an unloving, negative attitude to them. No, recognize with the eye of faith that they too are redeemed temples of the Holy Spirit, and if there is apathy, He is surely at work in them in His own way; and you will do more as a channel of the Spirit to them, if they are conscious that you are just loving and accepting them in our oneness in Christ; and that will give the bond of acceptance which will make it possible for them to have listening ears to what you share of the way the Lord is taking you and the burdens for others HE gives you. And that will rub off in the Spirit on them in a way merely a negative attitude of seeing their apathy will never do.

Thank God that Hound of Heaven follows after everyone, seeking till HE find!

Fancy you running into a poem of Studdert Kennedy. He was a living power in World War 1 as a chaplain. He was too liberal for many as he used to give out cigarettes to the troops, and there was a special brand the soldiers liked called "Woodbine", so S.K. had a nickname "Woodbine Willie"!! But he had a deep heart for need and seeing Jesus in needy people, "If you visit the prisoners, you visit Me"... And that comes out in this beautiful poem you quote. He has become a forgotten voice, and I'm glad to hear that voice again!

201

Well, darling, it is so good having these heart outpourings from you. Give Joyce my love and a kiss when you see her,
ever lovingly,

Norman

~~~

Aug. 30, 1974

Dearest Sara,

I was thrilled to receive such a wonderful loving letter from you today, and once again with this loving gift to my ministry thru CLC.

I will, of course, pass on yours to Bessie Adams. Yes, our closeness of fellowship with Ken and Bessie is wonderful to us. I always am so glad when a chance seems to come to "share" with them, they are so good to us; and so when your gift again comes directed to CLC for me, I just feel it of the Lord that I should do the same again and pass to them. I am sure you won't mind, as I so believe this is of the Lord, and in their having it, it is the same to us as our having it!

I can only also be thrilled that the Lord so comes thru to you in living light thru the books. It thrills me because I always knew in writing them that God had His revealing word thru them. They are not, of course, the kind of popular book (there is great room for them too!), and only really hungry "diggers" for gold will get into these; but I do have many evidences that God does meet folks thru them. It is wonderful to me that just our one visit should have been of living fellowship together. A new book is just on the way and should arrive from Britain in September, so I am fixing to send you one - called WHO AM I?

Yes, it's marvelous these days among the young folk. We have been on Long Island in the little home a dear friend, Marian Johnson, gives us each year; but folks have got to know about our visit and I have had half a dozen meetings, largely with these open-hearted young folks. They just grab eagerly at any crumb of new light.

Yes, as you say, and God has taught us together, we don't "see" the non-Christ part of our loved ones. We see them each as Christ in their human forms, though they may not yet know it, and what they are now is God purposed negative means of preparing them for the "moment of truth". That keeps us praising and learning by practice not to judge by appearance, but be "see-through-ers."

Thank you, dearest. Any chance of seeing you at Callaway this year?
ever with my love,

Norman

~~~

July 12.76

Sue dear,

I'm so glad you wrote and our precious Linda suggested it to you,
and as you say, it helps just to pour out our heart to someone.

Dear, there is no way but the "obedience of faith". That does not
mean a lot of things you have to "obey" and do. No indeed. But you have
to <u>believe</u>. "The obedience of <u>faith</u>". That means you have to collect all
your feelings in a bundle, all the sense that you are no use in life (no,
you're not if you see yourself as just yourself; but what a lie when you
<u>know</u>, as you do know, that you are actually Christ in his Sue form!),
and all feelings that you are alone, and have lost your old friends and
none loves you etc etc. You collect them in a bundle and recognise their
source. They don't come out of you yourself, your inner "I am" where
your spirit is eternally joined to Him THE SPIRIT. They only come from
your outer feeling level, your soul and body. And God can settle you by
no other means than that you are hurt and miserable and think you
hate yourself (Of course you do not!), so that you differentiate between
outer soul-reactions which can tear you to pieces and put their lies on
you, and your true still self where in your center you and He are one.

How do you do that? Right in the midst of all those disturbed
feelings, you affirm God's word to be true, and you say it is true – that
Christ dwells in you, and you and He are joined as one. You don't feel
it, it may appear nothing to you to say it; but saying it from your inner
centre, is the obedience of faith which takes God at His word. You
<u>can</u> do that, love. You can say it – read Rom.10.17. Repeat it over and
over again, if need be. Don't fight your feelings and thoughts of that
kind. Just replace them by turning your attention the other way and
recognizing Him by faith.

<u>What you believe</u>, and that just means you accept and state it to be
true of you, though you may feel nothing. It will, when the Spirit knows
the right moment has come, settle into you with an inner awareness.
You will know you are not just Sue, never again, but God in Sue's form;
and then you may refer any disturbing questions about your use in life,

your friends, or whatever, to HIM. There is no other way, darling. You must suffer until you recognise that this suffering is because you are believing your soul-reactions to be real, instead of just bluff; and you replace the suffering by believing which then becomes inner awareness and peace, and then freedom to share with others the great secret you have learned. As you share and love others, you will be blessed.

Write me again, love, and talk further with me. I am here to help and love you,

lovingly darling,

Norman

~~~

May 1976

Precious one, about your daughter. Of course when I saw and read the cuttings, I didn't catch on to whom they referred till I read your letter. Of course the shock has been great for you all. But, as you say, here is where what we know of God's ways of love, so puzzling or cruel to the flesh, but really His ONLY way of fusing us into our unity with Him, enable us to "see thru" and praise. Little Ann will know this also. We <u>cannot</u> in this distracting world be pressed into His arms and ways of <u>perfect love</u> except by experiencing in some devastating way what seems cruel and wrong and "why should it happen to me" kind of thing. True dying with Jesus to our human selves can only be by some forms of suffering or humiliation which don't seem fair or kind to us. <u>Then</u> we learn that accepting wrongs done us or unfair treatment is what roots us down and fixes us in daring to believe that everything that happens to me has been <u>perfectly determined</u> by my God of perfect love. By this means I get my practice in "seeing through" to HIM ONLY in ALL things, even when I can't at first see why. Then as I am fixed in a loving God in all my affairs and self, I can equally be fixed in seeing Him at His love-work in all people and things, including the one who has wronged me. And I am <u>not</u> afraid. I don't have to go round and protect myself for the future. No. God has me in His hands and everything that touches me is meant by Him.

The one most tremendously used in our WEC these years is my precious missionary "daughter" Helen Roseveare who was twice raped by the Africans, and her bold testimony and her return to love and serve them moves thousands. I will tell you more of her. Even the Queen read her story.

So I know you dear ones, lift up your hearts and heads in <u>praise</u>, and are not ashamed to accept for Christ what He sends and use the victory He gives me to help others equally "distressed".

Thank you for sharing this, darling. Give Ann my love.

So many hugs and kisses,

Your own father,

Norman

~~~

March 7, 1977

Dearest Sara,

That is good of you to write and send this loving gift, dear, which is a help. Thank you so much. As you say, we haven't seen each other for a long time, but we have this living link of love in our oneness in Christ.

This new magazine "Union Life" is having a wide outreach and bringing light to many in finding who we truly are - Christ in our human forms, and in the liberty of living freely in that inner consciousness. It is more than Christ in us; it is He the Real I indivisibly - as Paul said in Gal. 2.20; and I have great joy in going around revealing this to many struggling with the illusory sense of a divided self - and as the revelation reaches its fulfillment in God All in all - nothing but He exists - and that covers good and evil!

So thank you, darling, and I am so glad you are finding the same joy in being so occupied and knowing that all is He shining His light by us.

Lovingly and thankfully,

Norman

~~~

May 25, 1979

Dear Paula,

Our dear friend has told me of what you have been going thru lately. I praise the Lord for <u>all</u>. You are perfect in Him and are eternally bound to Him. And in ways He knows best, He takes us along paths which "seem" as if we have slipped from Him into some other power, such as you with heroin.

But there is no other power - only the One Power - HE. Nothing else has power over us (all destroyed in Christ's cross), except as we are deceived into believing something has a power over us, and it <u>feels</u> as if it does.

But no, it is being deceived into believing a <u>lie</u>. All that comes to us like what you have been thru is to give us practice in "the obedience of <u>faith</u>;" and that does not mean works or struggle, but the continued <u>saying</u> with the word of faith (Mark 11:23) what the Scripture says you <u>are</u> – "I <u>am</u> crucified with Christ", and that means I boldly say I am dead to sin and it has no "dominion over me," and "I have crucified the flesh;" and then at the same time go on to say, "Now I live, <u>yet not I</u>, but Christ lives in me."

You keep boldly saying <u>that</u> – even when at times you outwardly feel the pull of flesh-powers. Boldly see only Jesus in you as you, against all appearances, feelings and temptations, and you will experience Him delivering you, and I know you are experiencing Him.

So just keep on picking yourself up in faith and refusing condemnation or guilt, when you are tempted, and HE is taking you along with Him in His "highway" of victory.

Glad to have a word with you and that you have these loving links with our dear friends.

Lovingly in Christ,

Norman

~~~</div>

<div align="right">May 11, 1981</div>

Thank you, Betty darling, refreshing as ever! Yes, that's what we are doing, isn't it, having eyes to see all these beauties of the Living God coming thru to us in what to natural eyes seem only mundane things. There is no mundane, all is only HE as we have learned to penetrate the outer disguises, whether apparently pleasant or unpleasant. So Life itself is "exquisite beauty." Just as those lovely words you end with.

Loving you, darling, off all of June and half of July in England

Norman

<div align="center">~~~</div>

May 28, 1981

My dear Chris,

Just back from our third Union Life weekend - Simsbury, Conn., excellent like each of the others. I think weekend family fellowships are the Lord's special way by which folks who are becoming "knowers" can get to know each other, or themselves become "fixed". Our next visit to Hawaii will not be "general" but to a real group becoming seekers and finders!

And here was your next letter, Chris. It came in time for me to have it also Xeroxed, and the two, attached to my short note, are going to about 50 of those mostly part of us, so that they can see the fierceness this sharp-cutting edge of total truth has, not among the "pagans," but among the most devoted to Christ when still mixed with law. It will stir many to read it.

Meanwhile, Chris, you are "shut in" with God with even your employment taken from you. But I think, as you exposed your heart and mind as you write, the Holy Spirit is already settling you into that "single eye" you so preciously know. I see by the end of your letter that you have decided to sell the car and get one for which you have no further payments to make. "Owe no man anything." You are right there.

Of course it is not wrong to be "practical" and to reach out for a job, so long as first I already have the provision by faith, and reach out just insofar as the Holy Spirit moves me to do. Settled faith first, and then works which proceed from, not replace, faith. But as I say, you preciously know that already, and the Spirit fixes us still further by our soul-storms thru the negative. This is beautiful "training" for you, so we praise God together that He meant your boss to put you out. He was behind that as much as He was behind Pilate making the decision to crucify Christ (John 19:11) - so out of this practical "death" is coming not only the resurrection for you in your material needs, including Vivien and the children, but in what you will have to share with others thru all this and indeed by these present letters going out.

Meanwhile we shall be watching with you for this fixed coming provision, and as led, you will keep me up with the news.

Just one other thing. We rightly speak and see everything in terms of either Satan or Christ in action by us, and therefore you see what the pastor and people are taking as their antagonistic position towards you (and me) as Satan coming thru their souls, and thus like enemies towards us; but also be sure that you see it is only Satan in some of

207

God's precious people, being deceived into mistaking their soul (Satan inspired) attitudes as though from their Christ-indwelt spirits; and that means you perfectly love them and speak of them as HIS perfect body-members, just as much as you and I are, and thus you differentiate between their true selves in Christ with whom we are eternally one and their deluded soul-selves in their attacks on you. So thru all this, we only "see" oneness, the oneness eternally of Jesus' John 17 prayer. Also we see that, as God <u>means</u> everything, whether in appearance good or evil, therefore, God is <u>meaning</u> the pastor and church to take this opposing attitude and spread it even to your boss.

I find, right to the unsaved, it makes a big difference to see that every human being is a precious redeemed son of God (2 Cor. 5.19 & Rom. 5.18) if they recognized and accepted it by faith; therefore sinners are precious humans, seized and made captive by the false spirit of error since the fall, and Satan in them as them is the sinner and enslaver, and they only slaves. That makes it so easy to see and love all without judgementalism (as Jesus with the woman of Samaria, and the woman taken in adultery, and Zacchaeus, etc.); and though we do also see that there are those who refuse to come to the light of who they are and Christ is to them (John 3.19-21), and thus do act as and become devils and lost, and are really actually and practically identified as sons of the devil (rather than just children and slaves of the devil). Just this passing thru my mind and I see in your writings how clearly you do love your brethren as ever, even though they are really refusing to call you any longer a brother!

I enclose copy of what I'm sending round the 50 or so with Xeroxed copies of your two letters.

ever with my love to you both and keep me in touch with what the Lord is doing about a job.

Norman

~~~

Oct. 10

Sue Ellen darling,

Yours has just reached me. I can't write you properly while on this tour (I return home Nov.5) but just to say SEE ONLY PERFECT GOD IN <u>EVERYTHING</u>. Don't accept guilt or condemnation. This is God's LOVING WAY for you – the suffering only establishes you in who truly are – first in God as your one true love, & Orin as your true human love and just go on right as you are at present, including your job! ONLY SEE GOD in all that has happened and is now happening. Keep PRAISING – no matter what the soul-heart may be – you are He in your Sue Ellen form.

Always loving you & so glad that you share all with me. This is your being "stablished, strengthened &settled" in love – I Peter 5:10!

Loving you,

Norman

~~~

Nov. 20.85

Dearest Marge,

Good to get yours on laughter (and add to it God "laughing" at his enemies and their machinations, just as God has used Communism to stir faith in the world as never before - Ps. 2!).

Does look as if the Spirit is liberating you both for further scattering of our "Total Truth". I rejoiced in Bus sharing with me some new insights he had just had on "seeing thru" beyond appearances in people which may often appear queer - in us all - catching on to the meat meaning of Heb. 5.14, has taken me a long time to catch on to the subtlety of that verse. And now I like in your letter your bold statement "expressing Himself as me" - not "in" me. There is just the subtle difference which will bring us our good dose of persecution from our brother evangelicals! So as God is calling you this wider way, there will be a cross in it as well as the glory, even in faith for material living, and caring nothing but for the TRUTH to get out-DCD! So I'm hoping you may be with us. I think God is stirring the stew pot in you precious two, rather like old days!

So this with my love and thanks for all your ever-good welcome for me and the special gift Bus has in getting good companies together.

Norman

~~~

Feb.9.87

My dear Mark & Jean,

I was staggered when I received this loving gift from you two days ago from WEC. I had to go and share the news with Sandie. Thank you so much. It was wonderful the Lord putting it into your hearts to send such a gift. We just live by the Lord's surprises through His loved ones, and the provision that comes from them - but big gifts like this are always such a surprise. What strange people we are when we have the Lord's constant word to us, "Take no thought... Be careful for nothing", and yet it is always a thrill thru the years when we find He means what He says, and "your heavenly Father knows that ye have need of these things"; and there, it's always true! So bless you for your love.

So thank you with all our hearts,

Lovingly,

Norman

ഓ രൂ

EXCERPTS

No one can know the apparent "danger" of this kept freedom, until he has recognised, accepted and confessed his fixed release through the Cross of his precious human selfhood from its false owner, and his replacement by the True Owner. Then it is "Yes I AM".

~~~

I am glad that you are going on with the Lord. It is a very simple life when the one fact has laid hold of our hearts that Christ lives in us, as you say. Whatever situation we are in, we are then able to look away from it and recognize in faith that the Lord Himself has put us there, and is revealing Himself through us in it. He puts us in difficult places and with difficult people, just so that He can love them through us, and the faith that overcomes the world can be seen in us.

~~~

It is the Lord who is walking in her in this apparently strange path. He just forces us, doesn't He, to find out that nothing is really anything except Jesus only and Jesus is nothing but love, therefore He gives us plenty of perverse people as they appear to us to be, to expend His love upon through us. I know He is walking like this in and through her and Jesus only will be seen in her. She is on the solid rock.

~~~

Plenty open doors and hearts on our "Total Truth" level. Those who know become "gonners" - they just say "That's it and there's nothing else". How can there be when it is a revelation that there is only God in the Universe - All in All - and all perfect love.

~~~

Doris Ruscoe has this month published, (I urged her to work on it and she saw it as of God) a new book called "The Intercessions of Rees Howells" published by Lutterworth, and if I'm not mistaken is going to be a best seller opening many eyes to those "hidden secrets" of intercession by deaths to life, and will gloriously justify where folks still think he made a mistaken word of faith on World War II instead of this now turning out as the opening door "by the destruction of the dictators" to a worldwide sweep of the Spirit and spread of gospel unknown since the birth of the church! No, no, to us the point is if we make a statement of faith after serious waiting on God about doing it, we take it as saying something GOD HAS DONE, and no matter what the appearances, we shall see the thing done on the "exceeding abundant level"!

~~~

We all get it one way or the other, don't we, and you just now with your friend. We are just forced by Perfect Love to keep seeing GOD ONLY working all out in perfect love, when the externals are so imperfect. You and I know there is no other answer in the universe except "Nothing but God exists"!

~~~

We surely all go thru times when the outer conditions shout "darkness" at us, but once I <u>know</u> that inner Spirit-witness, that I am not really just I, as a human independent self, but I as fixed expression of Christ, then you and I know how to walk right on, don't we, and knowing that what looks like dark is "the shadow of His Hands".

~~~

To us the whole basis of Lanyon's writings is the continual "hidden" cross in which he continually "dies" and challenges us to be "dying" to all outer negative believing responses to things and people, and continual "resurrection and ascension" in Christ in his and our "seeing" (positive believing). Perfect God only in all.

~~~

We don't "see" anything but Him, do we, whatever the appearance may be, & as we see only Him and no negatives, He will appear with His deliverance. We draw to ourselves what we are "seeing" which is only He as found in all things.

~~~

We make the strong point of temptations being something to welcome as James said, because they are NOT SIN (the difference between Jas.1.14 &15), and accept (Agree with your adversary quickly!) as his right to tempt us; but then by such acceptance of the temptations without condemnation, having freed Satan to do his tempting, we are equally free to recognise that these are only pulls on our soul-body and give us excellent continued changes of reversing, in our freedom, those pulls for the recognition of who we now really ARE, Christ in our forms, and we then replace His love, purity, releases or what not for the pulls of the Tempter. So we joyfully turn temptations into fresh experiences of Him as us! And then we go further, and as we now see "all things worked after the counsel of His own will", we accept Satan's assaults of all forms as "<u>meant</u>" by God, and thus ever fresh opportunities for those positions and words of faith which are God's agents for turning every kind of Calvaries into resurrections!

~~~

It is <u>HE</u> who has committed Himself to us.

~~~

Glad the tapes are a blessing - my object was to shew there never has been any other final reality except He All in all, first in us, then in everything, and the opposite is only an "appearance veil," and we won't "judge by appearances."

~~~

That was your "dark night of the soul" when you wrote before, which has to be before the dawn. Soul never dies to external impressions in this dark world, so you will get other negative stresses, but they are gloriously our practicing ground for seeing HIM ONLY and helping others to that "single eye".

~~~

So it's always the same - we live life from within. We are and act by the way we see or believe things to be. If we see evil, we are held by it and contribute to it, etc. Whereas, if we see only "perfect God" in every condition (though outward appearance to natural mind sees only apparent imperfection), then perfect God comes thru somehow.

~~~

Let's keep stretching in faith, money is God's problem.

~~~

Yes, it's good God has put you where the Light is needed to shine - in your restaurant work. Don't be afraid, or condemned, by the fact that those with whom you make contacts in the love of Christ, mistake it or would turn it just into fleshly love. After all, when we are in the flesh we can only manifest or see flesh in others, so they are bound to misinterpret you. And you, as a human, may often yourself feel a natural human response. But God has His keeping hand on you, so don't hold back but be bold in making contacts given you, because what truly comes out of you to them is Christ's love for them and seeking them. God will keep you from misuse of the flesh.

~~~

We are <u>wrecked</u> on God, let us recognise it and wait only for Him.

⧼⧽

FAITH...PRAYER...INTERCESSION

You were that unique expression of light out of my darkness.

~~~

His meat was <u>faith</u> as it is now mine; and bless him, he has taught me so much about <u>faith</u>.

~~~

When I hear from you I always feel badly that I know so little of what God has taught you. I have reread a couple of your books this past month and am eager to be taught of the Spirit as you have been. I know you to be the only one who is a "father" to me, in the Lord. I am blessed that God has even let me know you. I respect you in every way possible.

~~~

A man of God with wide horizons and great depth of insight – full of Christ.

<div align="right">Rev. Armin Geswin</div>

ഗരു

August 15, 1956

Dear Mr.Culbreath:

Thank you for your letter. Concerning the prayer of faith for souls, I always look upon it that God gives us the authority of faith for those whom He particularly puts across our path and lays upon our heart. I take it that when God does that, He knows who is prepared and He moves us with a spirit of prayer and faith for them. I also think yours is a good suggestion that prayer is God's means of weakening the power of Satan.

As to the words for expressing such a prayer, I always go freely by whatever God lays upon my heart. I will consider the general promises of Scripture enough when it is a person or people to whom God particularly directs my attention for prevailing prayer.

Sincerely yours in Christ,

Norman Grubb

~~~

September 12, 1957

Dear Karen,

Praise God for the grand news of the flow of blessing, only remember that it passes on from blessing to Blesser! That is to say, there are times when God takes all feeling of "joy and praise" away at least from our exterior feelings, so that we are not walking by the highest forms of feeling (soul life), but by JESUS HIMSELF, as our joy, praise, and faith, no matter how He manifests Himself in our external circumstances (spirit life).

You ask some searching questions on Rees Howells. There are both types of prayer, what we might call responsible praying and co-operative praying. Responsible praying is intercession, for it means that God has so laid a thing on us that we know He is saying to us, "I will do it through you." That type of praying is the one prayer R.H. refers to, and it is accompanied by paying the price - whatever God may require of us in taking the place of those we pray for. It is when there is death that there is life, so intercession has a death in it, death to self that others might live. You don't make up that death, or think it out, but it is just something <u>God</u> gives in His own way, and not the least in our way, when He gives us an intercession. As the price is paid, the Spirit gives us the authority to claim the answer, even as Jesus had authority to claim the coming of the Spirit on the basis of His intercessory death.

There is also the other type of praying, the quick shaft of prayer for this or that, maybe the daily remembrance of things and people God puts on our hearts. I call that co-operative praying; and in the least prayer there is some proportion of travail and identification. I agree with you about the value of prayer, or even more of the attitude of faith and love to pass us by.

That is a good saying of Mme. Guyon - from surrender to abandonment. Surrender is mainly passive, I giving myself and perhaps hoping that God won't take too much. Abandonment is active, we expecting God to take us and share His cross with us. You don't have to feel that to be willing - that is soul-life; you just have to recognize that our highest call is when God can pour Himself out through us, as He shares with us His Self-giving Life; then you accept that by faith and ask Him graciously to make you one upon whom He can put weight. He will do it. Don't look within to take your spiritual temperature; look at Him, and boldly reckon that He will identify you with Himself in loving and giving Himself for the world through you. It is a simple life. It is all He!

My warm love in Christ,

Norman

~~~

September 11, 1958

Dear Phyllis:

I am so glad you have written, although you do present me with some tough nuts to crack! I had been hoping to hear from you, and wondering why I had not, and was actually on the point of writing to stir you up!

Thank you for your down to earth openness. You will never get through while you allow yourself to be controlled by yourself. Self is always a slave to one spirit or THE OTHER. You are bound to be hardened and bitter while you allow yourself to be governed by what you think and feel, because really that is giving yourself over to the hidden control of the evil spirit of unbelief, rebellion, hate of God, etc. There is no remedy for time or eternity except to bow our hearts and minds and take God at His word. That means that you step right over, in the obedience of faith, into the <u>fact</u> that you, as an independent self with your own ideas and reactions, died on the Cross with Christ, and thus you no longer recognize or admit the mastery of the false satanic spirit over you; instead, you take the place by faith that you rose with Christ in His resurrection, and that means that Christ Himself, the Spirit of truth and love, lives in you, and is your real new Self within you.

There is no other way. In all life we are not sure first, and then believe afterwards. No, we believe first (and act as believing), and then we become sure. Hebrews 11.3, "By faith we understand...", not we understand and then have faith. You aren't sure of the chair you sit on until you first sit on it! So God demands of you and me that we bow our hearts and heads to His revealed Word, even when we feel we have reason to think that He has failed us. We simply obey Him, and we do that by taking Him at His Word, right against every feeling of rebellion. It is <u>after</u> we have stepped out in faith, accepted the fact that we in our independence have been crucified and buried with Christ, and now He lives and thinks His thoughts within us, that we find the assurance of faith within us.

So will you not do this again, even if you have done it many times previously? Just keep stating the facts of your position in Christ, and He in you, no matter how many times you are tempted to disbelieve it. As you persist, you will become established in faith. So don't be surprised at <u>your</u> feeling hard and bitter. Of course you do in your independent self, because independent self is always the dwelling place of the spirit of hardness and unbelief. The tenderness and faith in you will be as you recognize Him who is love actually lives His life in your committed self.

Now let us go on battling this out together. If you can't follow or don't like what I have said, don't turn your back on me, but regard me as a brother in Christ, and don't keep me waiting a lot more weeks for an answer to this! It is just possible that deep inside you there is some <u>point</u> of resistance or rebellion, some undealt with sin that God has put His finger on, which keeps you fighting against Him. Are you conscious of this? If so, let Him deal with you on this, but if not, there is no need to be introspective, but just by grace to step out in obedience of faith as I have tried to describe it above.

My love to you.

Your brother in Christ,

Norman Grubb

~~~

October 20, 1958

Dear Mrs. Wilson:

Thank you for your letter, and for letting me know about your daughter. I am so glad that she is making steady progress. Please give her my loving greetings. We have got to learn to keep our eyes steadily on the Indwelling Christ as our physical life and health, even though we may be receiving benefit from this or that treatment. We do not live by the outward appearance or feelings of our bodies, but by the fact that the inward living and life-giving Spirit is within us. The same with the needs of our unconverted loved ones. We have rolled the burden of them onto Him and leave them with Him. We must not judge by appearances in their wanderings, but by faith boldly see them in Christ, held by Him and worked upon by Him, until the victory is visibly won. All these are means of teaching ourselves this wonderful walk and warfare of faith. So may God teach you these things, as well as us.

My warm greetings and thank you so much indeed for this gift enclosed, which I will put into the Lord's work.

Ever yours in Him,

Norman

~~~

Nov. 20, 1958

My dear Brother Norris:

How good of you to write in your busy life.

Alas, it has come too late. I am up in Canada through next week, or I certainly should not have failed to contact you when Jack came through. We fixed our meeting for the day before he flew, and had a grand three hours together, setting our doctrines right!

I am sure you have had a time of rich blessing here. This country is full of hungry people, because there are so many keenly evangelical and Bible churches where they give them the milk of the Word, but not the meat. I could spend the rest of my life taking the openings that come to minister on the life in the Spirit in the churches.

I think it is wonderful that the Lord has laid our children on you. Mrs. Grubb was thrilled to read this. Probably God has used the prayers He has prayed through you both in the children and in clarifying my faith. Our two children here, thank God, are now really going on with

Him. We are thanking God for them both. ONE is still far away, but I see him clearly, with the eye of faith, as already captured by Christ, and I walk in that faith till it becomes fact. God has made that position of faith clearer to me quite recently, that's why I connect it with your prayer. Thank you indeed, and I have been able to help others on this point of faith for their children. My old friend, Clarence Foster, the Secretary of Keswick, was writing me today on this point, because he has difficulty to believe for his three boys, and I was passing this testimony to him.

Warmest regards to your wife and loving greetings to yourself.

Ever yours in Christ,

Norman

~~~

January 24, 1961

Dear Mrs. Birney:

What a good surprise to get this long letter from you, especially when you tell me that you have a difficulty to see. I would never guess it from your writing.

I had wondered whether I should hear from you, because the American papers had in the news about Hedgson, and I commented at once to Mrs. Grubb that I thought this must be your brother-in-law. What a shock for you all, but I know you will all also praise the Lord for giving him this last highest honor of being a martyr for Jesus. He lived a wonderful outpoured life and then ends it with a martyr's crown. What an ending! One day we shall look back and see that he was more highly privileged than any of us — Phil. 2:17. C.T. Studd used to love and quote that verse in Lightfoot's translation — "I congratulate you and do you also congratulate me". It was always C.T.'s ambition to be taken to the Lord that way himself. So our praises overflow our shock and sorrow.

Yours in Christ,

Norman

~~~

February 7, 1961

My dear Suzanne:

I have you daily on my heart. God's wall of fire is around you and Satan will not be allowed to touch you through any of his agents; and at the same time, God's redeeming love flows through you to those who wrong or hate you, for they too are precious to Him as He died for them, and we say in faith that God is speaking to their hearts, including the woman who has been threatening you. I shall be glad to hear more of how you are proving the wonders of God's grace in this dark valley.

Will be writing again.

My love in Christ,

Norman

~~~

March 2, 1961

Dear Brother Adcox:

I have just returned from the South to find you letter awaiting me.

I think the point is that we first boldly accept the fact of the union with Christ by faith. That means we are really one, as vine and branch are one or head and body.

Accepting this fact, we take it for granted that the Motivator constantly motivates us. Being our Vine, He is bound to be pouring the sap of His vigor and thoughts and life through us. Being the Head, He is bound to be setting the members in action. These are the disciplines you refer to — not actions we take except that, as we recognize Him joined to us by faith, He just causes us to speak and act (Phil. 2:13). When we consciously turn from Him, not merely tempted, but responding to temptation, then we sin and return to Him in admission of the sin; but then we immediately move over in faith to the Reality of the Cleansing Blood, where all the past is blotted out.

I will send you under separate cover a small pamphlet called "The Key" which goes into some of these things.

I wonder if you know my beloved friends the Woods. I would like you to know them. They truly love the Lord, and I am sure you would find living fellowship with them.

Sincerely yours in Christ,

Norman Grubb

~~~

March 26.61

My dear Elaine,

I was very pleased to get this personal "inside" letter from you, and I am knocking this off personally to you. I always felt a bond in spirit with you and will always be glad if you regard me as a kind of "father" in Christ to whom you can so write from your heart.

It is precious that God is opening to you what He has been after in you. I have always been sure that God has a place for the rivers to flow thru you and your husband, and maybe each of you a "difference of administration but the same Spirit" in it. Intercession consists of distinct commission (standing in the gap); identification which means living for and dying for those for whom one has the commission; and authority in the realisation that the Ascended Christ is really fulfilling His intercessory High priesthood thru you, and what He does He completes in victory.

Write again and share with me what God is saying to you.

My love in Christ and to you,

ever yours in Him,

Norman

<div align="center">~~~</div>

Sept. 4.1965

My dear Leslie:

Finally, your leap, not into theology, but into faith! I greatly like your linking all of God's callings to Jesus to faith exercised by Him as a human. I never have had any doubt in my mind, and have often talked that way, that every phase of His affirmations of his Sonship, of Him being the fulfillment of God's Word through the prophets, of His death, resurrection and finally ascension, were all exactly the same leaps of faith as we make. It is only this that makes it thrilling and real to us, and still inspires us to follow along. I am impressed that in His last supper talk, John 14:17, he makes no reference to His resurrection. He was "through" on that. But all His thought is around the coming of the same Person into the disciples as was in Him. This is the product of the ascension, and the priesthood of Melchisedek. And He now fulfills this priesthood, not only in us, but by us to others. We share that priesthood - that is Hebrews 11. But I also like your thought, quite original to me,

that it was Melch who taught faith to Abraham or at least in its deep implications. Good. Spread this quality of faith abroad.
Much love.
Ever yours,

Rubi

~~~

Ft. Washington, Penna. 19034
September 8, 1965

My dear Brother:
Thank you ever so much for your letter. Your news had the appearance of being bad - but there is no bad news to faith. This is one way in which God's people in India are going to prove for themselves that they are strengthened with might by His Spirit in the inner man and to recognize their union with Christ, and many will witness a bold confession. So praise the Lord. God will be glorified through His church in India, and the gates of hell won't prevail against it; and a shining light will also appear from many hidden away in the more formal churches. God has never left Himself without His witnesses, as we are seeing in Rome itself these days.

But besides this, we stand straight against any such newspaper statements as you quote and God will not allow the Government to exclude His missionary servants. We will watch and see God blow on this attempt to close them all out, and He will preserve the way for His real witnesses to continue. This is our chance for faith and we take it.

Grand to hear of your constant witness in many places, and the blessing, and it was good to hear of you and Bro. Bakht Singh together. I am just starting out now for some weeks of touring in many places.
Warmly yours in Christ,

Norman

~~~

October 2, 1967

Dear Gene:
Delighted to get yours. That I should think "too unkindly" of you "for the intensity of the convictions"! What an idea! I delighted to find someone with whom I could talk these things over, and I saw it

223

concerning you, exactly as you are now saying - that it is not a turning from faith but a seeking of its higher dimensions. We are surely going up the same path!

So when next we visit your area, I do hope that we can be together. I start a month's tour in the South tomorrow. Blessing on you both - and He is always blessing.

Ever yours,

Norman

~~~

February 6, 1968

Dear Lanny:

Grand about the house. The only way of faith is to keep a single eye, and once one has believed, it is God at work, for we understand that our believing is really the faith of God, He thinking and speaking the word of faith by us.

Where there are apparent failures, such as with those two friends not coming back, still keep on believing ground - that God is doing what you asked Him to do and said He would do, though you can't at present see how that worked out. Just as Rees Howells gave a date for the end of the War which did not come off, but it was really God's way of setting the College aside to pray through the crisis battles one by one.

I don't personally date too much, unless I am pressed to do so. I just take for granted a thing will happen. It seems that mainly you have been disturbed by things not happening by the time you said in faith they would. Rather keep your eyes on the thing happening, such as that the porch will be completed.

Anyhow, it is good to talk these things over, and the great point is to let nothing interfere with our boldness of faith. There we stand square on Scripture grounds.

Love to you both.

Ever yours,

Norman

~~~

Jan.4.74

Dearest Sara,

I was just thrilled that you and Ellen could fit it in so that we really could have that lovely time and share together in the "secrets of the Spirit" - and there is no greater secret than that really nothing but God exists in the universe; and our temporary misuse of ourselves in our former fallen condition, and the distortions of our world as a consequence, are really only His merciful ways of pressing us out of our negative believings, by which we accept things in their outward appearance, and into the positive believings of seeing HIM only at the centre of all; and boldly using the authority of faith as His sons and daughters to bring into visibility what we need. How simple when all our part in it is to speak the word of faith - as Jesus and all the men of God in the Bible did!

Our dear Bessie is getting better, though there is still improvement needed. I have my precious Pauline in bed at present with ulcer trouble, but once again the Lord is the healer.

With my much love to you all. Did I give you this little leaflet. If so, forgive my repeating it.

Lovingly,

Norman

<div align="center">~~~</div>

May 19.75

My dear Ray,

I am so glad that you have written again and that occasionally you are moved to write and share like this. I am off this week for a three weeks tour in Florida, so will send you this line before I go.

I don't think we have to have a double vision on faith and works. I am to be occupied by faith which means committal to and consciousness of my inner union with God. But He is love-in-action by me, so that the conscious result of my conscious union is He moving out by me to unveil Himself to others. God works in me "to will and do…" Phil.2:13, so He is the doer also; and my job is not to assess the amount of the fruit, but to keep being what I am, which is He in my human form; and expressing myself (which is Himself) in whatever ways He takes me in ministry and contact with others.

Equally it is not for me to "judge" how far others appear bound in a mechanical or legalistic setting, or oppose or criticize. I am to see God

225

Only in all people, and He is causing them to be and react just as they are, whether negative or positive. Then I can accept them as they are, allow them to be or think as they are or do, and love them because they really are God in their human forms and maybe don't yet know it. Then I am free to be myself and go on sharing and giving what God gives me, whether they "hear or appear to forbear". If I judge another, I really judge and bind myself: I am seeing from my little helpless self-attitude. If I see God in another, when it may even appear it is more of the devil than God, then I am free to accept them and love them and just to give what God gives me.

As to whether opposition is the "obvious" sign moving you elsewhere, I would go steadily on, reaping the fruit where you are, and when God says, "Move", you will have no doubt.

Hold back nothing God makes real to you. Hide no light under a bushel, whether folks can "take" what you say or not. You can only truly transmit what is first living truth to you, isn't that so?

So the Lord is taking you on His perfect way - He will fulfill in you John 7.37.38.

Ever with my love,

Norman

~~~

July 24.77

Joan my dear,

I am so glad to hear again from you.

Yes, love, you must die out to the emotional soul-life (that's the meaning of Heb. 4.12), and it does take the form of apparent outer indifference to church-going in the old style (and thus lots of legalistic exhortations), also to praying prayers as of old, and reading the Bible as before. Now you are learning to BE. That is you and He in your eternal unity which is an eternal fact. There is a sense in which you don't "know" yourself, you just ARE Joan. In the same way you are now JOAN-GOD (hyphenated), and just BE. As you so truly say, you know beyond any outer forms you love the Lord and His Word and there's no other life for you. Precisely. And as you just affirm your love and don't try to examine, and still less condemn yourself, and wonder at not "feeling" Him, you will gradually settle into the kind of praying which is thinking things over with Him and speaking words of faith, and thoughts coming to you from the Scripture which are alive and not just outer reading.

Yes, you may sometimes feel it was nicer having more outer security in church, Bible, prayer, etc., but you will come into the permanent glory of the eternal union as you-He and live there. So you will keep going, darling, as He keeps His Own Self going as you and in you.

And we will hopefully look to being with you later. Yes, my son is about the same. It is GOD taking him HIS way - all is perfect, as with yours.

Lovingly, darling,

Norman

~~~

May 29.78

Dear Ray,

Many thanks for yours. It is good to keep sharing. I am now off on June 1 for England for those two months. No I'm not taking public meeting, - the first three weeks are our WEC Leaders Conference; so I'm not likely to see your brother. I will take his address.

Glad these "total truths" are settling into you. James tells us the negatives give us necessary background to "Patience having her perfect work!" which means being established!

The key is to build people by faith, not pull them down by unbelief. So keep seeing your folks as Christ in their forms, being formed in them as in Gal.4.19. See the discrepancies, "hypocrisies" etc as merely soul-diversions from who they really are. And we have plenty of them too, so need to keep removing our beam before pointing to their motes! Faith builds up!

And our "seeming to escape" our resting place is precisely what you say - only seeming – soul bluff. See how the Hebrews writer used that word "seem" in 4.1 and 12.11 - being caught out by bluff.

So keep "walking in the Spirit" -walking in the flesh is not gross sin, but just negative believing - as if we are not Christ, but independent selves with our own reactions.

My much love to you,

Norman

~~~

227

May 2.80

Dear Marcus,

    Thank you for your letter and I am so glad you have written. You are being taken by the Holy Spirit in you through your good and necessary education. Our rational faculties are a marvelous asset, but human reasoning can never prove a thing. Faith has to "leap" beyond reason, (though assisted en route by it), and attach itself to something outwardly "given". In this case the written word of God which I am so glad you search into in your morning QTs, is that outer given object. But faith means you have inwardly accepted what is outwardly presented as fact for you. And that fact is that the God of the Scriptures and the Jesus of history is inwardly The Eternal Person who permanently lives in you as you. You do get a "consciousness" of this, an inner "knowing" by the Spirit; but you do not even live by that (that "sense of His presence" you mention). No, you live by fact accepted by you as fact, and at times as now with you back in "confusion" and lack of "spiritual wisdom", with no reliance on your reasoning or feeling. This is this walk of faith - and your times of "confusion" etc. is the valuable means by which you keep practicing this walk by faith. You can never become "established" by any other way, because reason and feelings vary, but we live at our center where by faith He and I are joined (I Cor. 6.17); and as you do that, the inner "knowing" (the witness of the Spirit) does also settle into us in due course.

    I wish it was possible for you to come and see me again!

    With my love in Christ, He IS in you, the Real Self in your human self, whether you "know" it or not!

    With my love in Christ,

Norman

~~~

Dec.20.81

Sara dearest,

    How lovely to get such a "Spring-filled" letter from you, for we always live "in the dew of our youth", don't we, in our Spirit-union with Him! I still rejoice in the special joy of you being with us at Albany, and specially Charlie. Am looking forward to the weekend again next May.

Yes, as you say, "all our fresh springs are in Him". What a difference when clouds have finally disappeared for good (though there is often the "appearance" of them, but that is bluff to faith!), and all is ALWAYS HE, within and without. I like Ps 2 when God laughs at opponents, while we humans fuss about them, and then He used negatives just to set His Son more firmly on our believing consciousness, and in fact we are "more than conquerors".

With my much love and joy,

Norman

<div style="text-align:center">~~~</div>

Dec.31.81

Dear Nick,

I am late in answering your good letter, as I'm only now back from a 2¼ months tour of visits and groups on the West Coast. Touches of the Spirit everywhere of course.

I see you talk of going to live "on the streets": but I must take it this Lubbock address will find you. Yes, I will hope to be with you next Fall. Yours is the address I will use to make contacts for Lubbock.

I think the Scriptures must not go beyond the "you ought" level except by many hints for those who can "see," and evidences in plenty of Bible lives, because the moving-in to experience where "you ought" has permanently become "you are" can only be by our faith-choice. It is then we who turn the "ifs" (If we walk..) into "since we are walking...". It is only by the Spirit's eyes that the whole Bible to us becomes a book of "YOU ARE and you read every exhortation as positive "Yes I Am."

And sanctification is a finished condition of our BEING, for HE is that to us - 1Cor. 1.30. This is where the acid test of the reality of the replaced life in us is seen; for when we <u>know</u> ourselves as He, we have moved right on from progressive sanctification (cutting out the word "progressive") to involved intercession. Thus, those who haven't crossed that Rubicon by the Spirit confuse Paul's "not that I have already attained or were already perfect" in Phil.3.12 with Paul's sanctification, which he had left far behind as a finished fact in his first phrase of 3.8; and his reversed absorbed attitude as intercessor begins by his last phrase of that verse; and thus all his perfecting is concerned with the completion of his "high calling" as intercessor. The same as Jesus who was All in his confirmation at His baptism, yet went on to say He still had an unaccomplished baptism (Lu.12.50). So don't let those who think they have it all by outer Scripture confuse you and pull you back into those law-ways. No, all is now involved in intercession, including weaknesses.

Yes, spirit is <u>we</u> - Knowing (mind-set), loving, choosing (will). Soul is the reasoning faculty which seeks to interpret the Spirit mind-set, and of course emotions expressing the love-being. Most seem to have this mixed.

"Inner man" of Rom.7 of course is the only "real man" —spirit-man!

So, glad to chat with you, and write again. I rather think I sent you this on "soul-spirit" but enclose in case not.

The Sept-Oct issue of Union Life Mag is a masterpiece on lamb-intercessors.

my love,

Norman

~~~

Sept.18.82

My dear Marge,

Only after I had written you and Bus a line and closed the envelope did I note your comment on top of your letter on "WEC sharing" of needs. But I think I ought to "safeguard" even our precious WEC by saying that our faith basis, while it is an individual need, and not a general WEC one, is not by making the personal known, unless clearly guided, lest it really means that we haven't "got" the need already supplied by the faith which establishes us in the inner consciousness of having the "substance"; and the sharing with others is a kind of secondary means of supply! I think on the whole WEC has kept faithfully to this principle, certainly a 1000 times more than all the begging missions of all kinds with their "return" envelopes! I keep reminding WEC (and reminding myself) that I should never use the word "need" unless I am adding that my mention of it is only to underline the fact of the supply which I know to be there in the invisible and to become visible. Actually I am sure that is the word and expression of faith which God actually uses to draw supply into the visible, whereas expression of need, not swallowed by faith-supply, retards the drawing of the supply! You're an old Weccer and know this well.

So God is giving you the perfect basis to your wider sharing of Union Life in action by keeping you on the spot of apparently unsupplied need - and then the deliverance! And giving you also the sharing of the principle of intercession (which has been coming more to the fore just now again in our Louisville Weekend which was tremendous and glorious) in your "sufferings" by your daily job, and being wearied and "bored" in the soul-body, as part of your and Bus' intercessory "dyings" for your "union" ministry, and where folk see in you the glory which overflows the "suffering"! And it is interesting that actually in your own new Denver area Bus is already finding the harvest field. Give my love also to Darrell & Beth.

Just off next Sunday for England. Every indication in Louisville is that the Spirit's revelation by us is bursting out at the seams!

Love to you both

Norman

~~~

Dec.25.82

Dearest Joy,

This is a "joy" letter from you. I haven't written before because I have only now returned from my three months tour, which included our good hour together. So I've had to delay letters.

But yours is good, especially of course about your Mike. I shall want now to hear how he is established in the Housing job. I love to hear how the Lord got him off the green chair and into all kinds of activity, and behind it lay that you had learned the secret of releasing him, and not "trying" to do God's job in His ways with him; and when you were able to convey to him that you had released him and were trusting the Spirit to operate in his life, the changes began, even though he may not yet clearly realize their Spirit-source!

Yes, I'm so glad, dearest, that you three did make your way over and we could have that good hour, and could share how all is PERFECT, no matter what appearances are, and indeed the dark spots are deliberately given us by God to make the light shine out brightly.

So keep writing, dear. I have marked down seeing you when I do come B'ham way next.

That was good also how clearly you "saw" that job was for Mike when you first saw it advertised. No, I don't hope the Spirit leaves you quiet!!! I love to see Him moving us into all kinds of love-action. All folks are so desperately hungry for what is now glorious truth to us, and the Lord gives you boldness among your fellow church-people, as occasion arises, because only bold witness confirms us in our "knowing" and is the Spirit speaking to others.

Loving you,

Norman

~~~

Nov. 17.85

My dear Clarence:

Your letter, just received, means a tremendous amount to me, especially considering from whom it comes. I don't get a great deal of encouragement, not in any large way anyhow, in writing this kind of thing [Summit Living]. Yet I feel so deeply with what you say – that so much of the devotional reading does not go down to grass roots. And I find it tremendously in the evangelical churches here. Folks desperately hungry because they have been fed on the milk of the Gospel, but not on the meat of the deeper aspects of truth. They have a faith, but not an intelligent faith which has given them a foundation of understanding which cannot be shaken. Long ago I took to delving in the mystics, not finding what I wanted in modern devotional literature, with few exceptions. I drank deeply, particularly from that master of all of them, Jacob Boehme; then I had to go through years of sorting it all out and confirming it with Scripture. Now things begin to fit into place, and come clear and simple; indeed, I am already starting to jot down some more stuff, at least for something of brochure size, because a lot more clarification has come since the thing I sent you. I am deeply convinced, although it sounds awful to say so, that even our deeper life teachers are not really giving the clear foundations, and as a consequence they put many hearers into bondage, because their emphasis to exhort the believer to get on with his consecration, prayer life, witnessing, etc. (really an exhortation to a Romans 7 life!) rather than unveiling to him a Christ who is all, and will surely mould those who recognize Him in their allness in them, into the pattern of life He intends to live in them. But enough of this. Anyhow, you do encourage me, and I will send you anything else on this line that comes out. I find a great reception among these hungry folks, for it is possible to put this Christ-centered truth in a way which does not tie one to this or that "school of thought" or antagonize them.

I fear we have had a worse heartbreak with our one boy than you with your three, and he is still – in the visible – far away from God. But I equally have it clear, with the eye of faith, that he is already in Christ, and I hold him there by faith when I can't see a sign in fact. We have handed him over to God and His grace, and do not regard him as our responsibility, beyond maintaining the continuous attitude of "calling the things that be not, as though they were". I take it that when God puts a direct need or challenge in my path, such as of course my own children are, then it is God saying to me that He has already supplied that need in the invisible and is requiring the human cooperation of my faith (His believing in me) to bring the invisible into the visible. I don't feel that I need to know more of the will of God than the fact that they are my children. I take God's will not to be something that I have got to discover outside of myself as it were, but because He is living His own life in me, the road I walk is His road, and therefore I take it for granted that He already has the answer in hand for all problems I meet on it.

I really think the C.U.M.B. letter gets better as the years go by; but I was amazed at the ministry God has given you among alcoholics, etc. I did not know God had lead you this way. I would have much to learn from you in such a ministry, and how much God must teach you about taking the sinners place in intercession to go through with it. That is wonderful.

My love to you, Clarence, and many thanks, so glad the gift to Alan was a good sum. It was a good idea of Godfrey's. Warm greetings to Dorothy.

Norman

~~~

Nov.10.88

Dear Mary,

Good that you keep sharing. Once you see you never were "just you", but those fear-invasions to give you a clear insight into negative invasions, really from the spirit of error. Then what do you do with them? Struggle, fear, flight, desire to have touch with someone else were the old ways of escape. But NOW you are NOT MARY, but Christ in His Mary form. Therefore the value of the negative fear attacks since you were a child are excellent background training for you now to know their negative pressures on you, on your soul-emotional reactions, and so now clearly, having come by the Spirit to know you are Christ in Mary, you do not fight nor regret these assaults thru the years, you rather ACCEPT and thank God for them as background negative training. Then as you don't 'fear' these things, nor 'struggle' to get release from them, you are now FREE TO RESPOND, AS YOU ALREADY ARE DOING, BY AFFIRMING who you fixedly ARE as Christ-Mary, and know those negatives were the Satan-bluffer, formerly in you, but now only invading from without, and you STAND in who you are (as in Eph. 6:10,11 and then 14 onwards.)

So my dear, take no further note of such assaults. Don't 'fear' or anticipate them, but see them as good practicing ground for settlement in your Christ-self; and therefore good background negative experience you can use to help many other fearful ones from their past. Light SWALLOWS up dark! But you first must have some dark to be swallowed up.

So my dear, you are now well learning from your own past now being swallowed by the present, to have valued experience for helping many others!

Keep always clarified in the FACT of you never being again "just yourself", though it may appear to be so, but ALWAYS HE AS YOU, and then the invasions of the negatives on soul and body are recognized as where they come from – not to be 'feared', but accepted as Satan-bluff and replaced and the special value as an intercessor in helping so many others torn up by invasions from their past.

So just this with love,

Lovingly,

Norman

~~~

Mar.6.89

Dear Constance,

Deb gave me this loving gift from you. Thank you so much dear. The Lord is so aboundingly good and I am thankful.

I am so glad we had those hours together. (How <u>great</u> it is when the Spirit lights that light in us that HE is the Real One permanently in us as us, and we learn the precious walk by faith and not by sight.)

Thank you and with my love

Norman

~~~

Nov.28.89

Dear Emily and Wesley,

You shew so much caring love in your letter. You go thru much, darling, as you always have. How well I remember you back to your beautiful youthful days when you launched out for Asia. Wesley has been privileged to have you, and you faithful to him, and your two girls. I often think of you in your neat little spot and glad I saw you there. Slowly slowly we learn that we must be put thru contrary things to produce "passion" in our faith against appearances, the vast vales of "suffering", and the 'curse' and snare of the established church is making faith seemingly so obvious and simple thru infant baptism etc. that thousands "think" they are "Christian" by an elementary so called faith-attachment; but living faith lives because it <u>COSTS</u> to believe, as Wesley with his long struggles with Xtian Science and you in the physical. My one physical "snag" at 93 is arthritis in one leg, so I 'crawl' around on a "walker" but mercifully very little pain, and still "all clear" north of the neck!

Thank you for the word on our Phyllis. Yes, she sent me her newsletter and special letter with it, about the time "in the depths", so I shared with her about that, and now her arising again! <u>WE</u> know there is a "River" which always inwardly flows beneath all outer conditions, because outer sufferings are soul-body, though real enough, where we have learned to walk in the Spirit. And it is good to get that word about your loved Robert, and give him my love.

Meanwhile, my WEC goes greatly right ahead, and are preparing for their three yearly Intercon with 140 leaders from worldwide for three weeks in Kilcreggan. Our present Internat Sec Dieter Kuhl of Germany is good, and is putting our Third Pillar - HOLINESS - as the main issue. So I am writing them my grandfatherly letter as oldest living Weccer, with a MAGNIFICENT ARTICLE JUST COME FROM A PASTOR WHO with two others twice drove all night to have days of fellowship, and now says he first "caught on" to the reality of No Independent Self thru me "in the 1970s", but has written this tremendous thing on Evangelical Humanism, that lie of self-effort, which I shall send around as they have plenty from me in my Rom. 6-8 pamphlets, Paul's Key to the Liberated Life, and the YES I AM, my last book, and brochure I wrote for that leading Nazarene pastor who said they weren't clear on the self life; so this will be another voice for our Weccers instead of "just Rubi"!

So with all my love as ever and so glad we keep our love touch with both of you.

Rubi

~~~

Sept.21

Thank you, love, for your letter and poem, and all the love which always accompanies them. I am on tour and finding ever greater response, as I think we are able to put always more clearly this "exchanged" life. We go free now, able to accept ourselves and be ourselves because we know that He's "operating" us. So much of my old "prayer" life has been exchanged for a "recognising" of who we really are, Christ in our forms, and affirming those words of faith in Him in action in us by us, in all, rather than asking Him to be so! What a liberated and "sufficient" life, isn't it.

Glad, darling, of the good word on the girls, and that they hold in the Meth. Church as able to reach folk, though it so often means sitting under way out teaching from the pulpit, so much more law and self-effort, than our "enabled" life.

Love is the way and we love all as He does.

Lovingly

Norman

~~~

June 8

Judy dearest,

Thank you for yours. Always glad to get them!

Prayer to me is the inner consultation with Him as me, and then as I see things or people to be, I move into the word of faith for what is God in that situation or person. Then having spoken it, I "see" it as fact, and my repeat "prayers" are repeat recognition as fact. The parable you refer to is in Luke 11:5-10. It means persistence that the sleeping friend has the supply and he is going to give it to me! What do I ask or 'pray' for? I just inwardly consider what I would really like to happen or be, then I move in with my word of faith based on "my desire" – Mk.11.24!

Loving you, darling and always glad to hear. We are really bound in heart!

Norman

~~~

May 22, 1990

Dear Ones,

I have unanswered letters from you back to last December, though while staying with loving friends.

God knows His own loved ways for each of us, and that has included no less than 95 years for me! Since my 18th year, I have been full speed on the pedal for Him and have so much to be thankful for. But I think my last years at that kind of speed are ended and it looks like "wheel chair" for me! Pauline and I had 62 years together since we first joined her father in what we then called "The Heart of Africa" in the Congo with the Azandi "human flesh-eaters" tribe in 1920. She has now slipped off to be with the Lord eight years ago, and my loved granddaughter, Sandy, helped by my own daughter Pris, have been our God-blessed family.

But now swift changes have come with my Sandy having to take severe treatment in chemotherapy to thankfully remove signs of cancer. At the same time my own legs (not my brain yet, thankfully!) have so given up that I think it means a wheelchair life for me! But what can I say when my whole life has been loaded with open doors of Christ-witness in many lands! Even now, having truly a home away from home first with Tom and Page Prewitt, and now with old loved friends, Billy and Mimi Anderson. Don't we all learn that when "outer disaster" strikes, there is abundant Romans 8:28 awaiting round the corner! And this for me not a two weeks stay, but many months. Romans 8:28 is surely solid!

It gives me this chance of one more sharing in writing. I wanted to share how earthly hurtful frustrations and distresses are the very seedplot for surprising new ways of God for special further purposes. As with Jesus at the cross and Paul in prison, those living examples of Satan assaults are fitted back by our obedient faith into some unique opportunity. In fact, I have daringly illustrated this from my own 95 years in what will probably be my last earthly adieu, calling it "INTERCESSION IN ACTION."

My main purpose in doing this is to give us the constant practice in the meaning of trials as underlined by James in the first chapter of his epistle, and Paul in his first comments on his new birth (Romans 5). In my own case there have been six "could have been called crisis" which turned out to be life changing and Spirit planned career points. They left their plain traces in the riverflows that followed. I also like calling them "Obediences of the Spirit," the title Moses gave to that first great obedience of Abraham, our pioneer of Genesis 12:1. Always the cross was at the heart of these obediences and always there were costly launches of faith, but then always, sometimes years later, there was "the abundant fruit that remains."

So in this series of articles are the details of those "obediences of the Spirit." Each one was a challenge of faith by which some plain word of God headed up in a crisis of obedience. Then there followed in God's timetable a "there it is!" I start with my first youthful army obedience – a mark of the Spirit left with His C.O. (Christ's own) trademark on the battalion. Then the obediences of Cambridge days which have left their evident glorious Spirit mark on nothing less than the Inter-Varsity Fellowship world-wide. Then came the most permanent digging into my heart by the Spirit in my early days with C.T. Studd in the Congo, which put the most lasting birthmark of Galatians 2:20 on all my years of ministry right up to today. This was followed by the five years of translation of the New Testament and parts of the Old Testament into what we little dreamed would be the official (though doubtlessly largely improved) Bangala Bible Translation, for the whole of Zaire.

Then those years (how many, 35?) in the building up of the faith foundations of a total faith worldwide commission in the Worldwide Evangelization Crusade. We grew from one C.T. Studd to the 2000 fulltimers in WEC-CLC in 50 fields today! The book publications with the lives of C.T. Studd and Rees Howells followed, with both books still best-sellers. In the foreground have been some WEC biographies, and then the outreach of another dozen or so books – reaching out with the fullness of God revealed in scripture, most recently with <u>WHO</u> <u>AM</u> <u>I</u>? and <u>YES</u> I <u>AM</u>.

I have recently sought to share this fullness in detail in the pamphlet, "NO INDEPENDENT SELF" and the brochure "IT'S AS SIMPLE AS THIS." Then great light came on Paul's Roman 6-8 which I give in "PAUL'S KEY TO THE LIBERATED LIFE: ROMANS 6-8." I am finally so gratefully thankful that I can lay down my pen or typewriter, <u>YES</u> I <u>AM</u> being my final book – not simply because of the exhaustion, but also because the Spirit has gathered us together in increasing numbers and clarified conviction unto the end of our search! Though doubtless others will take up the pen to build upon it.

I know I am leaving with you our pearl of great price, so simply available to all by faith, and so totally completing.

With my love in our eternal bonds,

Norman

~~~

Ap.19

My loved and caring Fred & Gloria,

Gladys has just sent me this wonderful loving caring gift from you and it always is a fresh love-touch from THE LOVER through my fellow-loves. Thank you so much, when it means that I can't be sharing with you in your home and with friends. But thank God what & Whom we have is always living.

I am stuck to my typewriter and have finished a thing on INTERCESSION-IN-ACTION, which I ask my Sandie to send to all my Weccers and loved friends after I've joined "the cloud of witnesses", shewing how ALL SITUATIONS are ALWAYS places of HIS intercessory work by us as Royal Priests, when we <u>accept</u> our situations, no matter how unpromising they may appear as HIS Commission, Cost, Completion, just as Paul turned the hopelessness of being Nero's prisoner in Rome to being "the <u>Prisoner OF THE LORD</u>", and out came his witness and fruit among Nero's soldiers and those Prison Epistles to us all. So it is wonderful to have the constant practice of seeing <u>THRU</u> the appearance to always being HE in our forms! So it has to be with me and you when I can't be with you, but the typewriter keeps me busy, and life is ALWAYS FRESH AND ADVENTUROUS WHEN SEEN BY OUR EYES OF FAITH.

So thank you dear ones for such love and such a help.
ever lovingly,

Norman

~~~

May 8.
Winston Salem NC

My dear William,

Your letter has reached me here, and I can send a short line, but hoping to have "dialogue" with you in June. One thing I am sure of is that it is not <u>more prayer</u> that is needed, but more <u>faith</u>. Heb. 11 doesn't say "By prayer Abraham etc", and Jesus never urged the folk to pray, but to <u>believe</u>, and of course Mark 11.24 is key for us. There is much too much just "spreading needs before God", and much too little doing what God is challenging us with, identifying the specific need and then making our declarations of <u>faith</u>. In this, you are absolutely right that our old method of so-called morning meetings were first of strategy - what is God presenting us with? Then definition - what's the exact next step in achievement? And then with some Scripture inspiration from the men of faith, we go to declaration.

It was NOT prayer which was the genius of the Spirit in my day, but FAITH, around which all so-called prayer times centered.

Enough now and to be continued when we meet.
Much love,

Norman

~~~

May 20.

My darling Daughter,

It is so long since I've heard from or had news of you, but you and I have a love-bond which no length of silence can ever disturb.

Love, I have a sense that the Lord took you thru a rougher rather than your normally glowing, flowing stream of love last year. I did not get a chance of talking with you or sharing which I would love to have; but I know, precious, how we can sometimes be hurt, like Jesus, in the house of our friends, and it is a real hurt: but if so, darling, He has given you the special privilege of practicing, as you so often have (and I need plenty of practice at this too!), being hurt and really feeling it, and then replacing the temptation to see those who hurt me negatively which leaves me in bondage to my negative seeings, with seeing all our loved ones as they really only are - God's loving Self in their human forms and our total oneness, and not "seeing" the shadow which crossed us: and that is our freedom again to love and be loved. So go on being your Lover-self among us all, as you are to me, by "dying" to anything in any of our family which has come across to you as a self-shadow of the negative towards you. Boldly replace that in your "seeing" of them, by what you know is the reality of every member of our family, that they love you and you them. So don't let any shadow any may have cast on you remain as a shadow you cast on them.

My precious Pauline remains about the same, maybe physically somewhat weaker, but at rest sweetly as ever in the Lord and among us.

I just LOVE you, my darling, and please pass also a loving hug to your Jack.

Norman

∞

EXCERPTS

There are no limits to God.

~~~

Faith inwardly KNOWS, because it is HIS knowing expressed as us, so there is not that burden or fear in going thru impossible conditions, but zest and anticipation. That's our special secret, isn't it.

~~~

SOLDIER-INTERCESSORS (II Timothy 2: 2-7)

Finally I thought I would just remind you that we are all learning together that the topmost of our high calling is as intercessors, and the summit of our ministry is to know the biblical and spiritual reality of being an intercessor. A far cry from the normal concept of intercession being just intercessory prayer. The widespread book on the life of Rees Howells has opened many eyes to look for the right answer. I have written a pamphlet on INTERCESSION IN ACTION, giving the five main periods in my life when I knew the call of the Spirit to be an intercessor.

That death-life principle of John 12:24 and II Corinthians 4:11-12, which really is by grace the summit of our knowing and being who we are, He the Intercessor Spirit in us (Rom.8:27) and how we can now illustrate and explain this to others as well as knowing it ourselves in our own lives the meaning of Paul's final Philippians 3 word "This one thing I do forgetting those things which are behind, and reaching forth to the things that are before, I press toward the mark for the prize of the high calling of God in Christ Jesus". Which was Paul the intercessor to the Gentiles.

~~~

No dear, no journey is uphill. Only looks like that to negative believing. SEE that God <u>means</u> all that comes to you which might appear from Satan, then praise, rejoice and name what you want God to do!

~~~

I have never seen, even with my ICL links, their using the big OT prayer about a people repenting and getting right, because that does not apply to an earthly kingdom, but the Israel who were the church on earth until Christ. It was a call to believers to repent, not an unsaved nation!

~~~

We can claim Psalm 91 for ourselves and our houses. I remember I used to do this in the trenches in the last war, but felt a bit selfish about it, until I realised after all, the promises are open to all, therefore it's only our own fault if we don't make use of them!

~~~

The vision and commission He gave me that the whole church is to hear <u>who they really are by grace</u>, some rejecting, many precious ones accepting, as in all history of the movings of the Spirit in His body.

~~~

Once we are "caught", we are caught, and no stopping, and thank God there are increasing numbers of "caught ones" spread through this nation and on thru Britain. I see a million by faith, until that final day when "the earth will be full of the knowledge of the Lord as the waters cover the sea"! And we have the great privilege of being pioneers.

~~~

I know of Wurmbrand and everywhere I hear how greatly the Lord uses him. I would agree with you that the appeal to the government by these Russian Christians does not further the cause of Christ but there are always those who will resort to the arm of the flesh when they don't know the power of The Other Arm.

~~~

You won't like me nagging at you about mine on Intercession which you turned down as too egotistical. But the point which somehow must be made, and if you can't get it thru the Mag, we must try booklet form, as some are pressing. Maybe my epitaph!! You see the point is that most readers of Rees Howells are enthralled but go away saying, "Marvelous, but far beyond me". Now the truth the Spirit has impressed on me is that all born again are "Royal Priests", and I use my life to shew from that first moment when I gave up that girl for Jesus, the Spirit Of Intercession set me going full steam in the Brit army, and every incident in my life afterwards has been enlarged intercession. THIS IS NOT BEING SAID TO OUR PEOPLE. Of course it is egotistical. Was not Jesus? Was not Paul? But if there was a proper preface word, folks can be pointed to a real death in every intercession, and that is the point, and then the faith persistence till it is gained. So someone must get this out. You suggest another writer. But my experience after seven biographies, Fenton Hall, CT Studd, Alfred Buxton, Jack Harrison, Edith Moules, J.D. Drysdale, Abram Veriede, Rees Howells. In every case I have followed the line of giving their lives in their own quote, and every one has been a success except J.D. Drysdale, which I unfortunately named "Prophet of Holiness" and that frightened folks off. So I know by personal witness is the way.

~~~

The great center of Rees Howells intercessions was the clearness of the commissions he received from the Holy Spirit of the particular intercession he was then called to, and the principle by which there was always clarity in what the particular intercession then was, and always the 'coming thru' to the point of "gaining" it, coupled with the law of the "the first fruits always going to the altar". The prayer part always headed up in the "gaining" of it. That comes out clearly in the incidents in his life story and most particularly in the great final one in World War II which has now such a world outcome in the vast spread of the gospel. So Rees Howells lived in great liberty of the Spirit. I was like a son to him, and he lived what he called a perfectly 'natural' life except when the Holy Spirit was on him in those "gaining" stages.

~~~

I would like to make an unhesitating appeal to you to by no means to be moved from your calling. You are one of God's intercessors, set apart for the furtherance of the Gospel. Beware for Christ's sake and your own sake, from being turned away from this. God is allowing you to be tested in the fires. May the pure gold of the Spirit who goes through to the end, be found in you, not the dross of self pity or exasperation.

~~~

Indeed, I feel, that the whole thing is once again God asking us to launch into the deep, "not knowing whither". It is again the old time stride forward of faith. To accept him will be pure faith, with many points still unresolved. God has always set His seal to our obediences of faith, despite our weaknesses and fears. So it is true that I am "pushing". But I don't push finally against God!

~~~

So glad, my letter came at God's right moment - just after a "rough time": and every rough time is only to deepen the truth to me that nothing is rough except insofar as I see and accept it as rough in my inner believings. As a human I always have to start in this negative world by feeling the negative (the roughness): that's normal & right; but I am learning more quickly to replace my negative reactions of believing evil by seeing Him in His perfection meaning this situation to be, then I see Him only in and through it all, whether I can see the reason or not for the moment; and so I praise and the pressure is dissolved. That's our daily death & resurrection walk all thru life isn't it - it is Paul's 2 Cor.4.7-12.

~~~

Let's keep stretching in faith, money's God's problem.

~~~

On this "word of Faith"...The fact that it is a spoken word, is the guarantee that it is not a passing thought, but has therefore taken concrete form, and has as its background a true desire which comes from us (Mark 11:24), yet of course really issues from Him as us. Therefore it is not just a passing gust of feeling, and remains with us as something already done by God and seen inwardly as done by us, and we now watch Him for His manifestation. Isn't that about it?

~~~

It is just a fact that the Lord means us to walk through all kinds of valleys of shadows, to establish us in seeing negative as only reverse side of The Positive. James, the most practical, starts his whole letter off with bang-bang-bang- trials, trials, as "all joy" for they establish us by faith-practice in our maturity where we've found the lot and need nothing, because HE in ALL IS ALL.

~~~

But the principle is that we always start through soul or body negative feelings. JESUS was perfected as intercessor by "sufferings", and that was what perfectly suited God. See Heb.2.10 and indeed all Hebrews. So there are pains. The way never changes, does it. WE always start by "feeling" this or that and then, as quickly as we "see" it to be HIS way, we move to peace and faith. But 2 Cor.4:7-12 is the continual experience – for Paul said "Always bearing about...always delivered unto death"! So we will spend our lives passing through appearances of imperfection to actual perfection in the imperfection. No wonder Paul said that is "more than conqueror", because we are able to share that reality with others, and that is precisely why we are taken thru them, isn't it – intercessors "suffered being tempted" and thus "able also to succor those that are tempted".

~~~

It is the Lord who is walking in her in this apparently strange path. He just forces us, doesn't He, to find out that nothing is really anything except Jesus only and Jesus is nothing but love, therefore He gives us plenty of perverse people as they appear to us to be, to expend His love upon through us. I know He is walking like this in and through her and Jesus only will be seen in her.

~~~

I am glad you are going on with the Lord. It is a very simple life when the one fact has laid hold of our hearts, that Christ lives in us, as you say. Whatever situation we are in, we are then able to look away from it and recognise in faith that the Lord Himself has put us there, and is revealing Himself through us in it. He puts us in difficult places and with difficult people, just so that He can love them through us, and the faith that overcomes the world can be seen in us.

~~~

That academic question about if HE wills and plans it anyhow, what point in our believing; the Spirit always means us to be cornered on a reasoning level, to know truth and light are products of faith in action, not theories about it. He does just will and do, and we just also will & do! QED!

~~~

God has led me along these positive lines, as you recognize, although you are quite mistaken linking me with such men as Blumhardt or R.H. They were in a class apart, and knew the guidance and authority of the Spirit as I don't. In my general life and ministry I certainly find this positive attitude of constant recognition of Christ is all things and people, and of affirming the certain fact of His working in all situations to be the effective way. We see its results in our fiercest WEC storms and needs. But at the same time I recognize that many in the Bible carried burdens and fought battles in the Spirit in a way that I don't. The danger of the positive way is spiritual lethargy, or passivity as you call it. But still I go on the way God leads me, perhaps because so many fight battles and take tensions which are really expressions of Romans 7, rather than Romans 8 life.

~~~

Don't be a nibbler of the possible, but a grabber of the Impossible!

ෂ ෙ

MARRIAGE

Ever since you first visited our home, I have had the feeling that if I could ever get a firm grip on the reality of my union with Christ, it would change my life totally. The freedom and joy that I could see in you were the most convincing evidence of your argument.

~~~

Whenever I was with him I always felt the strongest of his characteristics—FAITH—LOVE and ACCEPTANCE—a truly humble man!

~~~

Thanks be to God through Norman Grubb, I have experienced a freedom that has continued to grow and develop into a faith that continues to walk in the light. Such insight this man had into truth.

~~~

One thing we remember most vividly is how Norman made us feel so loved and so valued.

ℰ◌ℭℛ

Donna darling,

I'm so glad, dear, that though you say you are not a letter-writer, you have so opened your heart to me. That is good, because we love each other and can share together.

Love, you are like that bride with her bridegroom in the Song of Solomon – called the Song of Songs! She sought till she found her beloved and entered into union with him "his left hand is under my head and his right hand doth embrace me". Those days of "the singing birds" had come to her with him, and they were at rest together "feeding among the lilies". And you, darling, have found your inner rest in and with Him and He is your heart's delight – Christ in His Donna form, as you say.

But you lose Him again and are not yet wholly satisfied in Him alone, and you, as it were, tell Him to turn and leave you and "be like a roe or young hart on the mountains". And so, as you say in this precious letter of yours, darling, you "are almost two people to myself". You lose sight of your true Mate (thy Maker is thy husband), and want an inner satisfaction in yourself, like the bride who was seeking her own self-satisfaction and so turned the bridegroom down when he came knocking at her door (chap.5).

You see your Heavenly Lover has deliberately taken you into a human marriage with a mate that did not physically satisfy you, nor give you soul satisfaction in a mutual understanding of each other. And you had lived your life "thinking the most important thing in life was to love and be loved and your True Mate was taking you a way in which loving him and being loved by him would be total satisfaction to you. "A garden enclosed is my sister, my spouse; a spring shut up, a fountain sealed...I am come into my garden, my sister, my spouse..."

But not yet finding your total contentment in your heavenly marriage, and not finding it with your earthly mate, you sought and found other men. Through them you were blessed with your precious children, but no "other men" can ever satisfy your true heart-hunger which is satisfied in your true marriage, but you are not yet settled in it – and to be the "garden enclosed" to Him alone.

So, love, you still "get lonely and want companionship with a male". You have a strong physical sex desire and want the satisfaction of completed physical intercourse (and so do I and so does any normal human, male or female); and you also want a male companion who can be truly companionable to you in normal daily living – a normal soul need.

But, darling, your True Mate lovingly won't let you find your human hungers be satisfied on a human level. He keeps you starved until you are so satisfied in Him that any human sex or soul-companionship can be done without, and if given, is merely secondary and no sort of rival to your true matehood. That is expressed in this marvelous Song by the bride's total rapture in her bridegroom, expressed in physical terms as "the altogether lovely one—-the chiefest among ten thousand", with his perfect physical presence; head, eyes, cheeks, hands, legs, belly – in chap.5.9-16. And he, marvelously, is totally delighted and satisfied with the beauty of his bride, also expressed in physical terms (4.1-7). "Thou art all fair, my love. There is no spot in thee" – and that is you and me, Donna darling, as he sees us!! – hair, lips, eyes, teeth, breasts "like clusters of grapes" – and even repeated in 7.1-7.

So this is total mutual satisfaction – we the bride with the Heavenly Bridegroom; so that we start by rejoicing in what He is to me - "My beloved is mine and I am his" and ends by my rejoicing in His joy in me - "I am my beloveds and His desire is towards me." Beautiful!!

Now, Donna darling, you see what Christ's love purpose and love aim is towards you, and He'll never be satisfied with less and never let you get away with finding an answer in a human mate, because He knows that equally can never satisfy <u>you</u>, for He IS your total spirit-soul-and body mate, but you have not yet come to the final settlement of your eternal mating (where you live in a permanent spirit-intercourse and climax).

So how can that become <u>the</u> fact of you, darling? Just by your one "obedience of faith" – which is already true of you, but not yet so finalized that it is never repeated. I mean by that "obedience", not some religious works or "trying" or prayer or anything – but the one obedience of <u>faith</u>; and faith means that you affirm a given fact from the heart-centre of your being, and do it once for all, so that you never allow a rival desire or affection of soul or body to have any footing in even your mind (2 Cor. 10.5), beyond what you can't stop, - the sudden invasion of desire or thought.

In a way you have done that, love, yet in a way you haven't or you wouldn't be bothered about seeming to be "almost two people" – and bless you for your precious honesty. You see such an act of "obedience of faith" (which merely means your one act of obedience is to believe He is to you what He says He is, and you know down in your centre; and you are to Him what you have long ago said you are) does include what Jesus said of those who were His disciples in Luke 14.25-33, ending in that last "whosoever he be that forsaketh not <u>all that he hath</u>, cannot be my disciple". And that means that, though you may not at all feel like it in your body or soul desires, yet you affirm by faith that you have forsaken all, despite any kind of human feelings or desires. In that case for you, darling, it means that you can and will live with no "companionship of a male". For it includes "all that he hath" and actually Jesus named human affections and relationships (in vs.26, 27).

Maybe you have done this, love, well then do it in such a way that it never need be repeated, despite wherever invasions of temptations.

Then as you do this, even if it is a repetition and you do it finally never to be repeated, you are also affirming your total marriage to our One Bridegroom - the altogether lovely one, and our true intercourse with him. That is saying in Paul's New Testament terms, we boldly say right out, we ARE dead to sin in Him, and dead to the law (taking any outer "you oughts" or false condemnations), and ARE as in Rom.8 "made free", and only "led by the Spirit".

And as you say that and stand in that once for all, never to be repeated, then you "have the witness in yourself" (I John 5.10) and the Spirit in His own way makes you know you are in this Soul Marriage and none other; and the normal human desires will never take over again. You CAN walk alone with HIM, and will If He so wills.

And then the answer to what you mention about "wanting as He wants" will obviously be that you only want (down in your spirit - no matter what soul or body wants are) what HE wants, which is your perfection and that is your perfect basic satisfaction in your union with Him. And then, as The Song says, we go forth with our Bridegroom "into the fields". We "get up early to the vineyards to see if the vine flourish" and we get talking about the needs of "our little sister who hath no breasts, and what shall we do for her"?? (7.11, 12 and 8.8); and our shout of joy is "love is as strong as death... Many waters cannot quench love".

So that is where you really are, Donna darling, and maybe you aren't even bold enough to affirm your own beauty as He sees it and thus you now see yourself, and that He is your all in all and none else; and you are free just to be yourself just as you are day by day, which of course, as you say, is He in your form; and you are loose from the control of any lesser human desires, because you are so occupied in visiting the vineyards with Him, caring about your "little sisters" and to Him "being" a garden enclosed of sweet spices, yet calling on and being ready for the north winds which will blow on your garden and the spices flow out - to the starved world. (4.16)

So, loving you, darling and glad to be able to spend another hour with you, though at a distance.

Lovingly

Norman

~~~

Dec.26.59

Dearest Margaret,

It was a great joy and interest to get your letter, though you might not think so with all the time it has taken to write back! I have carried it with me to answer - but!

It was lovely to hear of the Lord's presence at the wedding, and that your lives together are His. You will have trials to bring you more and more on to Christ only, but you will have a heap of the goodness of God outweighing everything else. You may be sure I shall not come Victoria-wards without seeing my beloved niece! We have enjoyed our visits through many years haven't we, and you have allowed me to be an uncle since you were - how old! But I have no dates bringing me west at present, maybe not before next fall.

Yes, marriage does not alter self. Only Jesus does that, and then not by changing us, but by being Himself living in and thru us. We shall always have to walk in the Spirit with Him and with each other. Marriage is a wonderful bond. How God beautifies <u>everything</u>, spiritual, mental, physical, all have their touch of heaven on them. But the bond is only truly strong and blessed when it is in that order. Learning first oneness in Christ, letting Him have His say in everything, coming back to Him and to one another in Him, when we get at outs with Him and each other as we do. Then minds can meet and reach out in a multitude of interests, for everything is God-given, when they are first sanctified by His indwelling. In Him we can have a heap of interests and activities, such as the pictures you mention. Then in our bodies we are equally made for a union which has the full blessing of the Lord in it: that side of sex has been so smeared by sin that often the Lord's people have felt there was something questionable about it. But no indeed, as the Bible makes clear. It is part of the wondrous beauty and joy of all God's gifts, culminating in the little family God may give you.

So glad of the good word of your Father. I am busy about this country with endless openings. Pauline and Priscilla and the grandchildren are pretty well.

With much love, and looking forward to meeting Austin next visit.
ever your affectionate uncle,

Norman

~~~

April 5.61

My dear Barbara,

Thank you for your letter. It is just what I would have hoped for from you, next to talking with you - you have just opened your heart, and not "kicked back", but lovingly shared with me a glimpse of the Lord's dealings with you and George. Thank God! What married couple, including ourselves, does not have to find a walk together, both in Christ and in the flesh, in this most intimate of human relationships? It is lovely to hear you say that this has been God in you both, using your married adjustments to center you more completely in Himself, as well as in one another.

Don't bother otherwise about what any of us think or say. How slowly we recognize it is GOD who is conforming us to His image thru the various problems and battles we all have. Just be ready to share with others how Christ is being formed in you as the ALL in all through your experiences in marriage and otherwise. That's all that's needed!
ever yours in Him,

Norman

~~~

June 22.

Dear Kelly,

I am so glad that our "Elizabeth" has become linked with you, when you both start as having your real "marriage" each to the Lord, and then only secondarily to each other. My Pauline and I had that settled before we married, and kind of went thru an experience of "dying to each other", so that we were then always free in our 62 years together to have GOD's interests and ways first in our life and activities. That's the only

key to a real marriage, and then our spirit-bonds to Him and thus to
each other stand steady when soul and body bonds get tested when we
really live together.

So the Lord will now keep you two dear ones first for Himself
during your waiting year (I think you said you were not marrying for
a year), and then when you are together, and HE has, according to Eph.
3.10, a perfectly prepared life in which His "rivers of living water" will
flow out of you to many, and then when you look back as I now can, how
thankful I am HE kept me through many tough spots and had His plan
for me. So also for you two.

ever with my love

Norman

<div style="text-align:center">~~~</div>

Dec. 2.70

Bonnie darling,

Well, how good to get yours, dear, and to find out that it was
running about after me, and that neither of us had forgotten the other-
impossible – we are in each other's hearts.

I can't "take" divorce as something we should kind of toy with as
a way out, love. I still stick to Bible foundations on marriage as "one
flesh" and the children the products of the union; and to contemplate
divorce, unless forced on us, is to lower our sights to what appears to
be a human way of escape for us; but once we accept that we are God's,
we have to accept the "death and resurrection" relationship where the
verdict on our lives is with Him. It isn't basically a merely horizontal
bond between man and woman, but a vertical, or triangular one, with
God at the apex. I believe, love, this is the ultimate test on who we really
are – He living in our human form, or just we humans. If we take the
latter way, we find we move from mess to mess, rudderless.

It is tough to say this, darling, and easy to say it when I have a good
marriage; (but God in His own way differs with each of us) has to corner
us to where the ultimate choice is made between self and God. However
tough it is, married love is ultimately a matter-of-fact bond after the
first passionate period quiets down, and is a workaday family life with
its self-giving aspect on being the home for the children. Intercourse
should be the physical binding factor giving pleasurable fulfillment
to both, and mental and spiritual companionship should be the other

binding joy; but even if these are both absent (as maybe largely with you now, darling), still the bond was made before God and sealed in the birth of the children, and I don't see how we can deliberately look to break it, however lacking in the above respects, unless GOD steps in and the break is not of our doing. You are one of three, darling, in my own links of correspondence and love, who are going thru this battle, and in each case the wives would wish to leave (but there has been no "other woman") and are, I hope, holding on and going thru, this being where they are really finding the death-resurrection way in God we all have to walk to find true living.

So there it is, little love. Can we talk further when I come? Just anyhow, whether you dislike what I say or no, lean back for the present on God, and keep your mind on Him bringing His ways to fulfillment for you and your husband.

Then if there is an uncertainty in your heart about your marriage, does this open a dangerous door with Daniel, or is there nothing in that? I note he has gone to be with his wife. Is all ok between them, or might there be danger of passion taking over if you meet, and the two marriages being broken? If you have it fixed in your heart and mind that any meeting is going to be thrilling and romantic, but not going to bed with each other, or future plans in that direction, then ok, and the keeping power of God in you can just be a revelation of the power of Christ to Daniel. I have also just heard from one of our workers, single, sorely tempted by a charming army officer when they got a bit cozy together and then him asking for intercourse, but she stopping at that and explaining why, and he understanding, and he being a young Christian, this is probably just what will shew him the different drive that possesses someone in whom Christ lives, that, though we can enjoy human pleasure, our selves and bodies are to minister self-giving love, which is transmitting God in us to be God in them, which alone is true living, rather than being driven by our own bodily self-satisfactions.

Thank God, HE has you, precious one, and I love to be poppa to you; and God will keep His strong hold on you.

This with all my love, precious and a big hug,
Your poppa

Norman

~~~

Aug.21.72

Karen dear,

I'm so glad to hear from you again and some of your news. It is
good the Lord kept you His way about Wayne and I am sure that is
right. It is good that He kept His hold on you while you were with him,
as permissive sex has got such a hold these days, and our bodies are
temples of the Holy Spirit and only to be given in sex to the one mate
God gives us in marriage - and then the physical union is the perfect
symbol of the one eternal union with Him.

You speak of being able to "discipline self" which seeks to destroy
or devour our real self. The way of deliverance is not to keep negatively
believing in the wrong ways the human self can take us, for what you
believe in holds you and you build it; but replace negative faith with
positive believing and recognizing that your human self with all its
appetites and potentials is joined to Christ as branch to Vine, and
your humanity is the necessary means by which He manifests Himself
in His deity. Then you don't fight or strive against natural desires or
reactions, but you recognize that our human selves are always subject
to temptation because that is what keeps us alive to reckoning on God;
and when tempted, you simply transfer your believing from the fleshly
reality of the temptation to the true fact that Christ is the Real You;
and as you recognize Him, Spirit overflows flesh. And when we do
fall into sin, which we all do, then quickly replace the sense of guilt
and condemnation with praise for the precious blood and immediate
cleansing. Then we are not negatively fearful of the wrong uses of
our human self, but positively thankful that it is God's means of
manifesting Himself as the Vine thru the branch!

Much love dear and write again. I liked your little x slipped in above
your signature and I return it!
Lovingly,

Norman

~~~

May 3. 1978

Dear David,

I feel privileged that you should share your heart with me at this
time, as of course I know and love Sue (and had heard of your married

difficulties), and have met you. Your letter reached me on tour two days ago, and I returned home yesterday.

David, this is all God's perfect way of love for you both, so as James says, "Count it <u>all</u> joy when you fall into diverse trials" (though you can't feel it joy!).

You see God has already brought you wonderfully, He in and as you, by your continuing in your love relationship with Sue, and you knowing she loves you, though in your soul-human reactions, as any husband, you are hurt and wronged and can feel unforgiving and bitter. Yet you have come far in knowing who you are – Christ in your David form, so that you don't confuse your natural human soul-reactions with your true Self, Christ loving unconditionally by you, where love is not emotion, but the fixed spirit of self-giving and other-loving.

But there is one final recognition of who you are, when you know you are totally God in your human form, therefore accept with praise (though not feeling it!) that He at present means you to accept and love Sue even without the normal physical and emotional love-relationships which we are normally meant to have and enjoy with our mate. This is "the obedience of <u>faith</u>" which affirms Him as your Real Self, and you do not "see evil" in her in this present condition, but only God being Himself in her in this condition at present; and boldly affirming that He holds you steady, though without the fulfillment of your normal human desires. This actually is His planned and love-way of fixing you in Himself alone as your all in all – nothing but God in our universe – by this shared death and resurrection with Him. This is the riches you will be able to share in the future with many in their desperations, having gone that way yourself. So it really has an "intercessory" purpose in it.

Meanwhile and from that place of "reigning in life" and free in Him, we take also the position in faith that He in Sue is in the process of restoring her, by these radical lessons, to knowing true love (He in her) which is simple self-giving without any necessary emotion towards those God has given us to live for them, and that is she for you; and to know once for all how to discern between soul deceptive "love" and the only true love, God loving in and by her. So we see her back with you in true human love-relationship, having got true love into focus.

Sue has written to me in past days, so I will be bold to act a "father in God" and write her. I hope you both may be free to share with each other the two letters, just as I am so glad she honestly shared with you her dairies while going thru this soul-attachment.

So you ARE what you are, David, total God only, and we are given this priceless marvelous privilege of living, not by self-effort and all their fruitlessness and labors, but by boldness of recognising and confessing, without feeling, our crucified and risen and ascended position – He having replaced me in my inner centre, and we "walking" on the water (not sinking in it!) in Him.

Again I say I am glad you have given me this opportunity of talking with you and I am also so glad you had those times with our precious friends, John & Linda and the others.

with my love,

Norman

~~~

May 3.78

Sue dearest,

I know and love you, so that I can write you as precious to me. You will realise that I have heard something of the ways <u>the Lord</u> has been taking His Sue, and now I am so glad that David has written me. He hasn't suggested I write you, but my heart and Spirit suggests it! I hope that it may be that you will share the letters I am writing to each of you.

Dear, this is all God's <u>beautiful way</u> to give you such a settlement in HIM Alone, that all that has been happening is great riches in the help you will be to others going thru the same things in future days.

You know, love, we all have to go thru love "affairs" in some form or another, because human-love is the strongest form of our being created in His image, who is love; and the great lesson so many thousands need to know is the difference between soul-emotional and physical love which is just human outer covering (though very beautiful), and true love, which is simply one <u>thing</u> only, or I should say One Person only, GOD who IS love. So "love" is the inner spirit of being for others, with no necessary emotion attached, though emotions may follow along with it. But its basis is in "I will". "I will" praise the Lord etc, as the psalmists were so often saying when they were feeling all caught up on their soul-body level.

So you see, darling, God loving by His Sue form is, in the special marriage relationship in which most of us live, a fixed giving of myself to and for my mate, with nothing primarily to do with emotion or the physical, though that beautifully follows along with it. But if I never "feel" or even if I "feel" antagonistic to my mate, I love him (or her) and belong to him and to his interests, no matter how I feel. You <u>belong</u> to David and he to you!

Now you, love, have been thru some recent experiences when you have had a real "love" or even passion for other men. We can have "safe" loves for others of the other sex once we are finally and for ever settled in the one love, which on a male-female level is given to one only, symbol of our eternal one-to-one marriage with our Heavenly Bridegroom.

You have had to go thru some rival loves (so did I with two times of "inordinate affection" as the Bible calls it), and this has been beautiful for you, to settle it once and for all in you that soul-body love is outer (and often lovely) attraction, but is not to be confused with our one total spirit-love which may at times be with no feeling. And remarkably, as if to settle that true spirit-love in our "whole man", we are given total physical union with all its ecstasies to be also only fulfilled with our mate. That's why Paul says union with someone outside of marriage is the one sin of the body, different from all other sins – (I Cor.6.18).

So you see I am glad you have gone thru this, and glad David knowing who he is as Christ as his form, has stood steadily by you and it has even confirmed his true love to you and you to him; so that you may really now learn the difference between soul-self love which is only appearance-love, death-love; and I am glad that God's overshadowing love has been on you so that these loves have been broken, without the ruin of your two lives being broken. I know you will have felt the pain, and may still do, and you will "appear" to have love for that other man; but, darling, you KNOW God, and therefore you KNOW that true eternal quality of love which alone is true love, where HE <u>gives</u> Himself for us; and now as being us we <u>give</u> ourselves for others. So you know that that other love, as I knew also, which grabs us as a kind of driving passion is a false thing; for true love is freedom. And the other is named and is adultery and false.

So, love, give yourself back to your David in the full symbol of your physical union. The Bible says plainly in marriage the wife's body is not her own, but the husbands, just as his is not his own but the wife's (I Cor.7.4,5). So quite apart from any emotional feeling on your part (because if this other soul-flesh love has been recent, it probably has occupied your emotion) give yourself to David as belonging to him on that physical level. Emotion will return later. You can do this, because you are not you, but Christ in your form and therefore you are <u>able</u> to do what you know is HE in you.

Well, dear, I am glad to have been able to talk with you, and God is bringing you thru to a marriage-union in spirit, soul and body which will bless many.

Just always loving you,

Norman

<div align="center">~~~</div>

May 31.78

Sue darling,

I'm so glad you've caught me just before I fly tomorrow, and I'm so glad, love, that you have shared your heart with me as far as you can. How I would love to sit down with you and if I wasn't going to England, I might try to find a way. But that must wait.

But anyhow, precious, you've told me just how it is with you as far as you can by letter. Yes, of course you have the answer right – all is spirit, and you are in Spirit-union with Him The Spirit.

Confusions are on the soul level, and don't try to find answers. Accept being in confusion on that "reasoning" level, until the Spirit clarifies.

You say, love, that you are "tired of hanging on by faith". Then don't, love. You are HUNG ON TO by Him, whether you do any "hanging on" or not. Just BE. If that means "feeling" in darkness, and "feeling" with no answers, accept that, on your soul-reasoning level. Faith as I say, is not trying to hang on, it is just AFFIRMING FACT, though all hell seems against it.

I would gather you want to have answers, and folks of course seek some from you, and this is what puts you in the tailspin. The present answer is that you have no answer, and won't try to find any until they come as "light from above". It may appear to leave you looking like a fool or zombie, ok, that settles you always more completely in GOD ONLY. You are right, this is His PERFECT AND GOOD WAY TO do this marvelous "fixing" in you. So get it, love. Disregard any desiring for answers and thus "confusion" when you have none. Praise God that you and HE are eternally <u>one</u>. HE in His Sue form. Stand there and as Eph.6.13 says, "Having done all stand"! Regard all negatives as just illusion and bluff. BE STILL and know that I am God – in His Sue.

As to David, darling, probably this is confusion and problem for him. Now don't resist his maybe negative attitudes towards you, if these things have happened which you can't explain yet. Accept that he has a right to have what attitudes are real to him; but your answer is that you can only be silent until GOD gives you any further answers. Conflict comes out of opposing, so that is why you acknowledge his right to be disturbed; and only that you can remain "Still" until God gives further light.

Only with that, love, don't cut yourself off from being his wife, as I wrote you before. Be in all normal ways the wife you are pledged to be; only you cannot give answers beyond what the Lord gives. So SEE CHRIST in your David too, and we praise God that all this is settling him also more totally in the Lord.

I wish I had the opportunity of talking longer with you even by letter. I shall so much want to hear how the Lord does what He is doing, establishes Himself in you. It is all perfect, for you are perfect in Him.

I love you, darling, and even this short chance of talking with you.

Norman

~~~

Oct. 78

Dearest George & Rita,

You know I love you both and rejoice in the secret that we share together of Christ being our real inner selves, and we each forms of Him. But I have kind of taken you both in my heart and faith to Britain because I heard, though of course only second hand, that you had a sin problem with a couple of your friends and also things were not too happy in your own marriage.

You have allowed me to be close to you in your own lives, so I am hoping you will let me be the same again now: God in His love and wisdom means us to go through our negative patches (and we all have them, myself included), as the necessary negatives to press us in and settle us in Himself, where we no longer see negatives, except as these pressure points to give us constant practice in seeing HIM ONLY in ourselves and each other and in all, doesn't He.

I was recently with a couple of old friends in Boston whose marriage about twelve years ago I had a good deal to do with. They both know and love the Lord, she a nurse, he a businessman, and with their three children. They go ahead together in their nice home, but we open our hearts to each other and they have their clashes, mainly temperamental, he rather sharp on the kids when he returns from work, and she not as responsive as he would like in sex – nothing major like leading to a crack-up, but of course disturbing happiness. I think, or hope, that they saw, as I have constantly to see, that God means us to be different, and it is to give us practice in seeing each other as Christ in our forms, and being thankful for all of Him we do see in each other; and then at the same time, as best we can, accepting whatever is the rough edge in the other as also being meant of God; and as we accept and love, as we are more concerned with the uprising of negative attitudes in ourselves than in the other, God does His changing work in the other one also! The meek inherit!

So I am just writing this to say that I love you, and see you in faith held together, each of you knowing Christ in yourself as your Real Self, and then seeing Him and nothing else in each other, and so bound together as a witness to Him and the children in your united lives.

I just see one chance by which I might see you. When I return in November, I am making some visits south. I might drop off just for a night and be with you. If that were possible, I would love to be with you.

ever loving you both,

Norman

<div align="center">~~~</div>

Jan. 26.80

Sue darling,

I'm so glad you've written and we can be in touch. Evidently it was not of God that I come when I had planned. Love, if there was a real necessity, I could possibly "make it" in Feb, but I don't think there is that, as your present way seems fairly settled.

Darling, divorce for us who know Christ as us is not for us. We don't accept it because love is nothing to do with the soul-body kind of passion which David is now mistaking for love with this woman, or that you had, though I reckon you did not know then the difference between soul and spirit – which you do now.

So, I would be saying you were wrong if you yourself were wanting and choosing the divorce. But if I get you right, you accept that God had given you your mate in David and you should not move out and have tried to continue on these visits; but the real reason is that David had this adulterous passion and chooses that, mistaking it for the Spirit-love which is meant to bind you and overflow all soul-drive. And you are only going along because that is really his choice. I hope I'm right in this, darling, and that it is not you who are deliberately choosing and wanting the divorce (except maybe in your own soul-reactions with D. loving this other woman). I hope I've got this right, and that you would stand to your marriage, but D. won't have it, and only in that sense you agree. Take that stand, darling, as Christ in you. David, I believe, does know the Lord, but if so, he is in for a tough time, because he can't be going into this adultery deliberately, and choosing this soul-flesh passion in place of his true mate-love for you where he is for you and the children, and God's way for him, rather than for himself. And it is a problem to see how he can be again in a right God-relationship when he "exchanges" wives like this, and continues in it without repentance. I shd have to say this to him, but the Lord is not at present putting me in touch with him, but with my darling Sue.

So I think that's all I can now say, love. You call it turmoil and so it looks like – but it isn't. It is God's perfect and beautiful way for you so long as you are just having to accept the divorce, and with whatever hurt, you are going right on with the Perfect Lord walking in you, and in union fellowship with all of us who love you.

Always loving my Sue and will love to be with you!

Norman

~~~

Aug.21.80

Charlotte my darling,

This is a wonderful letter from you. You are taking your place right in among the Heb.11 faith-victors! Darling, you are fitting in with those women who "were tortured, not accepting deliverance that they might receive a better resurrection". I mean GOD HIMSELF (and what a joy to HIM!) is taking you right thru the soul-agonies of contemplating Charles leaving you, and all that means of heart-tearing for you (even to the very spot in which you wish you could get away from God and thus keep Charles – and you CAN'T – Beautiful, glorious! And how the Father rejoiced over that one!!). And darling, this has meant for you and all of us who can share the intimacies of your "fight of faith" (not fight to seek and find faith, but to affirm it), a clear settling into what IS and in the heat of the battle to find that it IS - that you have ONLY HIM in the universe, and HE ONLY IS your Husband; and in that seeing of Him only, even when He comes to you in a disturbed Charles form which might even mean him leaving you, and the effect on your "reputation" and home life and everything, you have released all (not without pain and constant soul-surges), and are detached from your human husband, and <u>free</u> in Christ walking His own free way in His beloved, and equally freeing Charles to go whatever way God in him is taking him, as yet unknown to him that it is God, and in whatever suffering ways (a hell suffering while yours is a heaven, intercessory suffering) at last to bring him to himself. Beautiful, darling!

Fully praising, and many must be refreshed by sharing your glorious faith walk!

Norman

~~~

Dec.6

Julie darling,

That's a beautiful letter that came yesterday, way the most beautiful I've had from you, and if you're saying Brad is pure gold, I know someone else the same - and of course because it is ONLY HE as us!

So how I go along with all in this lovely letter. You are RIGHT, and as the years pass, you will say as C.T. Studd did, and I too, that our joy is not having refused to do what God gives us to do; and I bear witness with CTS in my older years that you look back with greatness of joy, and you say, "Yes it was just the Lord taking me HIS PERFECT WAY". So you say that now, darling, in your younger years and about dear Brad. This fiercest battle when you just steadily affirm that GOD is your total sufficiency, not Brad or any man; and, love, you'll look back, no matter how difficult to do just now, and you will say "I being in the way, the LORD LED ME" - just as CTS and I do. I look back amazed at the tricky ways the Spirit has taken me, ways I shd never have gone but for His overruling guidance, and how they have turned out to HIS glory and my joy and privilege, and so for you, precious. And I hope this means that you can find another "lover" in me in whom you can confide your heart. Darling, you're a GREAT AND PRECIOUS ONE in the Spirit, and I know far better after this letter.

Yes, you can't touch the inner knowings. I can only say somehow you just wake up one day and say "Of course it's He as me!" Took me two years. Stand by I John 5.10 and leave the Spirit to give that witness. You just rightly ARE.

Darling, there's no place where on earth we are free from doubts, questionings, pressures of all kinds. We live in 2 Cor. 4:7-12, but we learn not just to accept, but to embrace the tough spots (though they will always start up feeling tough), as our faith-opportunities.

Just loving and hugging you. I'm having such a good time 'down here' sharing living bread, that I know with Him is "far better", but here is good – with persecutions and sorrows also!

LOVING YOU

Norman

ॐ

EXCERPTS

Yes, don't be concerned about these marriage problems. The Spirit has to get at self-reliant self by all ways. In earlier days marriage was not a way, because it was a "done thing" – for all marriage problems to be covered and the couple to go on together "enduring". Now a breath of honesty has come in and marriages are questioned. Ok, let them be and praise and thank in every case, even if it has been adultery. We have to get broken from our unperceived self-sufficiency. Firmness I suggest comes in where there is any who justifies and deliberately continues in a sin-relationship: to fall is one thing; to remain in it by choice and not wanting the Lord to change things is another. But I have even to say this that I know couples who have broken up, remarried, and go on with the Lord. I am for remarriage. I am not for promiscuity.

ॐ

HEALTH & LOSS

He could bear us up in faith, encourage us in dark days and stand with us in the all-embracing darkness.

~~~

All difficulties were to him an opportunity.

~~~

Through the many years I was involved with Norman touching peoples lives he always used the Bible verse, "God is All and in all." There was always the message you are loved.

~~~

Norman, in death as in life, you will forever be our frontrunner.

~~~

Lack of supply was always seen as an opportunity to see God work.

രു ഇ

August 7, 1956

Dear Mrs. Allen,

I heard of course from your sister about your operation. Thank God you are one who is prepared in the Spirit to take all things from Him. I would gladly accept your invitation to be one of those who shared in laying hands on you and praying for you, but my problem is that I am not back until after Sept.4. Probably you will prefer to gather a few friends at an earlier date. He is our life and thank God you dwell deep in Him and He in you. These things that loom up as much as big tests when we are up against them will seem very small when we are at once ever with the Lord. All that really matters is whether we have the faith of God which is unto praise and honor and glory in our fiery trials, and I thank God you have that. Praise His Name.

Ever your friend in Christ,

Norman Grubb

~~~

November 4, 1958

Dear Brother Floyd:

It was a great shock to return today and find your letter. It hardly seems possible that your wife has gone to be with the Lord. I fear it must have been very sudden and the grief must be very great to you. I send my deepest sympathy and love.

You have proved, I know, and will prove, that our times of greatest difficulty and shock are the very means God uses to root us in Himself. As you say He is in you, living His own life in His own way in you, and just where you find it most difficult to see the next step, you will find God leading. Looking off unto Jesus, "the Author and Finisher of our faith." So I praise the Lord with you, that just now, as never before, you will know Him with you and in you. I shall be keen to know and have fellowship with you in whatever way the Lord leads you.

Affectionately yours, and with much sympathy,

Norman Grubb

P.S. I will send the book on to you, and please accept it as a gift.

~~~

Box A
Ft. Washington, Penna.
December 18, 1958

My Dear Kathleen,

I have only just heard that you have undergone a serious operation. So this is just to send my sympathy and love. How well I remember those wonderful days of fellowship we had together in your home—we never stopped talking!

It makes all the difference, doesn't it, when Christ is our Life for spirit and body. So you can relax on Him. He is your Life, no matter what the physical appearance may be; and when He lives His life in us, well, He just lives it in whatever condition He takes us through. It is JESUS ONLY.

My love to you, I shall soon be sending a circular with our more general news,

Ever yours affectionately,

Rubi

~~~

November 3, 1960

Dear Linton and Mrs. Woods:

I feel terrible to have arrived back yesterday from my six weeks' tour in the West to find that I have not written you about Mrs. Woods. I was caught up with big and useful changes which took place at our Annual Staff, also my preparation for the Western Tour and Mrs. Woods affairs. I have meant to write you and thought I had. So very sorry.

She went quietly Home after about three days in coma. The Lord had wonderfully provided. The lady staying in the house for the last month was both a nurse and a Christian. Her niece also was with her, and of course, Mrs. Morganweck continually over. She passed on without any special time of suffering — a glorious end to a soldier life for Christ in which she never faltered. Her mind was razor keen to the end.

At her request, we buried her body, (not herself) in a beautiful quiet spot under a glade of trees in the big Philadelphia burial grounds. I read the main part of the funeral service from the Anglican Prayer Book as she requested (and it is mostly Scripture), but I also took the opportunity of giving a word to the handful of relatives and friends about how she found her Lord and followed Him and I prayed as God

267

gave it me at the end. Some said it was the most beautiful service they had attended.

I enclose a letter which I prepared for friends.

Ever yours in Christ,

Norman

~~~

November 7, 1960

My dear Mr. Campbell,

I have heard from Arthur Davidson of the way the Lord has suddenly taken your loved one home. It will have been a great shock to you, and we do send our sympathy. Thank God your intimacy of fellowship with our perfect Lord all these years will mean that though your heart is so saddened, you can accept it as from His hand of love. How good, as the years pass, as we look back, not on sorrow so much as for wasted years as on the abundance of the grace of God which has been so manifested in yours and Mrs. Campbell's lives. How much we ourselves owe to your fellowship in Christ. So I know that you do not sorrow, thank God, "as those that have no hope" though the loss and shock will be so very real to you. His comfort will much more abound.

With our sympathies and love in Christ.

Yours in Him,

Norman P. Grubb

~~~

General Secretary,
Worldwide Evangelization Crusade.
January 25, 1961

Dear Mrs. Cooper:

It was good to hear from you today, and I was so glad to get your news. The Lord is entrusting you with some very heavy trials, so He is giving you special chances for faith and praise.

I was so glad to get the news of Jim. God is wise and good of taking us along our paths of disobedience to their ultimate ends, so as to open our eyes to the real results of sin. Romans 11:32. It is wonderful that He should have used this means to bring Jim within the reach of this minister, and then to open his eyes and heart. It is lovely that you had this word from him. I shall be glad to hear how he goes on, God willing, yet use the testimony of his dark days to the blessing of others.

Then you yourself have been through such deep waters physically. We mustn't condemn ourselves for having fear and shrinking. We are meant to feel like that as humans, so that we can be cast on God alone; and even when we move over to faith in Him, it by no means always means that the fear or sense of pressure goes. Often we have to walk in faith in our fears. But praise the Lord for the real touch He gave you, and the joy in your heart. You have taken His as your life for body as for spirit, and in this special condition, well then, we must learn to keep seeing Him only as our inner resurrection and life, although constantly we may be tempted to the visible appearance rather than the invisible fact—Christ our healer.

Let me hear from you again. I am on the move going around on meetings for some weeks now, and then over to England for three months but letters catch up with me. It is so good that the Lord, almost casually, gave us this chance of contact and fellowship with you.

Loving greetings to you both,

Yours in Christ,

Norman Grubb

~~~

October 25, 1968

Dear Mr. and Mrs. Johnson,

Your letter came today. No, I shall not be over on the west coast this year. I usually visit for a month's tour once a year, but will have to miss next year through going to England. So I fear we cannot arrange a meeting.

I think the great permanent fact is that we always have the perfect eternal healing in our union with the risen Christ, and the body is a temporary tabernacle. The Spirit often quickens that also, and there are wonderful physical healings, but as Paul says we do remain mortal in this life.

Sincerely yours in Christ,

Norman Grubb

~~~

1965

Dear Lanny,

I won't say anything more now except that I MARVEL at the way the light has shown like a midday sun in you. We can talk all over; but I see with you on this healing business. We are not bodies, but <u>spirits</u>. What matters what happens to our bodies, which are only temporary tabernacles (2 Cor. 5:1)? Death (the physical) was conquered long ago and has no sting. WE ARE in the eternal life and health NOW, and the point is to get folks off bothering about their bodily condition on to BEING in their eternal unity with HIM. You hit it right, and faith-healing is only second class deliverance, and very unpredictable. Spirit-healing is eternal and unconquerable.

No more now, not that your letter is not worth a lot more; it is pure gold, but we can talk soon. So leave time for us to talk as well as the other folks. Let's also be selfish!!

Loving you both,

Norman

~~~

1972

Dear Lanny,

I know no way except what I told you when with you—all our pressures of all kinds are sent and directed and willed by God Himself in love, because we have never found our eternal foundations until we get the habit by constant repetition of transferring our attention (believing) from what appears to be so real to us to the <u>real fact</u> of our being in Him fixed in eternal health. That does not mean that we do not take any medical helps, we should take all within our reach because all from Him; but despite any continuance of the problem and the sufferings or strains entailed, we keep our attention on our eternal unity with Him, and our perfect perfection, including the body, in Him, and declaring (as you say) the spoken word of faith that we <u>are</u> healed. I know no way but this. I do not look down to see how He manifests His healing. I go on believing, praising, and accepting my present condition (with any medical alleviation) as from Him; and He manifests the level of healing as and when He will.

Even when you have spoken the word of faith, I would never say that means that I cannot use the Dr. or medical advice as when you had a sore throat.

I fear it is a fact that the bible believing Christians, unless they have moved right over to a fixed recognition and realization of the union relationship, when by "the baptism of the Spirit" or whatever term they choose to use, it has become fixed in their consciousness that Christ is living their lives, they are Christ in their human forms and thus held by Him rather than holding on to Him, then their only substitute is fierce forms of legalism. That is why we have to face the fact that we are outsiders and go beyond the danger point and are not acceptable. Even in the end you cannot sit on the fence; and if you haven't jumped over, sooner or later shew up as being still on the legal side of the fence, though you will never admit it and use most of the deeper life clichés! And thus can quickly sense it when a teacher, even with a big name, is still playing around in the shallows.

Glad you are taking Joshua. Can get some good stuff out of him, though be sure to keep clear that he was on the self-effort side thru his early years with Moses; you can trace it in his words and acts up till Kadesh Barnea. But then he had his "crisis" experience and came over in spirit to his promised land. He was with the 11 spies in their unbelief, except for Caleb. That was his Waterloo—Num. 13. And after that, thru the book of Joshua, he operated in the Spirit in power and victory, though each time he had to walk through his primary human negative reaction and be brought thru to faith. He was called by Moses "a man in whom God is."

Well, here we are- home for two weeks, then off to Bermuda and the south for four weeks. Shall welcome any further news and letter.

Ever lovingly,

Norman

P.S. About your business boss, don't you think the point is that you accept yourself as fearing, having no confidence, not being natural leader; this is the very weakness through His strength is made perfect. In other words you go ahead affirming God as your sufficiency while feeling the opposite. And including fear of your job. Accept that also, but then say, "But I know and affirm You have that perfectly in hand".

~~~

Jan.2.78

My dear Joe,

Thank you for your recent newsletter with your personal note
added. So glad to get it and I follow closely your good outgoing letters in
CUMB. It is a rich ministry.

I didn't realise you had this cancer trouble till I got this letter. I
am so glad we see ourselves, even in the physical, as in His risen Life,
(where Rom. 8.11 operates) as you are experiencing. Faith is the victory,
where how we are inwardly "seeing" controls us - either unbelief
(negative seeing on the physical-material level) or positive seeing
which is He in love-action in the situation or condition! Even physical
healing may have self-interest as its base, but Paul's "that Christ may
be magnified whether by life or death" is true healing, isn't it, and it so
often, as you are experiencing, includes the physical "quickening".

But my real point in writing was to say I am pleased that besides the
"Everyman" with its widening world ministry, you have completed the
Memoirs. What God did by you those early "Ruanda" days was a special
operation of the Spirit with its permanent message for, and illustration
of, the way of the Spirit in what we call "revival" – not just in some
sudden outbreaks, which are precious, but as a living permanency in
the Body. That's why "Calvary Road" has had such world ministry, but
we should have the record in the words of the one God specially used
in it. What you sent me, as I said, has its place as the background of the
Spirit's early beginnings in you, but wasn't sufficient by itself, and I
didn't see how it could be prepared without reference to where it would
fit into the whole. So I sent it back at your request, and take it that it
arrived. So I believe it of the Lord, Joe, that you have this published.

So glad of your word on Yosiya, how well I remember him and
William coming to WEC and with a permanent touch on several lives.
And other things of much interest you mention. A friend pushed me
into doing tapes on lives of men of the Bible, and then later on several
of the epistles. I did see aspects of the same Spirit in these lives which
I don't think have been brought out enough, and in the epistles I was
seeing from the point of view of Him Who wrote them (the apostle being
"the pen of the Ready Writer"!), rather than from THE POINT OF VIEW
OF THE READER (sorry I slipped into caps - I'm no typist!!), and again I
think the Spirit has spoken. CLC may put them into print one day.

My Pauline remains physically weak, but her "Real Self" resting in
the Lord and lovingly cared for by one of our precious older Weccers,

while my daughter Pris looks after the home and me. So we are rich - and I can get around some. Will be over next June for WEC Leaders Conf. to which they still invite their Methuselah!

ever with my love and thanking God for you both,

Norman

~~~

Oct. 7. 81

Dear DeeDee,

Thank you for your loving card and word of sharing on Pauline's "homegoing". Jesus spoke of His death as "glorification" - John 12:28, 33. Also 13:31. Then He said we believers "never see death"- John 8:51 & 11:26. We have really died when we have entered by faith into our co-death with Him: 2 Cor. 5:14 & Col. 3:3 etc. So why talk about our body death as death? Paul called it something different in 2 Cor. 5: 1-4. And we are already glorified - John 17:22 and Rom. 8:30. Don't attempt to reason about it, just believe and accept it, and then use words of praise and faith. Of course we are already – in spirit – members of His glorified body and have already come to Mt. Sion – Heb. 12:22-24.

Of course death is not body-death, that is just Paul's 2 Cor. 5 sloughing off corruptible awaiting the incorruptible - 1 Cor. 15; and real death disappeared for us in Christ and we are with Him in Him in the resurrection.

So we are always praising, aren't we.

Lovingly, my dear

Norman

~~~

June 23

Rhonda dear,

Yours has reached me as I have just arrived home. Glad to keep touch with you, dear. Glad you liked the little SIMPLE brochure. Pick up from p.29 onward, love. <u>We can only shine or see light when there is dark, so your physical problems are GOD'S DARKNESS FOR YOU, DEAR, TO PRESS YOU INTO SEEING ONLY HIM thru it.</u> Accept your physical kidney weakness. Don't fight it or resist it. Don't fight fear or try to be rid of it or take condemnation because of it. Fear is faith reversed into believing evil. So accept the fact of your fears, and then say to yourself and God, "Those fears only come from my outer physical condition, but I am YOU AS ME, and what comes to me through physical deterioration, is PERFECT from YOU." So offer the "sacrifice" of praise - <u>praise when it hurts to praise</u>.

And, dear, HE is being greatly glorified while you praise Him, when it is difficult to praise. You are accumulating pure gold. See 1 Pete. 1:7 – that believing is your eternal gold! And, love, while you believe and praise against outer appearances you have "the treasures of darkness" (Is. 45:3). And read again those pages about trials and temptations.

So, love, you may continue to have fear, but then you don't fight it, but accept it and then swallow it by believing HIM.

Write again,

Loving you,

Norman

~~~

June 30

Dear Rhonda,

God is well establishing you in who you are, dear, nothing less than Christ in your form. So, love, if you have the gift of prophesy, good, you will use in freedom what He expresses by you and as you; but in the end there are many gifts, but ONLY ONE GIVER, and you are HE IN YOUR FORM. So it is all important just to BE who you are – He as you; and gifts are valuable, but secondary.

Also I'm glad about your kidney troubles. GOOD! I think the Spirit has been teaching you just to accept your body condition, for it is only clothing and be thankful for every healing touch in it such as you have now experienced in this kidney deliverance. Meanwhile we go as HE AS US, spirit joined to Spirit, and just thankfully use our soul-bodies as outer means of expression. You are right, love, to be ready for whatever the Lord had for you through the possible surgery etc, and as you freely accepted, He did His quickening. So we live, not bodily minded nor body-fussers, but Spirit expressors!

Loving you, dear, and always glad to hear from you,

Norman

~~~

June 29.

Betty dearest,

Your "pink one" has lovingly reached me here on my seven week tour with my granddaughter Sandie. Yours is precious, as usual, but your word on our precious Tommy specially touches me. Dear, you speak of "low grade malignancy" and then add "is disturbed by this recent discovery."

Dear, it may be that you just did not add the further vital word, that with this "soul disturbance" he is fully praising our perfect God for His perfect way including malignancy- for we hopefully like you and Tommy and me, have moved on to that maturer "seeing" of good and evil Paul speaks of in Heb 5:14 as good and again with Paul our one hope is that our Christ is "magnified" by us whether by life or death (Phil. 1:20).

You see I have that touch of concern that in earlier years Tommy "drank" from "total truth" when he "received" from me (as he then said) when I had a series with him at a Ormand Beach CFO. But I have felt since his Aqueduct days he has rather moved back to the "normal" teaching levels (including much on physical healing-and what's that worth??!!) and not gone forward in our radical total. And so with this present real "disturbance" you speak of. If you could have added, "Yes, real soul-disturbance (which we are all meant to get when a humanly unpleasant negative hits us), but combined with a perfect praising that this "evil" is part of God's perfection, to magnify Christ in him". And when we accept and praise for a shock and a negative, we live in 2 Cor. 4: 8-11 so that it is worked out in vs. 12!! And when the negative is received from <u>God</u>, we are free to add that often Ro. 8:11 is operative while we are steadily believing in ourselves in God's perfect health, and not believing in the appearance-physical illness. So now, I watch for this highest in our precious Tommy.

Rivers are flowing over here - travels producing births.

Lovingly, darling

Norman

~~~

Aug. 15. 86

My beloved Roy,

I only heard yesterday from one who is in your fellowship that
you told your folks on Aug. 3 that you have cancer of the liver, and she
added "apart from a miracle, he has no hope. But he's trusting the Lord
for a miracle." And she was saying how the Spirit is making her an
intercessor for you.

We have had such years of precious fellowship on our wonderful
depth reality-that we are not "just we" but actually Christ Himself in
our human forms, so we are really Christ, and ourselves by grace just
the lamp for His light. And what a total difference that makes when in
our sudden human shocks which temporarily pull us back to the fears
and reactions of our deceived independent selves, we move back again
to who we really ARE; Christ as us: and then we are able to say with Paul
about our mere temporary human 'clothing' of our bodies, his and our
"earnest expectation and my hope that in nothing shall I be ashamed,
but with all boldness as always, so now also Christ shall be magnified
in my body whether it be by life or by death". What a glorious word!

So now, dear Roy, it is with you (and in a way I might say with me
at 91) that I know that HE is being magnified in your dear self so that
what happens to my body (whether by life or death), is a mere detail;
and we actually daringly praise Him that you in this way, after your
years of faithful witness of our total Christ in us as us for us, are now
manifesting Him, and the folks seeing Christ and not a human physical
Roy, in your present humanly physically hopeless condition, and really
we do not care what happens to us physically so long as HE is seen in
us in His completeness, even as you have been shewing Him as total all
these wonderful years of ministry.

It is indeed radical but so wonderful when the 'heat' is really on,
just to know "I am not I, Roy or Norman, but I AM CHRIST AS ME" and
so what happens to my outer self is what Peter called "the sufferings of
<u>Christ</u>" in my form and as he said, then "the spirit of glory and God is
on us!"

So I am just with you in spirit and love, Roy, and faith for the one
fact that really matters to us, HE manifested in my mortal human body.
And then I also see and believe, when our physical condition is not what
occupies our concern, and in that sense, like Paul, we don't care except
that all see us as Christ in our condition, then so often that "quickening
Spirit" does do a quickening work in our body, because to us that is of

less importance than that HE IS being the Quickened Spirit in our inner selves and spirits and all see Him.

So I know this is that with you, Roy, and I bless you in this privilege of this sudden sharpest of trials and "tests of our believing", and that it is for us that "faith in trial' of I Pet. 1. which though "tried by fire" is more precious than gold that perisheth... Unto praise, honor and glory at the appearing of Jesus Christ".

So I am with you in love and faith for him magnified in you as in me when my turn comes, and maybe also that physical quickening.

Ever loving you,

Norman

I always think Jer. 17:8 is a great verse-"shall not see when heat cometh"!

~~~

July 21.88

Thank you, darling, for sparing the time to write. This fire-test, as about the surgery really burns thru to our total, where nothing less stands - so when we KNOW that we are only solely expressors of him as us, and all He is and does is perfect love, then we can stand in the storm of negative fears about surgery, and be looking for the "good things" as in Rom.8.32 in all that happens, and the "bad" is not in our vocabulary as per Rom.8.28. That is where the light so shines out to a world constantly knocked over by apparent outer tragedy, where we STAND UP STRAIGHT because we know it is HE standing in and as us! Not without human disturbed feelings, but they are just what gives us our place of "overcoming" - by faith-fact in place of soul feelings!

My, when the storms blow how we find out ours is TOTAL TRUTH. Wow! What grace! That is the Sermon on the Mount house which stands in the storm, built on THAT ROCK.

All love darling,

Norman

~~~

277

Ap.17.89

My dear Eldean & Merry,

Good to hear from you, as we no longer meet by those good visits when you always made me so at home. My travel days are done except when someone drives me to weekend Fellowship, so I don't expect to be with you again.

Merry dear, Paul tells us plainly our outer man perishes and so we get physical sufferings, I do with arthritis in one leg, the one wounded in the war, so I 'crawl' around with a stick, but like you, I have the Lord's keeping power and that is all that is promised us - plenty of tests and trials, but "more than conqueror" as Paul said, because we are not "just we", but the Living Christ in us and HE is our life, when outwardly we may appear done for. So we have no shame about our physical weaknesses but make our boast in the Lord's quickening power. You have suffered plenty, Merry dear, but on you go in the power of God! You seem busy on the new home and have strength enough for that. I am pretty useless at 93 except for my typewriter, and how I praise God for my faithful Sandie granddaughter who so wonderfully cares for Pris and me (and Pris helps in many ways too), while Sandie also does a computer sec. job.

So I will be hoping to see you again.

Ever with my love,

Norman

<div align="center">~~~</div>

May 21.

Thank you, dearest, for your letter. Yes, I heard about Ruth, I did not know her beyond a handshake at a meeting years ago! Praise God for PERFECTION, and that includes at least physical deterioration for us all (Paul's II Cor. 4:16,17). But we see the glory right thru what may be Christ being magnified in our body by <u>death </u>(Phil.2.20!). I'm expecting that "glory" any day, but the Spirit seems to keep me going! I'm sure Ruth will be praising! I was visiting another just suddenly struck by terminal cancer and also praising in pain.

Loving you, dear

Norman

<div align="center">~~~</div>

Norman dictated the following letter to Harriet Wearren, one of the women who took turns staying with Norman's beloved Granddaughter, Sandy, in her final months. It was written shortly before her "homegoing." Neither of them was able to go and speak to the other, although they were in the same house, because of their physical restrictions.

8/4/91

Darling,

It may be that we are both en route to our eternal perfection – the words of the last verse in Psalm 16, "Thou wilt show me the path of life: in Thy presence is fullness of joy; at Thy right hand there are pleasures for evermore."

I shall never forget, through eternity, of the miracle of the Holy Spirit as He revealed the love of Jesus to you, and caused you to come back home to us and give such loving care to your Grandmother and all of us and the thrill of your offer, under the guidance of the Spirit that you yourself would take care of our precious Pris or make the arrangements by which she is lovingly cared for and has her rooms to herself, just as she has here, when you and I are together where David said in Psalm 16 that with Jesus we live in pleasures for evermore.

All my love and I can never say what the Lord made you to be to me all these past years. You have been God's wonderful gift to me and to Pris.

All my love and we will be always together in Jesus.

Poppa

~~~

P.O. Box 1707
Fort Washington, Pa. 19034
January 1992

Dear Marcus and Jean,

I had a big and wonderful surprise, little knowing its outcome, about ten years ago when my granddaughter Sandra turned up one day to say that she'd had a sudden revelation of the love of Christ and would therefore like to join in the care of her dying grandmother. My precious Pauline, my wife, did die a little later, and then Sandra, whom

279

we all called Sandy, stayed on with us, and opened my eyes to her extraordinary efficiency in running our home affairs.

That soon came to putting everything into her hands, but much more than that, I couldn't drive a car, but Sandy had for years been an expert driver. So we moved into a travel plan which must have come to at least 200,000 miles all over this country, taking me to homes where I could share what I call the Total Truth, and this we did for about five years through all the states of the U.S.A. And we got bound together in closeness of heart so much.

Then came the shock about two years ago of Sandy's having symptoms of cancer of the lung, which later spread through her body. This meant that these last two years were under drastic hospital care for her, and finally to the great shock and sorrow of my life, because I have such a love for her, the cancer won its way and she died a few weeks ago. My joy in the midst of perhaps the greatest sorrow I've had is that I knew she was going to the Lord.

Several close women friends spent whole weeks here being with Sandy; and when she spoke to one of them about death, she raised both hands, not just one, because with me being 96, she was expecting that the Lord might even take us both about the same time.

But I'm still here, and have copies of a lovely last picture of Sandy, one of which I enclose for you with this letter, and with it also a copy of what I have named as: "My Last Word" under this title of Total Truth.

Now with this, I am thanking you for yourself sending us such a letter of grief and love, and this is my only way of thanking you, as my hands are now too crippled to write or type.

What an enormous difference, when I now see how those ten years ago, by some means the Holy Spirit laid hold of Sandy with this renewed love of Christ and turned her whole life around from a secretarial job to joining herself to Pauline, and then to me.

You can therefore realize what an open sorrow I have in her dying these few weeks ago, and yet my seeing that it is only another confirmation of Paul's Romans 8:28, when "all works for good." And that good meant this practical ten years of closest cooperation for myself with Sandy, which obviously just fit in with the Lord's foreseeing that He would take her to Himself after these years. Meanwhile, combined with our travels, including weeks she spent in England (she retained her British nationality), her loving spirit made her a multitude of devoted friends, whose sorrow is surely like mine, swallowed up in knowing her joy in being with the Lord.

So, I thought you might like this picture of her, our last of her until not too long a time for any of us when we shall be together in everlasting joy and fellowship with the Lord Jesus Christ.

Thank you for writing and for many various comments in your letter and about your own affairs, which I cannot answer as I would if I could still use my typewriter. So this is written in the culmination of much sorrow and yet the flood of joy which swallows that up, because it is for her as hopefully it is for each of you to whom I'm writing, our own way of passing from the "light affliction which is but for a moment" to the "exceeding and eternal weight of glory" (II Corinthians 4:17).

So I write this to you with much love and thankfulness, which includes my own precious Priscilla, as she and I are the only two left at home of the earthly family. I am so thankful for Danny, the son of my Dan, and Danny's wife, Marlene, and their family for welcoming Pris to go and live with them when the Lord takes me. It is always all things working together for good, isn't it, for those who love God — Father, Son and Spirit.

Lovingly,

Norman Grubb

෨ ෬

EXCERPTS

I just walk in the fact of God's health and don't put my believing in physical appearances, though they are there alright to appearance!

~~~

I advise go slowly on the question "breaking the appointment with death". Others have said that, and they've gone. It is better to stand by Scripture as Paul in Rom. 8.23-25, or Heb.9.27, or Phil. 1.20-23. It is a diversion to get folks hassling about the body. Who cares anyhow – whether physical healing or death? 2 Cor. 5.5 is good enough for most of us. Keep on the spiritual!

~~~

My precious Pauline keeps going by the secret she knows so well. "My strength is made perfect in weakness."

~~~

We see continual identification with Christ in His death, both in our initial entering in to our union relationship with Him, and then in all the "pressures" of daily living as a permanent daily sharing of His dyings whether in large or small ways, but it is to us the hidden background to living in resurrection reality in and as Him, and on into ascension. We see this is precisely the whole glory tone of Paul right thru his great intercession letter of II Cor, and particularly given us in the victory paragraph of 4.7-18. We go along with C.T. Studd (a great "sufferer" in human terms as I lived with him in Congo) who wrote "Take my life and let it be, a hidden cross revealing Thee". And you see, we have not been seeing the glory, as with Paul, but almost total emphasis on your sufferings, which make us regard them as not the true sharing in HIS SUFFERINGS. BUT RATHER flesh-sufferings, not "died to" as the Scriptures shew us to do in our union reality with Him.

~~~

It is good to know that we first accept sickness as "meant" by Him, then as we don't fight but praise, we have freedom in faith to affirm HIM as our health, and then often His quickening Spirit in us- Christ anyhow magnified "by life or death": as Paul said- for we have "died" long ago, what we now call death is only "expansion", as Paul said in 2 Cor. 5.1-8.

ॐ ೧

BOOKS & WRITINGS

Your book is going to be such a blessing. What the atom did for conventional weapons, your book will do to theology.

~~~

Whether listening to Norman or reading his books I've always found myself silently saying Yes! Yes! Yes! It was as tho after years of looking at copies of a great painting, I finally saw the original.

~~~

I have never met you and I doubt you will have ever heard of me, but I feel constrained to write to you. It is merely that I would like to thank you for the blessing and inspiration that I have had through your writings. It is not so much quite what I have learned, for the Lord has taken me somewhat the same way of faith, but I wish to bear record to the touch of God on the page. Many a time I have put the book down either to lift my hands in praise to the Lord, or to sit and weep before Him.   a Pastor

~~~

Some of my most highly prized treasures are books from your pen.   Paul E. Billheimer

~~~

We are greatly blessed in our perusal of your books. They are indeed—acres of diamonds...

ജ ഇ

July 12, 1956

My Dear Godfrey:

Eric Cosden has done a beautiful job. I enclose a tentative Foreword. If my facts are not always correct, will some J.E.B. expert kindly alter as you please. Don't bother to send me over any proposed alterations or additions, just put them in. On the other hand, if you folks feel that this Foreword does not exactly meet the need or fit the book, please be truly free to do as God leads, and replace it by an alternative. All that matters is that God's will is done and that He is glorified. He is certainly glorified in the story to the real exclusion of man, especially missionary man—a real exception in missionary literature! I am sending the MS back by registered sea mail.

I have inquired of C.L.C., but I knew they would not be encouraging on the sale of small missionary books by authors unknown in U.S.A. They find no market for them of any size at present. Probably they will handle a few copies, but not a special edition.

The same about THE REWARD OF FAITH. They have some on stock, and they go slowly, but it would not justify them ordering a larger number. Spiritual life books are the best sellers from Britain, or biographies people know in U.S.A., or that have something special that catch their attention, but I am so glad that it is reaching the end of its third edition. That is good, and I feel glad that I have a little hand in introducing you to Lutterworth. I have not been so successful over J.D. Drysdale, which is really an autobiography. I knew I was taking a risk, and did it out of love and reverence for this memory, but for the first time I fear I have let Lutterworth down.

Ever yours affectionately,

Norman

~~~

September 11, 1958

Dear Brother Sternall:

I read through the articles. You reach to the heart of things with your emphasis on the Christ-in-you life. Your emphasis on "the enabling command" of God is really good and illuminating. I have not seen that truth put so concisely before, differentiating between a command responded to by the flesh or Spirit.

When it comes to publication in book form, I think is a different matter. I know there are preachers these days who just plunk a hand full of sermons in between two covers; but that doesn't really make a book. A book is a living unity, and must be written with a purposeful continuity from first chapter to last. It must have a clear thread of teaching running through it. You certainly have rich material, but have you anything which builds into a book? There are a good many books on the deepening of the spiritual life, and so another one must have something original about its emphasis and presentation, such as your "enabling command" article. Also I note that you have the same bad habit as myself. You don't lighten your text with illustrations–putting windows in the walls! Nor do I. I like just to concentrate on the meat and matter of my message; but I am sure it makes it heavier and less readable for the average reader, who isn't trained to think inductively into a subject.

That's about all I can say for the moment. Perhaps we can get a chance to talk. I think it would be difficult to get someone to rewrite your material. Nor do I really see why it needs it. The style is good enough; it is just the matter of having a sufficiently concentrated and expounded message to justify a book.

Sincerely yours in Christ,

Norman Grubb

~~~

October 1, 1958

Dear Dr. Henry:

I have been tremendously pleased with <u>CHRISTIANITY TODAY</u>. I have longed, in England, for a paper of that type which combined scholarship with spirituality and loyalty to the Scriptures. I feel you just "hit it," and am glad to note that you have many links across the ocean. I pass my copy on to one of our conservative Bible Colleges in England, of which I am a Committee member–the All Nations Bible College.

I am sending you under separate cover a little book just out–THE DEEP THINGS OF GOD. It is more of the devotional than academic type, but I sought to think things through a bit more to their foundations.

I know your British correspondent, <u>John Pollock</u>, very well; and I am also interested to see that G.W. Bromley had joined the Fuller Staff.

He was one of the best conservative theologians in Britain, and his contributions to THE LIFE OF FAITH were always good.

God continue to bless your ministry.

Sincerely yours in Christ,

Norman Grubb

~~~

November 4, 1958

My dear Samuel [Howells]:

I have now got the answer from Martin Lewis of Lutterworth. [RE: Rees Howells Intercessor] I am so glad that we have this friendly personal contact, so that we can tackle points like this, "unofficially."

The point Lewis makes is that normally they would not be reprinting because the sales have "dried up" in Britain. But because of close affiliations, they do not act towards us simply as a business, but always inquire first whether we want to continue a book for our own purposes. C.L.C. here has a steady sale for it, so they answered Lewis ordering another 1,000. (I have no doubt that we shall need a number more 1,000s in due course for sales here. It is amazing how I meet with folks, sometimes churches of them, who have been laid hold on by the book.)

I am sorry for the rise in price, because it is bad for England, although I don't think it will make too much difference over here. I say we must keep the book going, there is no other like it in its ministry, and so many say that of it.

So I don't think we need to regard it that Lutterworth is putting anything over us, but rather that they are doing a kindness in continuing to produce small editions, when a merely worldly firm would shut down on it. So I will hope to hear from you in due course, and then get touch again with Lutterworth.

Just back from a grand month's tour.

Much love,

Ever yours,

Norman

~~~

Feb. 7.1960

My dear Nan:

I am soon after you!! It was lovely having the closer fellowship with you. I did enjoy it and thank God for it. Hope you had a good time singing today, and maybe at the WEC meeting.

But my question is this. The friends who mimeographed that "Key" talk I gave you, now tell me they have another 100 copies I may have, and that clears them out. They then say they will also send me the stencils.

Now I very daringly ask you, on the basis of your loving offer, whether you think it could be possible or worthwhile to send you the stencils, if you could make more copies. If you could, of course, I will be responsible for the cost of the paper and anything else. We could also staple them together down here.

Anyhow I thought I would write and ask you. Of course I will understand if you do not feel free from the Lord to do this, or if it really is more work than you should undertake, because you have plenty already with your singing engagements.

One friend has asked for 500! That's a mouthful and we could persuade her to take less, and she offered to cover the expense (though I told her the Lord would see to that); and then there are others coming in.

Well, there it is. I love you all three in Christ anyhow, whether you can do this or not!!

your brother in Christ,

Norman

~~~

March 2, 1960

My dear Samuel:

Thank you ever so much for your good letter. It is always refreshing to hear of the Lord's working with you. So many ask me is the College still going, and how it is going, and it is a great joy to be able to testify to them that you have the same Lord as your Father! It is amazing how the book goes over here. Again and again people come to tell me that they have had nothing to touch it in all their lives. One of the members of Dr. Ockenga's spoke to me a few days ago, and that is about the leading evangelical church in the country, saying that he had never read anything like it before and his life had been revolutionized. That is the constant testimony. Sometimes I meet whole groups of people to whom

God has been speaking. It is really wonderful. It just goes on its own impetus over here. I still believe that it has a never-dying value, and absolutely unique as a testimony to the Holy Spirit in a life.

How much I miss my hoped-for visit to Britain this spring, and a day or two with you. What refreshing times we have had in the past. I shall never forget the days of doing the book with Mary, and the daily walks you would take with me and our fellowship together. Most precious. We are indeed bound in heart together.

Just back from the Washington Conference of the International Christian Leadership. I think I sent you a copy of the program. It capped everything this year. There were about 900 at the Presidential Breakfast, and my table, being No. 10 out of 120, was just beneath the dais where the President and speakers were. The great point was the ringing testimonies of the grace of God that the speakers gave. There was a famous Metropolitan singer who sang "How Great Thou Art", but before he sang, he said he wanted everybody to know that he was regenerated by the grace of God through our Lord Jesus Christ, and that you can't counterfeit that joy. Then others followed, each giving testimonies to their changed life through Christ, and one of the best was an M.P. from England who flew over for the occasion, Mr. Cordle. His testimony was excellent, and he turned to the President and told him the greatest ambassador this country has ever sent in our generation across the waters was Billy Graham. So indeed, that great crowd of Cabinet, Senators and Congressmen got the pure Gospel of the Lord Jesus Christ at that meeting. I have enjoyed writing Abram Vereide's life. It will be quite short and won't have, of course, the heights and depths of the great life, but it will have a living and unusual testimony through the types of people he contacts.

I am off now for a six weeks tour in the South. The trouble is that we can't begin to take the opportunities that are open. I will be sending a circular in a few days with some of our general news.

My warmest love to you and your dear Mother, as well as to all the beloved College-ites. I can just see you crowded together in the dining room on that Christmas evening, and I can see ourselves with your dear Father singing "By and By We Will See the King."

Ever yours affectionately,

Norman

~~~

April 12, 1960

Dear Mr. Michael:

Of course I am delighted to hear that you are planning a pocket book edition of "Mit Studd im Kongo." We have just heard from the Moody Press here that they are suggesting doing the same in an English edition.

I think you will know that the copyright of the book belongs to Lutterworth Press, 4 Bouverie Street, London EC, and you will need to get their permission.

With reference to the questions you asked me. Most certainly and make any shortenings you feel right. I know you only publish books for the glory of God, and that therefore any alterations will be what you think to be best, so that the reading public may meet Christ through its pages.

Yes, I will be glad to add a new chapter on the development of the work in Africa but it would help me if you could give me some idea of the number of words you would wish, and by what date you would like to have it. I have, like most of us, a pretty crowded program, but I will make time when I know your dateline.

Thanking God that He has put it on your heart to do this.

Sincerely yours in Christ,

Norman Grubb

~~~

July 11, 1960

Dear Mr. Robertson,

Our beloved mutual friend, Dr. Jackson, has sent me on your letter. Thank you for it, and it is good to hear that the Lord has blessed this little pamphlet "The Key."

How whole-heartedly I agree with you that none of God's servants have a right to copyright what they write, because if it is a word from God. He is the Writer, not they! We have trouble with books, because the publisher demands the copyright, but with pamphlets like these, we are free.

Most certainly do as you are led about printing in smaller form. If you do do this, then I will be most grateful to know, and to be able to order and buy some from you. The Christian Life Magazine is going to publish it in two sections, and that will make a demand. A friend had already mimeographed 1000 copies. But a large number of these are gone.

Yes indeed, I remember our previous correspondence.

Sincerely yours in Christ,

Norman Grubb

~~~

August 5, 1960

Dear Brother,

I couldn't make out your signature, but I'm sure I'm safe in calling you a brother in Christ!

Here with the extra chapter for "Mit Studd im Kongo," be free to use it as you like.

Sincerely yours in Christ,

Norman Grubb

~~~

Sept.3.60

My dear Irv,

Many thanks for yours. You will have a great time at Elgin House.

I am writing at once because I had not forgotten your suggestion of a chapter out of the A.V. book for the Magazine. But the only complete copy of the MS is now being inspected by Fleming Revells. The only other two copies (incomplete) are with A.V. and Marian Johnson. In addition to that, I would find it hard to know what chapter to choose! I would be very glad, when I get the MS back, to get some idea from you of what you would think suitable - such as maybe the Seattle chapter, and very glad for you to have it. I am all for ICL-FAW interpenetration! We can discuss it further at Princeton. Christian Life wants an article from me on AV & ICL, but I am leaving that too until the book is finally in the hands of the publishers.

Much looking forward to our meeting. I will come by train. You mention meeting me at Trenton. That is kind of you. I remember coming before to Princeton. So I will probably look up a train that takes me there and let you know.

ever yours,

Norman

~~~

290

November 7, 1960

Dear Joan,

It was just great to see so much of you and the other friends. I had hoped to get perhaps one glimpse and a little fellowship with you, but by no means all I got!

Herewith that heretical document you asked for–The Dark and Light Principle which I sent under separate cover. I only hope I have your address right.

The price of the Article is that you write later and talk to me about it! I would anyhow like to keep up an occasional correspondence with you.

Your brother in Christ,

Norman

~~~

January 20, 1961

My dear Bob:

Zondervan's have just accepted the Vereide manuscript, and I am working on a few final additions, so that the MS will be in their hands in about 2 weeks. Vereide plans to have some printed notification ready for their February Conference though it may be that publication had now better wait until the summer. I don't know about that. But if you want something on Vereide, I don't know what your right procedure is. Do you get permission from Zondervan's and then do you want yourselves to run through the MS and select, or will you wish me to write something or what? One difficulty is that MS has been rather built in sections (as it passed through the hands of critics) and I haven't got a complete second copy.

I heard, by the way, yesterday from Washington that Billy Graham had just been talking to Vereide and telling him that he had a wonderful six hours with the new President, and that Kennedy asked him to be an advisor to him, and that Kennedy is coming to the President's Breakfast on February 9th when Billy is to be the chief speaker. Of course you keep that under your hat!

I don't think you have ever got anything yet, have you, on that remarkable work of the Spirit connected with Ruanda. I visited there when last in Africa. To my mind it is the most permanent form of revival I have seen, and you will know some of the men connected with it who have been used world wide-Roy Hession, Dr. Joe Church (through whom it started), William Nagenda (the African).

Trace it down, and you find that a great many of the movings of the Spirit on mission fields have been sparked off by the visits of some of these.

God's blessing.

Ever yours,

Norman

~~~

February 6, 1961

Dear Brother Young:

Thank you for your letter which has been passed to me. Of course you are welcome to go ahead printing "Throne Life."

A friend in Los Angeles printed some thousands a few years back. These have run out and I am occasionally asked for some, but have none; so I would be grateful when you print if you could spare me a packet of them.

God's continued blessing. I am getting into print this year a book called "God Unlimited" which will deal in more detail with this whole subject.

Sincerely yours in Christ,

Norman Grubb

~~~

February 14, 1961

My dear Abram:

Thank you ever so much for allowing me once again to be with you for those magnificent meetings, and for giving me the lovely room in your hotel. When one sees the rising tide, it makes it pretty sure that we shall not have difficulty in getting the biography out.

Could I trouble you to pass the following on to someone who could kindly supply me with these:-

1. All the photos taken of you with the President and Billy, all of just you and the President so that we can make a choice.

2. I shall have to ask for the loan of that signed photo of you with General Grunther on the wall in the office. I will preserve it carefully but we shall need the original.

3. Is it possible to obtain from one of the newspapers (New York Times had it and doubtless many others) an original of the picture of Billy and the President, etc. in prayer?

4. Can I have a copy of anything put into the Congressional Record which would give the speeches of the Pres & V P from which I extract a statement or two?

5. If you have a copy of the Herald Tribune with the article by David Lawrence, I would like to borrow that also.

Sorry to bother you with all these things, but I leave for Texas tomorrow for two weeks; then I only come back for four days at the beginning of March when I see Marian again and run over the MS for the last time-then to Zondervan's so I haven't much time to spare.

Perhaps you could kindly pass this to someone who could see to these things and send me.

Ever yours affectionately,

Norman

~~~

April 4, 1961

Dear Olive:

Thank you for your letter with this loving invitation to undertake such a privilege as your Mother's life story. I just don't see how it could be unless the Lord opened quite an unusual door. Besides, the two books just coming out, one on the life of Abram Vereide with whom I work in close fellowship and who is so greatly used ministering to the Senators and Congressmen and other national leaders, and the other a book on my own line called "God Unlimited". I have also been asked to write one on our beloved friend, Eva Stuart-Watt, who worked among the down and outs in Ireland and was in close link with us, but I doubt whether I shall get to that one. It is a question of one of C.T. Studd's quotations, and that seems far distant also! I would love to accept your offer. I love to bring out a book which points to Christ. God has given me no gift of brilliant writing, but I do enjoy gathering together and presenting the richness of the Christ life in and through people. That is up my street. But this is the situation. It could not be done unless I paid you a visit and I see no prospects of that unless God opens quite an unexpected door. So I can only say that you had better be looking to God for the one of His choice and moving in to others with the invitation if God leads you to others. Meanwhile, if God does the unexpected and the indication is plain, you may know that it will be an honor for me to do it. I love you in Christ and what you are doing ever since God gave us that peculiar bond of fellowship and understanding in the visits I paid to you those days. My feeling of union in Christ with you has never altered since then.

So let me hear further from you about any guidance God gives you. My love in Christ,

Ever yours,

Norman

~~~

December 14, 1962

My dear Steve:

Many thanks for yours. I could not answer before as I have only just returned from a tour. The C.L.C. tell me they have sent off the Pember book. Please accept it as a very small gift, but it comes with much love.

I laughed at your reaction to the "Law of Faith" appendix! Maybe you would like to see a mimeographed manuscript which I share with an inner circle. The appendix was really a shortened form of this which I refer to as "The Dark and Light Principle." I have a few copies left, and can send you one, but I expect you have enough to go on with Pember.

I wish I could see you again. I always enjoy fellowship with you. Our hearts and minds meet. I have to go up to Gray Ledges to finalize the 1963 program. I wish I could come down through you, but I doubt if I can. I will let you know if I can.

I wonder if you had the talk with the Norwegian brother-and got his knots untied?? My love to you and Bertha.

Ever yours in Christ,

Norman

~~~

February 16, 1967

Dear Neil:

Ma Rubi tells me that she talked with you about an article called, "The Intercessors" published in World Vision Magazine and that you said you might consider printing it as a booklet.

I have now received permission from World Vision for us to do this, if we're led to-adding the credit line: "Copyright 1966 by World Vision Magazine. Reprinted by permission."

Now I don't know how in your huge load of work you could ever really get down to this, but anyhow I send you this kind permission from them.

Love to you and all blessing.

Ever yours,

Rubi

~~~

April 17, 1967

Dear Brother Frank:

It is very kind of your sister to send me this gift for the books. Please thank her for me. I shall soon be starting a series of visits both to the south and the Midwest which will take me into July, and it is during the visits that I find most opportunities for giving the books.

I visited Washington last week and met a lady whom I have not met before who had been reading, "Spontaneous You" several times. She has close connections through her husband with the Senate and House of Representatives, and is one of the only two who is not a wife of one or the other, but is free to attend the weekly Bible and Prayer Meetings of the Senators and Congressmen's wives. She has asked me to autograph a hundred copies and send them to her for them, though in this case, she's able to pay for them herself.

I've always taken the 144,000 to represent the redeemed because Paul calls us "The Israel of God".

Warmest greetings, and again thanking your sister so much.

Yours in Christ,

Norman Grubb

~~~

295

June 10, 1967

My dear Brother Frank:

I've just come home for a few days and found your letter here, with this further generous gift of $12.00. Thank you again ever so much.

I was able to give half a dozen copies of "The Spontaneous You" and several Rees Howells to various folks as God led, and I told each that this was a gift from the Lord made possible by a brother in Christ. A Rees Howells was to a live Baptist minister in Memphis whom I saw greedily looking through it. A "Spontaneous You" was to a business man in Hendersonville, N.C. who leads teams of witness with much blessing to churches. He immediately ordered several signed copies of "God Unlimited" for some of his friends, so it has been wonderful to be free to give these here and there when the Lord showed they were the right people. Another was to a minister of an independent church in Memphis.

These have been thrilling days in seeing the Lord work miracles again for Israel equal to the Old Testament. I'm so thankful that both USA and Britain have no hesitation in publicly siding with Israel. Both our nations through the years have been blessed of God because they have been kind to His people. God has all these things nicely in hand, hasn't He?

Ever yours,

Norman Grubb

~~~

July 5, 1968

Dear Brother David:

Thank you for your letter about the "True Discipleship" booklet. C.L.C. says it is out of print, and is not being reprinted. But certainly you are welcome to duplicate it.

I have not any other booklet just on this line. I enclose one that a friend prints, and God has blessed to many - "Throne Life".

Then there is another called "The Key to Everything" of which I have a number in mimeographed form and would send them to you for distribution, if that would be of help. Again it is a different type of message, and I enclose a copy.

Sincerely yours in Christ,

Norman P. Grubb

~~~

Till Aug 28
c/o Mrs. Aymar Johnson
Box 144
E. Islip, New York 11730
July 30, 1968

Dear Mr. Foxell,

You may remember our interchange of letters towards the end of last year on a possible MS of my "Memoirs." I was not able to get it to you then by your February date, and had to put off its completion till now.

But I now have it done and am writing again to ask whether you will consider it, and if I shall send it.

It is rather longer than I like-at a rough calculation around 70,000. Of course, I know it will only have local interest and sale; but I think, with my WEC friends and readers in England-not too many, but with my larger reader public here, at least while I am still able to get around on my meetings tours, and I hope to for another year or two, I could guarantee a first small edition and maybe one impression of a few thousands, at least enough to cover expenses.

Probably you are on vacation, as I am-where I have had the quiet enough to complete it; but I will await word from you and then send if you wish. I have only the one completed copy, not as tidy as I would like, but I have sought to make each word legible. I plan to call it "When God Takes Hold." I don't think it will need pictures beyond maybe one as a frontispiece. And would it not, if you accept if, be better just as a paper back of that rather stout kind like the good production of the paper back Rees Howells? That would keep the buying price down.

With kind regards and best wishes,
Yours sincerely,

Norman P. Grubb

~~~

September 30, 1968

My dear Cecil:

I don't remember whether it was you who asked for a photo for the Lifestory, so please excuse if I'm sending them wrongly to you.

I'm never great on this photo business, but I enclose one in a cardboard frame with my hand on my chin, which Pauline and I suggest for a frontispiece. I have not the original and the print appears a bit light, but is all I have.

Then there is a print of a portrait of me painted by a friend of mine who is a portrait painter, James E. Seward of Cleveland. His name is on the back of the photo. It is the one with me in an open shirt. We suggested that this might be suitable for the back of the dust cover.

I send one more–a smaller photo taken in York, England when I was last over, and this might be an alternative for frontispiece in place of the one with my hand on the chin.

Any advice on these? I should think that is all that is necessary for the book, isn't it?

Pauline asked me to ask if we can have the one with the hand on the chin back again in due course as it is the only one she has.

Ever yours sincerely,

Norman

~~~

Oct.1.70

My dear Joe [Church],

I don't know whether I am on my head or feet when I return today from a short tour and find your letter here. I can hardly believe it. I suppose I ought to give time to wait on God, but somehow I get used to jumping right in when I sense the freedom and seal of the Spirit. Joe, I would <u>love</u> this, but it is quite another matter whether really I would be God's choice to do it along with you. It does seem that God has given me a good many opportunities in putting together what He has been doing through various lives–C.T.S., and I loved doing Rees Howells (which folk don't like too well in Britain, but makes an enormous and continuous impact on lives here), and then Abraham Vereide, founder of the Presidential Prayer Breakfasts, and dear Alfred Buxton, Edith Moules, etc. It seems just to be along my line (and God seems to have sealed it) to catch on to what God has done through other lives, and specially when I am able to use and quote much of their own material and own words; and I usually find what warms my heart warms other folks! Then with that comes, as I think you know, the deep conviction which has never left me that God gave you to be the channel for one of His outstanding movings of the Spirit in our generation with it own special ways in which He has worked and which God has then used all over the world, including to me and WEC and CLC.

But there are snags. The first is the time. I have booked, as I usually do, tours which take me through next April. Actually, I could cut any of these out, but don't wish to if possible. I had left my programme open after April with no engagements (except one week at end July), and was watching to see what the Lord might have including possibly a visit to England.

So really I could consider it with you for next summer, but is that leaving it too late? I note you are with Hodder & Stoughton, good, but I would be 100% against them being allowed to touch any way in which God led us to present what He has been doing. That is why I have liked Lutterworth-not so good as Hodder for publicity and sales, doubtless, but they have never once raised a question on even a sentence of what I have submitted for publication! But maybe Hodder to whom you are now obligated would not wish so long a delay.

Then further, if this was to be of the Lord, Joe, finance doesn't enter into it. Let the Lord have all that comes through it and I certainly would only wish to attempt it in full collaboration with you and nothing published which had not your OK, or was actually a kind of combined production.

Then finally if there is anything of the Lord in this, I should somehow have to be able to get at all the material written or otherwise that you could supply, including, I suppose, most important, these "Wesley Journals."

Well, let's keep batting this along to see what God really says; but I only say I would count it the highest honour. Here surely lies a record which once again would be a stream of blessing to thousands.

So that's all I'll say at the moment. How wonderful to be brought to this closer touch with you after all these years. Yes, I am always thankful for CUMB, Alan and John E., and always miss Clarence.

My love to you and Decie from Pauline and myself,
ever affectionately,

Norman

~~~

June 23.71

My dear Bill,
You overwhelm me when you write, and I do appreciate your finding the time to do it. Of course, it is a thrill to me when I know we so flow

together in what we convincedly see to be God's truth (or at least the tiny facts that's shone to into us), and when you say these things of the books "A wealth in each sentence," and "truth has its own way of setting us free". Well, it does seem like that and I get many evidences of it. Of course, this type of book can never be the "popular" one, I have no gift of the kind of illustrations which take the weight off and make it more readable for many; but blessings on those who have, and each of us cobblers stick to our own last! I really would like to write a little more on a few aspects coming even more strongly to me, such as on the purposed unity of the universe, and exactly where and why "evil" fits, and so on. Only underlining what I am saying. I have been at home this month, thru not going to England, and of course, there is a good daily flow of mail and many letters take time (and I love it). I did even start a sheet of MS, but dropped it. Don't think the time has come, or I'm too lazy! But I do know things need to be said which others don't say. I say practically nothing original; only what I pick up from some favorite sources, but I seem to have the gift of being able to digest it and put it in readable terms and maybe add a little spot here and there.

And while we are on the books, Bill, there is no need for you to have to pay CLC prices. They always give me 40% off, and if I know what you would like, I can order and send to you. So please don't get involved in such expenses again. Send me a line of any you might like.

Yes, by the way, you are right-CTS and Rees Howells never lose their cutting edge. They are far more than mere biographies.

Much love, dear friend, you are a constant thrill, blessing and encouragement to me.

Norman

~~~

Jan.26.75

My dear Joe,

It is good to be in correspondence with you again. I much enjoyed a time I had with Roy here, and it was he who again brought up the matter of your Memoirs.

I have not answered your first letter of Jan. 7 because you told me to await a further one with copy of yours to Edwin.

Now I think some things need clearing. First, my impression is that your earlier pages (60), which is really autobiography on your earlier life, Cambridge, CICCU, etc., can only be effective as the first part of the full story of the movings of the Spirit in which God gave you such a vital part.

This, as you say, is already autobiography. Actually the way God has lead me in producing various lives such as C.T. Studd, Rees Howells, several of our own WEC folk such as Edith Moules, also Alfred Buxton, and the founder of the International Christian Leadership (Presidential Prayer Breakfasts and the hundreds of such breakfasts now all over this country) Abraham Vereide has always been to let the subject of the book do all the talking possible in his own words, and I being really merely a connecting link, with comments and clarifying explanations here & there, and God seems to have blessed it this way. So your earlier years pages should only need some "editing" of that kind.

But then you also add to this the suggestion of something more written on those early Cambridge-CICCU days. But as a fact, Joe, I would have little to say on this, because my own part in it which God did graciously give and seal with His Spirit is highly individualistic, really only my own personal experiences of witness and some fruitfulness which did lead on to the vision of a world IVF. But I was actually only at Cambridge Jan.-Dec. 1919, supposedly for their short pass degree they handed out on a platter to those who were going up before the war and then joined the army–and I spent more of those months in witnessing than in studying, because a Cambridge Pass-Degree did not take a monumental amount of study, especially as I didn't like my liberal Theo. lecturer, though I heard later he found Christ! Godfrey was CICCU Pres. then and Clifford Martin took on from me as Sec. when I left in Dec. for Congo, and Murray was next Pres. So you see I would actually have very little to add, certainly not enough for a book. Also we must remember that God's working in revival those days, and with the CICCU-IVF since are not precisely the same emphasis on the Blood in brokenness, cleansing and witness which God so used in the African Revival.

So I would not think, Joe, there was sufficient in your memoirs of your early years, moving on to Cambridge days, for a manuscript in itself, except as a vital opening part of all that God would give us through your whole Memoirs.

Another point I would add, however, is this. I note you speak of the MS which you call "rather historical" written for the Makerere; and then elsewhere you speak of your "Memoirs." I take it these are not the same, but the former based on the latter. But surely the Memoirs are what is vital. My original thought was to see to what extent they could be prepared or abridged (with as little change as possible) for the authentic history of those days. Now does it mean you have your Memoirs as quite separate from this "Historical" MS?

I would also like to raise this. God has given Edwin a specific ministry in the church of our day with his presentations of the workings of the Spirit in Revival through the whole history of the church. This is his "area." But I would rather feel his interest in preparing any of yours for publication would be just to fit in to his larger interest in revival in general. And might that not take away from concentrating on the unique story and message God has for us all in what God specifically did through you all in Africa (and including, as you say, your further world journeys?)

So that is how I see things at present, Joe. I just wanted to be ready if by any means I could help you to share with the church what God did and does as given you to see it-I being just "the voice" for the one speaking the real word. (And incidentally, I don't go along with those who say there might be too much Joe Church in what you wrote. What God does has always to be through His Paul, Moses etc., but HE is seen magnified by them!)

I shall love to see you if I come in the Spring, (though we shall be corresponding before then!) But I am waiting to see if I feel I can leave Pauline to cross the ocean, and she has been through a rough time, the Lord wonderfully bringing her through, but is still weak and feels my absences more these times, when she had so willingly given me through the years. Thank you so much for offering me to come and be with you.

Ever with my love and the Lord will take us all His way,

Affectionately and to Decie,

Norman

~~~

Dec. 26.77

My dear Wallace, Frances, & Marian,

I have now read through all the material, letters, etc. you gave me, Wallace, and this is what I want to say:

First, I am confronted with a surprise blank spot which I think makes any going forward impossible-and it is this. I did not look at the copies of the tapes we made together, Wallace, until I took them out of their envelope three days ago and now I find they are only copies of our talks about your involvements in Europe, but those first vital tapes on your own early experiences, and the Lord's dealings with you are not there! Supposedly not transcribed. And though, you do give some fragmentary accounts among your set of eight or so "set and valuable talks," those are nothing like sufficient to build your life story on. I think it would be impossible to proceed without the transcript of those tapes–which were your real warm self. So that at present, it seems to me, makes it impossible to proceed.

But, having first said that, I now want to say that I find <u>much</u> very moving and of value to be extracted (with some difficulty) from the letters and records. I only see one possible way in which something could be put together, (at least as I could do it), and that as the very personal record of God's ways with you, Wallace, personally, and what He has done by you in ICL ministry.

Some things much move me. There is your own continued insistence and exposure of your personal sense of weakness, inability, often failure & fears, really a down-grading of yourself which has its beauty (when I am weak...") and from my personal outlook too little bold consciousness of your sufficiency in God, but that's as I see it. But with that, and perhaps because of it, an <u>enormous</u> and beautiful and God-glorifying appreciation of <u>others</u>. You openly talk of yourself as a behind and not front man, and with that a constant underlining and appreciation of what Marian is to you and Frances personally in your ministry, and indeed as the lynch-pin of the whole ICL through the years (and indeed I love your letters to her which give by far the greatest human insights in to yourself in the ministry, but also your freedom in challenging her when you feel she is tempted to pull back from full backing of ICC through disappointment or through diversion into some over-emphasized aspects of the ways of the Spirit.)

But then, more important than your relationships to one and another, there is this remarkable love of men you have in your desire to see Christ as a reality in their lives, which I think is the outstanding characteristic of the Spirit in you and that includes your marvelous love-understanding, indeed almost love-affair you have with the French, with your constant almost unique appreciation for Minister Michelet almost like a European Abram. But not only this, you have a love-understanding love approach to all men, including those of other faiths like Islam, which appeals to me greatly as a missionary, than the bash-at-em attitude we missionaries and "soul-winners" usually have, majoring on winning confidence with those you are in touch with before presenting a flat-in-the-face "gospel challenge"–which I think results in never any letting down by you of the only saving gospel in Jesus Christ, yet rather a hopeful search for and emphasis upon any indications that these important men you are in touch with, when Christians already have some faith which needs encouragement-making your emphasis more the up building of incipient faith than straight "evangelism."

I think also you shew much hopefulness in your British contacts and certain definite backings from certain leading men such as George Thomas, Caldecote, Greenwood, et al. Indeed, all told, I think it wonderful what response you shew so many evidences of in leading men, not only of France & Britain (France always being your favorite), but in many other countries.

You touch also on the return to Abram's original simple approach, both in your own convictions and in Doug's, though I don't get it clear enough to put into words what the basic change of attitude is from ICL to "Fellowship Foundation," but I haven't studied your own outline of ICL history (which is very small print), but which I think you originally put together with a possible view of publication, which in brief reading gives me more an impression for a document for internal use than for public reading, but of course, I would need to go through.

So my present position is this-that anyhow I could approach nothing without your early-life tape that even then it would really be a chore, but possible, to extract from the papers & correspondence a workable presentation of how God has prepared, led and used you in European ICL (I have at present just lined in red for my own use a heap of remarks that to me have life and insight in them, especially in your Marian letters, and they certainly would not easily be brought together, but I guess could be.) Also I note that in the opinion of Europeans (or maybe all?) the AV life did not sufficiently portray his battles and struggles rather than successes. There is more of that in your material, but I don't know whether I could adequately bring it out. Again I would say it would have to be more a personal life account than an overall ICL "history," and therefore more I take it of a local appeal.

That brings me finally to my own position. I have not been able to get to it at all till a few days ago. I am now at home for parts of Jan-Feb (with gaps of a week away on meetings here & there). Then in Feb. I have a program which takes me right through December of the coming year, and indeed, really over March 1979. So with the present lack of that first tape, it doesn't seem that I can do anything now (I always find I have to build from the bottom up.) So it looks again as if there must be delay, and I don't know how it would fit in my program, but I would say something is still possible of a more personal nature which has a living word and blessing in it, and so I would like to leave it open and still see how the Lord leads.

Much love to you, I'm sending a copy of this both to yourselves, Wallace & Frances, and to our loved Marian.

lovingly,

Norman

~~~

Bristol

July 6.81

Dear Les,

I am so sorry to miss seeing you, and Ken Adams also said you had a copy of his MS for me, but our plans have been somewhat disrupted by the breakdown of the car lent us. I am now spending my final days at the Bible College, and my sister in Salisbury, and WEC. Anyhow I can see the MS when I return USA 20th.

But may I take this chance of asking whether anything might be possibly done to make a few copies of my books which CLC in USA are reprinting available in Britain? I find different folks who ask, for instance, for WHO AM I, and are told by you it is out of print. As a fact, as I expect you know, CLC USA have brought out impressions with their own newly designed covers of most of them –

Law of Faith
God Unlimited
Spontaneous You
Liberating Secret
Who Am I
Touching the Invisible
Rees Howells

I think the problem may have been that Lutterworth had published them and more recently given permission to CLC USA to reprint, so from Lutterworth's point of view (and therefore maybe also CLC Britain) they are "out of print". If you could even have a few copies of at least WHO AM I, there might be some small sale or orders of them.

But now also we have my new one coming, printed in USA by CLC - YES I AM, maybe coming out in Fall or round December. There would be some small sale for these if you could hold a few.

But even more important you may know Rees Howells is a big seller in USA, and there are so many enquiries about the meaning of Intercession as taught and practiced by Rees Howells, that Doris Ruscoe (sister of Alfred and older full time co-worker with Rees Howells and principal of his Missionaries School), that after I had put it to her last year, got it from the Lord to write a further book on Intercession with its scriptural backgrounds and illustrated by Rees Howells' teachings and life. You may know that CLC USA have accepted this (and also possibly Lutterworth, but I am not certain of this). Samuel Howells, Rees Howells son, is along with her in this and we shall both write forwards.

But Samuel also has offered to pay the expenses of advertising it, so I am hoping to consult with CLC about doing this in USA and getting notices of it to all Bible bookstores as Rees Howells sells so well. Now do you think it might be possible to consider some adverts over here in evang. papers, and that there will be some, even though much fewer sales over here. I would much hope you could do this. I think the book will have a message of the Spirit to readers.

So I am sending you this line as I don't think I shall see you, and with this, also thanking God for His riches of blessing on CLC worldwide, and on Ken's new book stimulating further interest, and yourself as CLC God-given leader over here, and indeed for the splendid spirit of co-operation between WEC & CLC both sides of the Atlantic.

With my much love,

Rubi

<div align="center">~~~</div>

Sept.4.81

Marj my dear,

I don't know why the Lord has suddenly made me like an old bothersome housefly buzzing around you – (but I shall be well swotted anyhow after this weekend, as I start a three month tour with Sandie). But here for the third time I am sending you what I know you already have – this time those two Japan enclosures! (Actually the Japan folks have done the very thing I mean – their report used to be so dull and usually negative in their difficult field, but they have had the quickening stroke of the Spirit somehow to turn their center into THRILLING WITNESS! This story of this ordinary girl pressed through by the Spirit into our first woman pastor in our Jap church fellowship is REALLY something! And worth any Mag headline.

It may be the Spirit has given you a different objective in publishing out THRUST, but, as I already told you, I always saw our magazine as a means of capturing readers, startling them and imparting some living touch of the Spirit to them – but NOT informing them as my chief objective.

I suppose I'm prejudiced because God shot me into WEC wholly from that little live "Heart of Africa" heart-shaped mag Mother Studd began by putting out. I was wounded and in hospital in World War I, a chaplain dropped the mag on my bed, I read of CTS all thrilled by his forest contacts with his "Black Gold", and the Spirit got me – and here I am still a burning-hot WECCER after 64 years!

So when the WEC mag was thrown in my lap in 1931 I built it straight into something which would catch readers, first of all by startling unusual <u>headings</u> and then by narrative which equally stirred and startled them! And by that means the mag began to increase into thousands.

Another thing I did was to "instruct" and inspire our field workers not to send me dull newsletters and reports, but just any special tid-bit which hit them in the Spirit, personal victories, exploits of faith even in "small" ways, field incidents and above all God working in nationals – put then on a piece of paper and send me. Also especially I urged new recruits, before they get flattened out by critical oldsters, to send me their new fresh impressions and on that sort of thing I built the WEC Mag, with Charlton Smith's enormous living help on the art side. Rusico followed that by our WEC "newspaper" over here, which looked rough enough but had LIFE. Then Earl Frid did an equally marvelous job from Reamsville.

So that is why I jump on these "tidbits" when I read field letters etc, and have sent these samples to you. I realise almost all turns on STARTLING HEADINGS, but this of course, followed by living incidents. And with that of course I kept the mag wholly loose from the report type of issue which really can only "feed" those already WEC or certain fields interested.

However, my dear, you can bypass all this, but somehow I have been "stirred" to send you these. My spirit burns to see WEC still a burning fiery furnace, and not just what it tends to have become just "another faith mission"! So please put up with me, and then drop this in the trash can.

With my love as ever,

Rubi

~~~

Feb.11.

My dear Stewart,

Yours came thru to me here to-day. First of all I want again and continually to thank God for the preciousness of our living trusting fellowship, both in our attempts to present "the way of God more perfectly", and in our practical co-operation in our heart's desire to see the Holy Spirit in the fullness of His activity by us in WEC in all the dangers of having become a large organization as well as an organism. I love to hear what you say of this "keynote address" to British WEC (of which I had already heard exciting favorable comments, and your glorious "cutting edge" emphasis so well received, which is my supreme burden; at the same time I really laugh at the Spirit's 'daring' by you that just when you are our I.S. you boldly present for publication these daily readings, when we know various Weccers wonder where I've wandered off to! The great point is that you have that larger spirit, (which CTS sought in vain with the printing of the DCD), of those who saw the greatness of what he was trying to put over and would not join those Isaiah said "make a man an offender for a word". And we do that. Just got yesterday a pamphlet which treats us in Union Life as dangerous enemies with our "heresies", and I have written the author that we really are brothers in Christ, and I think the Father will welcome us both on That Day! And in your glorious presentation to WEC of the total Holy Spirit pattern for which the WEC came into existence, I surely don't want to say anything, when you all are giving me the privilege of a morning talk in Intercon II, (I only want to underline what the Spirit is saying by you), which could divert into dead letter controversy doctrinally.

Therefore, as concerns the Readings, of course what you wish goes thru, because as author you must be wholly happy with what you selected, and we will drop my alternative suggestion. Also I'm glad you like the forward. <u>Maybe you yourself will also be writing some personal preface</u> as the background to the reasons for your producing this. I'm sure that will be a necessary introduction.

While I'm at it, because we have this understanding spirit between us, I feel I can say one or two things about your comments on what you are asking not to be put in.

First, I see the full sense of your point that being daily readings, it doesn't fit to leave one day's reading needing the next to explain it. Good point.

308

But I would like to say that somehow we are desperately leaving folks with a horrible misrepresentation if it sounds as if by saying this truth is "total", "Why do I ever sin"?!! Our whole point is that because we humans express the nature of the Deity indwelling us, that is our normal expression. But while we live in a world of a rival Deity, we are always open to his enticements: in our lost condition, the Holy Spirit "tempted" us back to God: in our new creation condition, Satan tempts us back to himself. We did respond totally to the Holy Spirit, and thru Calvary Christ replaced Satan in us. We are now constantly enticed by Satan (Jas. 1.14), & know in general how to exchange that enticement for Christ in and by us; but we can sin (v.15), and then move into I John 1.9 by grace.

No, the curious thing is that it is here precisely we differ from the holiness brethren. I will send you a reply I've just written to Ted Hegre, who kindly wrote, because it hits the very spot. If we humans have a nature spoiled by sin, then sanctified by a second work of Grace, then how do we sin again without becoming unsanctified? That is why they are accused of "sinless perfection". But we are saying that we in our humanity can respond, because it was not a change in us which took place, but in the Indwelling one in us (Rom.8.9 in place of 7.17). Then I grant you the way of saying "as us" does raise questions such as you say, implying "obliteration". But we might say Jesus saying "<u>Ye</u> are the light of the world" is about the same, when we are in reality only lamps manifesting the light. And such phrases as "ye bear fruit", when it is the Vine's fruit manifested in us the branches etc. And our main point is, as you know it well enough among our Weccers, and far more so among millions of believers, they stumble along in maintaining an abiding relationship as two related to each other, and it is only those in whom there has been the revelation of a fixed inner union consciousness, who freely say and act as spontaneous Christ-expressors – the "abiding" being merely a recognition of an experienced fact. Paul again says it, "I live, <u>yet not I</u>, but Christ liveth in me". He admittedly kind of contradicts himself when he adds "liveth in <u>me</u>" when he had just said "yet not I": but that is just the almost impossibility of expressing a paradox; and we in "union life" move more strongly over to the emphasis that we <u>are</u> He in our form, He as us; for then we are equally spontaneous in us "<u>having</u> the mind of Christ", and we willing and doing because it is He willing and doing in us. I know it is a fine point, and open to question; but we see the whole Bible full of men, and finally Jesus Himself when The Dove had entered Him, speaking and acting as speaking the words of

God (Matt.10.20), and doing the deeds of God (John 5:17,19). And as for saying "we spontaneously operate Him", again it may be a clumsy effort for saying that "we have the faith of God" (Mark 11:22); and what else is it if <u>we</u> say to a mountain "Be thou removed" etc. We <u>are</u> operating as God, He at our disposal! Again maybe too crudely said, like DCD! And here is my urge, just as yours is in your terms, that recall our Weccers to that daring solid attitude and action which caused Caleb to say "<u>we</u> are well able", and Elijah "no dew or rain but according to <u>my</u> word", and Peter "such as <u>I</u> have give I thee". You know this well enough, but it is the root source of our "extreme position" in Union Life, and we can but glory in it.

You know I'm not saying this to bring any influence to bear on you, I just delight in our spirit-co-operation, but just to comment on those points which you raise. And indeed the same about using the illustration of our profession. I am not referring to its continuity but to that undoubted fact that we humans are empty at that level, commit ourselves to obtain what we have not got (medical, language, what not); experience an inner "take-over" by that particular know-how, and then we come back in full action from being like a empty vessel as we started, to be an active person in full human action.

I see your point on the phrase about bringing Him to humans who are redeemed, but don't know it. A better phrasing would be good. I've always had careful revisers of my wild sayings!!!

Well, I just write this, though we are agreed in not inserting these passages, but just to share with you personally areas which have not meant to you what we mean, and in the joy of mutual sharing, though I'm asking a lot in your present big schedule to spare time to read through.

I'll pass the Forward with your correction to Kath.

ever with my love,

Norman

~~~

Nov.20.85

My loved Maynard,

How glad I am to get your Sept. letter, though that is long enough ago! But I wrote you on your retirement from the Flame, but only had your Southport address, but the faithful P.O. has returned it "Address not known", so I was stumped till yours came. Thank you for it.

Thank you for your precious words in your letter. It's your breath of love which has been such a blessing to me, "a Burning and shining light" since our earliest contacts with CHC, and we're about the only ones left of the old guard. Marvelous the keeping power of God till we have our glorious gettings-together with Him and each other!

I had touch ten years ago with the Nazarene pastor of the largest church West of the Mississippi in Denver – a wide-spirited brother, Don Wellman. We had touch then about using the word of faith in building the biggest church in Denver. But he also said recently, "We know our theology, but will you write your understandings on Anthropology". I said, "Those technical words are beyond me, but I suppose you mean on the self-life". So I've done that, about 50 pages, calling it "To All Believers, It's Simple As This", but am also bringing it out as a brochure. Sort of shortened form of my last YES I AM book.

I still eagerly read The Flame, and hope, that living warm touch Centering more on the Sanctifier than on the Sanctification will be continued. The life of the Spirit is wonderfully flowing worldwide these days.

Ever with my love and thankfulness for our bonds in the Spirit all these years,

Norman

~~~

May 8, '87

Marian & Ray darlings,

You both are OVERWHELMING. No other word I can use.

First I had just heard two days ago, that you have actually got in touch with Duane about his son and that he is coming to paint the house! What can I say? I felt like Keats says Cortez felt when he first saw the Pacific - "silent upon a peak in Darien"! I feel silent just like that. What else can I say, but MARVEL, AS I'm getting into the habit of marveling at God's unending outpoured love-gifts - a MARVEL which will continue through eternity. I can only say, Thank you. Who ever thought that when you came at such a sacrifice to have those days with me, and we had such precious living fellowship, this would be one marvelous love-outcome! So thank you, thank you.

Then Marian darling, your beautiful letter as beautiful in handwriting as the computer! And you have sent me back these MSS. It's taken me a day or two to get my breath back. But I have begun to glance at some (first time for years) such as Hebrews and James, and I have to say they do HIT THE SPOT. God did give light which kind of surprises and captures me now! I do think they have Spirit-revelation in them.

And now, darling, this means that you have copied and kept copies and lists of what you have. Thank you just for that also, as I get muddled. If the time ever comes, that they can get out in pamphlet form, I do believe they have "total truth" in them about the Spirit in these "men of the Bible" form, which does hit the spot and can reach folk. Even your own mother is a beautiful evidence of that! Thank you, dear, for telling me about her, I loved the way she would read that rather long one on Job and light kind of settled in and it held her attention. Just precisely what I think it will do for many.

So I'm so thankful, darling, that you have this in beautiful order, so that folks can know where the MSS are.

I have also the WHAT IS THE HUMAN SELF? and THE LAW OF OPPOSITES and more recently THE OFFENCE OF THE CROSS (from 2 Cor), then there is the INTERCESSION IN ACTION which I think you have. All these could be usable for pamphlets later if needed.

Also that first one you, Ray, dipped into FIRE AND LIGHT, the first I ever wrote. Also I have all the talks I gave to the missionary body in Karuizara, the vacation center for the missionaries in Japan which someone took down and I have in typescript form.

Then it is wonderful that you have already dug in and got Underhill's MYSTICISM. Yes, that is the key book. And even Bullinger's Lexicon which I did not know was still in print. The other we all ought to have is THE PILGRIM CHURCH which is the perfect book which gives the underground stream of the Spirit thru the centuries of which we are now the present stream!! I must see if I can give you the author. It should be STANDARD for us all.

I'll now have a look at Romans MS and 2 Cor. "Light is sown" is the queer phrase James uses, and we are doing this "sowing" and the harvest surely follows.

How I love you both and thank God for you,

Norman

~~~

Aug.20.87

Dear David,

I greatly appreciate such a letter from you and the CLC. It has been my joy and great thrill to see the Lord's greatly expanding seal on CLC all these more than forty years since that 'historic' moment when Ken & Bessie launched in faith in the little bookstore in Colchester in the midst of World War II, joined by such faith stalwarts as Pa Why and Phil Booth and Dorrie Brooking and others – and now indeed worldwide and walking faithfully on the same standards of faith and sacrifice as when you started. Where could you find an earthly business making it's nearly twenty million a year in sales, and none of the dedicated and called workers making a personal profit from it. Living testimony and glory to Jesus in its expanding outreach!

Thanks also for the further clarification of Lutterworth Press and discount. It takes some time for these business details to get into my thick head; and it seems that the reverse is also true, and it takes a long time for my thick doctrines to get into business heads!! I mean by that the poor folks who stick it out in my conference series in various churches!

I was sorry to miss Foxell of Lutterworth, as I had to be in New York that day. Yesterday he phoned saying that the Evangelical Book of the Month people here were considering "Deep Things" for their next book, which would be 10,000 copies. But the snag might be not that it was too expensive at $2.00, but too cheap!! So it is still uncertain.

Then also I am thankful that you have continued producing my books, and even striving to maintain a few rags of orthodoxy on my back! Thank you for the "defensive" leaflets enclosed. My sorrow is that so many of our evangelical Bible-believing brethren seem far more anxious of preserving the false garments of independent self-relying selves seeking to maintain our relationship with God, even when born again, than boldly moving in with Paul and John (and Jesus in John 15) into a fixed union where HE does the maintaining and preserving and fruit-bearing, and we are the spontaneous enjoyers and expressors of that glorious grace-relationship, as John says, easily and normally "walking as He walks", "knowing as He knows", "loving as He loves" as in I John 4:17. Great abounding life! As that naughty C.T. Studd said, "Evangelical believers are more concerned with preserving their sinful imperfection than enjoying at least the outreach into sinless perfection"!! No wonder they "cast him out", but you in CLC have helped preserve the witness of that Wildman, and equally Rees Howells, and patiently endure me, Thank you, and praise God.

Lovingly and enthusiastically as ever,

Rubi

~~~

June 10, '89

My dear Mary Alice,

What a letter! And your handwriting so perfect thru all those pages, whereas I had to give up writing by hand because you Americans said you couldn't read my stuff, and yet my amateur typing is not much better! So thank you, thank you, and for your own picture from your hide-away with your husband!

Of course I am greatly moved by the way the Spirit 'caught' you in the reading of the Rees Howells life. He had an enormous impact on me. I had learned total abandonment to Jesus thru C.T. Studd, my father-in-law, whom God told me to join in the heart of Africa after World War I. I also wrote his life and you should have it if you have not seen it. It was for long a best seller and went to about thirty "impressions" and in about ten languages, and has been an enormous challenge thru the years. One lady printed 20,000 as a special edition for American students. Then to the revolutions in my life thru my years with C.T. Studd in the Congo where first the living reality of Christ came real to both my wife and me thru a five hours session by ourselves in a banana plantation in the Congo we laid hold of Gal. 2:20 by faith and the Spirit bore witness. I have written my own experiences called ONCE CAUGHT, NO ESCAPE.

But then another enormous impact on my life was when Rees Howells was led to ask me to visit him in his then newly acquired first building of the Bible School by faith in Swansea. On that first visit and a walk with him, a clear stream of the Spirit poured into me as he talked while we walked, and I recognised I was privileged to become linked with a second MIGHTY MAN of God, and I drank from him, specifically on the life of intercession in action. So then I was privileged to write that second "best seller" and the Rees Howells book is still a best seller. I could not say how many people have said to me that they never read anything else like it outside the Bible. Jerry Falwell's life was transformed by it and he gave 50,000 copies of it thru his Broadcast.

Yes, I've written various books, though those two biographies have been outstanding as best sellers. I enclose a list of others.

My most recent book on this list is <u>YES I AM</u> and that most completely goes into what the Spirit has been revealing to us thru the Word. So that is piling various good things on you, or putting them with-in reach.

Yours is a great letter, my dear, and these flowings of the Spirit. All thrilling.

My love,

Norman Grubb

~~~

May 17

Rhonda dearest,

Good to hear again from you. You ask about the mystics. The standard book which can be got in paperback is MYSTICISM by EVELYN UNDERHILL. That will really open them all up to you. They are hungry desperate folks, (of whom now Rhonda is one) who will not take a No, and pay any final lying independent self price to KNOW. Mystics were usually former Catholics and came thru the harder way; we understand the Pauline reality of the total FAITH KEY, but there's much more to be learned from them when you have a heart hunger.

I'm having such a great time down here with the rivers flowing, that it's good, like Paul said to the Philippians, that he was in a quandary to "depart and be with Christ far better" but to remain good for them. So on we go!

Dearest, get off God perfecting you. Say rather you ARE PERFECT because you are not Rhonda-I, you ARE Christ in Rhonda form, and stand by that and don't be confused or put off by your humanity which must have its reactions to be human, but sin is only when I deliberately mean to do the wrong thing and do it. One good sharp friend said to me, "When I am really angry with someone and I say, 'Damn you' and hit him over the head, is that sin?" The damn was ok, I said, but the hit goes a bit too far! But we often take false condemnations because of our "damns"!

Glad you speak out among your church folk. Love them, appreciate them, but stand at all price for what you know is TOTAL TRUTH and there does always include a "sword"!

Let's hear again from you. WE are putting our south travels off to the Fall, but hope to have a visit soon.

my much love,

Norman

৪৩ ଓ୫

EXCERPTS

Your touches on philosophy are interesting. That recent little book, "THE DEEP THINGS OF GOD," is in a sense Christian philosophy, because I tend that way. It ought to be called "THEOSOPHY," if a false cult had not pinched that name or equally "CHRISTIAN SCIENCE" if that had not been misused. The profoundest Christian philosopher who ever lived is to my mind, Jacob Boehme, the German cobbler. His English interpreter, William Law is also great.

~~~

I laugh also about this SUMMIT BOOK, so completely without my having an inkling, Stewart was doing it and that's a real labor, really based on him using my books all these years in training schools of WECCERS. But I laugh, because I enjoy reading these snippets, and I see it as God's joke, as I infinitely prefer to serve up massive prime steaks; God knows that most folks can more easily enjoy a "hors d'oeuvres". And I am not selling or advertising, yet it is running around and reaching folks.

~~~

So you will see that nothing we can ever put out in print can better hit the spot that Paul named as "determined not to know anything among you save Jesus and Him crucified". But by that means as in Gal. 2:20 our faith identification with Him personally is that old enemy is out in the "I am crucified with Christ" and in place of him "Christ lives in me". Glory!

~~~

You have really taken me by surprise about the book. I am such a pessimist that I never think a book will go, whether mine or anybody else – and then they do! Then I really am thrilled and amazed to hear of such a rapid sale and immediate reprint.

~~~

It is better to major on many letters full of deliverance with more of the gold than the dross. So many good things pour in for publication. I know the value of those sort of living extracts, because I rebuilt our small failing WEC Mag into a strong circulation by picking out from our pioneer missionaries' letters all those outstanding experiences, which I mingled with the spiritual life articles which were ultimately published, and still run around under the "Touching the Invisible" title.

~~~

Glad you liked the Moses tape. I have the inner conviction that God has enabled me to put total truth in the terms of the lives of those men and thus take them farther than in the normal OT biography, and in due course they will be published.

~~~

But now for God's JOKE. Stewart, these DAILY READINGS are running all over the place with not a word of push from me. The joke is that folk are loving getting me on the hors d'oeuvres level when they can't yet stomach my T-Bone steaks: and that clever clever Spirit knows what's what, and surely "drove" you - (HIS NATURE IN YOUR FORM"!!!) to take all those many hours in doing it. Stewart, I just MARVEL AT GOD and marvel at Him driving you like this. I must admit that as I pick the book up and read excerpts I ENJOY THEM!! Surely God laughing at my heavy stuff compared to these short sharp shots. Stewart, it shews every evidence of being a big seller over here and lasting when my big gun stuff dies out! Just one point, I think you said you would put the royalties into WEC. Well, may I make this wish as involved in the background -please use what comes in as <u>GOD LEADS you</u> and don't just lump into WEC, and use as personal if ever needed. That's my contribution, please!

~~~

So I have to write like this, and as Paul said in his writings on occasion, "I think I have the Spirit of God".

80 03

And from Norman's *final* letter to us all......

"BY **FAITH** MAY YOU FIND THE ANSWERS
THAT THE LORD HAS FOR YOU...MAY YOU
ALWAYS WALK IN FAITH UNTIL WE MEET IN
THE GLORY OF GOD."

Norman Grubb

December 1993

NPG Writings

Biographies...
C.T. Studd, Cricketer and Pioneer
Jack Harrison, Successor to C.T. Studd
Alfred Buxton
Edith Moules, Mighty Through God
J.D. Drysdale, Prophet of Holiness
Rees Howells, Intercessor
Abraham Vereide, Modern Viking

Books & Booklets on WEC...
After C.T. Studd
Christ in the Congo Forests
With C.T. Studd in Congo Forests (U.S.A. printing)
The Four Pillars of W.E.C.
Mountain Movers
Spanish Guinea
Ivory Coast
Penetrating Faith
Ploughing Through
The Price They Paid
A Mighty Work of the Spirit
This 'n That

Books ...
Touching the Invisible
The Law of Faith
The Liberating Secret
The Deep Things of God
The Spontaneous You
God Unlimited
Who Am I?
The Leap of Faith
Continuous Revival
The Willowbank Story
Modern Crusaders
Nothing Is Impossible
Yes I Am

Booklets...
The Key to Everything
Romans 6-8
Are We Still On Target?
Throne Life
It's as Simple as This
The Secret of Suffering
No Independent Self
Intercession in Action

Magazine articles...
Worldwide
Christianity Today
Floodtide
The Evangel

Glossary

AV......Abraham or Abram Veriede

Camp Hill......WEC Headquarters in the U.S.

CEI......Christian Evangelistic Institute

C of E......Church of England

CEI......Chicago Evangelistic Institute

CBMC......Christian Business Men's Committee

CFO......Camp Farthest Out

CIM......China Inland Mission

CHC......Christian Holiness College

CLC......Christian Literature Crusade

CMG......Commander of the Order of St. Michael and St. George

CMS......Church Missionary Society

CTS......C.T. Studd, founder of Worldwide Evangelization Crusade

CUMB......Cambridge University Missionary Band

DCD......Don't Care a Damn...booklet by C.T. Studd

DV......God willing

FIEC......Fellowship of Independent Evangelical Churches

HAM......Heart of Africa Mission

HT......Hudson Taylor

ICL......International Christian Leadership

Intercon......WEC leaders' conference held every six years to review strategy, policy, etc.

IS......International Secretary of Worldwide Evangelization Crusade

IVF......International Varsity Fellowship

IVCF......International Varsity Christian Fellowship

JB......Jacob Boehme, 16th century mystic

JEB......Japanese Evangelistic Band

JW......Jehovah Witness

KCMG......Knight Commander of the Order of St. Michael and St. George

The Life......Bio C.T. Studd Cricketer and Pioneer

Missionary HQ......Missionary headquarters

MP......Member of Parliament

MS......Manuscript

MTC......Missionary Training Colony

NA......North America

Pente......Pentecostal

PG......Portuguese Guinea

PPB......Presidential Prayer Breakfast

P & P's......WEC's Principles and Practices

QED......Asked and answered (Quod Erut Demonstrandum)
RAF......Royal Air Force (England)
RC......Roman Catholic
RH......Rees Howells, founder of Swansea Bible College
Samuel Howells......Rees Howells' son
The Seven......The Cambridge Seven, missionaries to China
SCM......Student Christian Movement
UL......Union Life
WEC......Worldwide Evangelization Crusade
Xtian......Christian

&) CR

Endnotes

[1]Norman Grubb, *Once Caught, No Escape* (Fort Washington: Christian Literature Crusade, 1982) 28.
[2]Grubb 50
[3]Grubb 70
[4]Grubb 183-184

છપ્ત

Printed in the United States
122522LV00001B/82-147/A